MW01180560

ADVANCE PRAISE FOR
SAVING GLOBALIZATION—WHY GLOBALIZATION AND DEMOCRACY OFFER THE BEST HOPE FOR PROGRESS, PEACE AND DEVELOPMENT

It's typical of Mike Moore's intelligence and courage to come forward precisely at this moment of international crisis—that is, when his voice is most needed—with this well founded and finely expressed defense of globalization. It's encouraging to know that one of the true champions of inclusive interdependence is not second-guessing what both practical experience and serious reflection have instilled in his actions as a national and international leader. Please read this excellent book.

Ernesto Zedillo
Director, Yale Center for the Study of Globalization
Former President of Mexico

The book reflects the qualities of the author—a direct no nonsense confrontation of the major challenges facing the world today and an attractive incapacity to abide sloppy prejudice from whatever quarter it may come. Mike Moore brings an acute historical and theoretical perspective to his treatment of these challenges but his great strength comes from his political experience at the highest level and subsequently as head of the WTO—he communicates on complex issues in an eminently readable form. He argues the case passionately and convincingly for globalization: "It is not a policy... it is not a regime imposed by some Wall Street conspiracy... it is a process that has been going on ever since our ancestors stood upright." Moore concludes by describing himself as a "reckless optimist." Reckless or not the world needs more optimists. The optimism of *Saving Globalization* is balanced, well-informed and well reasoned. I, who tend slightly more to pessimism, highly recommend it.

Robert J. L. Hawke
Former Prime Minister of Australia

Mike Moore is among a select group of people who have shaped globalization as we know it. As Prime Minister of New Zealand he helped redefined the functions of the modern state and as director-general of the World Trade Organization he steered the process of definition of the global trading system. I learned of his compassion for the poor and the excluded while working with him in the UN Commission for the Empowerment of the Poor. Mike is a champion of the poor who is passionate about bringing the benefits of a truly global economy for their betterment. Despite the gloom and doom painted by what he terms "enemies of reasons," Mike is driven to see the marginalized empowered and democracy to succeed. In his latest book, *Saving Globalization*, Mike makes a compelling argument as to why globalization and democracy offer the best hope for those who truly want to improve their lives. This is a must-read for those committed to eliminating poverty through creation of wealth.

Dr. Ashraf Ghani
Former Finance Minister of Afghanistan

Saving Globalization: Why Globalization and Democracy Offer the Best Hope for Progress, Peace and Development is a truly excellent book. This is hardly surprising as there can be few better equipped to write it than Mike Moore. Those who know him will recognize in his writing the lucidity of thought, the pragmatism and the idealism that characterizes him. While the central thesis, evident from the title, is widely accepted, the understanding of the issues is often less than adequate. While, as Moore says, the system provided by the World Trade Organization "is holding firm," there is no doubt that the current economic crisis is causing strains and there are legitimate fears of a creeping protectionism and nationalism undermining the great achievements of recent years. The book is accessible and cogent and presents its case admirably. It will have lasting value.

Peter Sutherland
Chairman, BP plc and Goldman Sachs International

Michael Moore, having been Prime Minister of New Zealand and Director General of the World Trade Organization, has chalked up extraordinary achievements in public life. He is also an astonishingly gifted writer. In this masterly book, written with a lifetime of experience, he addresses many important issues, particularly the advantages of an open world economy. If only his eloquence had been emulated by the G-8 leaders when endorsing trade liberalization and opposing protectionism. Moore's book is indeed a *tour de force*.

Jagdish Bhagwati
University Professor, Economics and Law, Columbia University
Author of **In Defense of Globalization**

From his vantage point as former Director-General of the World Trade Organization (WTO) and Prime Minister of one of the world's most open economies Mike Moore is uniquely qualified to describe in great detail the transformational power of globalization and political pluralism and why these processes are so often misunderstood. *Saving Globalization* also provides a timely and chilling warning of the threats facing globalization as Western political leaders are tempted by short-term political expediency and struggle to adapt to the rapidly changing global economic architecture. Mr. Moore then applies the full force of experience in describing the policies, institutions and strategies required to continue broadening the benefits of globalization throughout the developing world and to maintain prosperity in the West.

Stephen Jennings
CEO, Renaissance Group

Saving Globalization

WHY GLOBALIZATION AND DEMOCRACY OFFER THE BEST HOPE FOR PROGRESS, PEACE AND DEVELOPMENT

Also by Mike Moore:

- *On Balance*
- *The Pacific Parliament*
- *Fighting for New Zealand*
- *Beyond Today*
- *Hard Labour*
- *A Brief History of the Future*
- *The Added Value Economy*
- *Children of the Poor*
- *A World Without Walls*

On *A World Without Walls*

Mike Moore makes a strong case for the benefits of free trade and open markets. But he warns that global governance needs to be rethought to cope with the challenges of globalization. A wide ranging and thought-provoking book.

George Soros, author of *George Soros on Globalization*

A World Without Walls is excellent at giving a glimpse of what goes on behind closed doors in the negotiating process, viewed from the position of an official mandated to bring together the different parties and to secure an agreement.

Times Higher Education Supplement

On *Children of the Poor*

POOR Mike Moore; he has a gut level empathy with the poor that many politicians spend years cultivating, but he holds the unfashionable yet sensible view that the best way to improve their lot is to have more faith, not less, in the market economy.

The Dominion Post

Mike Moore draws attention to the appalling neglect and maltreatment of children in New Zealand and points out that this will lead eventually to social catastrophe. The statistics are depressing and getting worse—crime, drug use, under-age pregnancies, truancy, youth suicide—all the indicators are pointing the wrong way.

The Southland Times

On *A Brief History of the Future*

Mike Moore is an irrepressible optimist, and his prognostications are far more pleasant. He has a clearer picture than any politician I know of the productive and prosperous place these little islands could enjoy in the next century. His message is one to be heeded.

The Press

This book reflects an unashamedly internationalist outlook. As such, it is not just a job application but represents the expression of an outward looking politician in an increasingly isolationist political context. Moore makes his case that if New Zealand is unwilling to adapt and change to international realities, it will follow in the footsteps of imperial China and Spain.

New Zealand International Review

Saving Globalization

WHY GLOBALIZATION AND DEMOCRACY OFFER THE BEST HOPE FOR PROGRESS, PEACE AND DEVELOPMENT

Mike Moore

Former Prime Minister of New Zealand
Former Director-General of the World Trade Organization

WILEY
John Wiley & Sons (Asia) Pte. Ltd.

Other Wiley Editorial Offices

John Wiley & Sons, 111 River Street, Hoboken, NJ 07030, USA
John Wiley & Sons, The Atrium, Southern Gate, Chichester, West Sussex, P019 8SQ,
   United Kingdom
John Wiley & Sons (Canada) Ltd., 5353 Dundas Street West, Suite 400, Toronto,
   Ontario, M9B 6HB, Canada
John Wiley & Sons Australia Ltd, 42 McDougall Street, Milton, Queensland 4064,
   Australia
Wiley-VCH, Boschstrasse 12, D-69469 Weinheim, Germany

Library of Congress Cataloging-in-Publication Data

ISBN 978-0-470-82503-7

Typeset in 10.5/13pt ITC New Baskerville by Macmillian.
Printed in Singapore by Saik Wah Press Pte. Ltd.

10 9 8 7 6 5 4 3 2 1

To honorable public servants, elected and otherwise.

Cowardice asks the question—is it safe? Expediency asks the question—is it politic? Vanity asks the question—is it popular? But conscience asks the question—is it right? And there comes a time when one must take a position that is neither safe, nor politic, nor popular, but one must take it because it is right.

MARTIN LUTHER KING, JR

Table of Contents

Foreword

I have yet to meet anyone who has more practical economic and legal experience in the politics of international trade than Mike Moore. I have learned much from him—and this book has taught me more, particularly about the history of global trade, all the way back to antiquity. The book's common refrain is "this is not new in history" and the author explains with impressive facts, figures and anecdotes how economic migration, expanding local markets across national borders, and other earlier forms of "globalization" have led to greater economic growth and prosperity for ordinary people, particularly the poorest among them.

I first met Mike Moore in Geneva in 2001 at a meeting of the Inter-Parliamentary Union on how to make international trade more equitable and just. We were both keynote speakers, but Mike gave a better presentation—smart, entertaining, and, above all, an impassioned case that free trade was not just about competition and increasing productivity but could be equitable and "good for the people" of poor countries. In those days, advocates for the poor were not supposed to be proponents of globalization. It was a bit of political correctness that annoyed me, a fan of markets who had spent decades working to reduce poverty in my own country, Peru, and in the rest of the developing world. In fact, in my first book, *The Other Path*, originally published in Peru in 1987, I lamented the inadequacy of the debate over development: those on the left who cared about the poor knew nothing about the market, while those on the right who knew their economic theory didn't seem to care much about the poor.

At that IPU gathering in Geneva, I had finally discovered a fellow *rara avis*—an ex-Labor Prime Minister of New Zealand, who as a young man had worked as a laborer and social worker but who had also participated in major trade negotiations around the world as his country's Trade and Foreign Minister and then as WTO Director-General. When I was asked in 2005 to co-chair (with former U.S. Secretary of State Madeleine Albright) the Commission for the Legal Empowerment of the Poor, I nominated Mike Moore as a commissioner, and there was not a dissenting voice. He emerged as our best speaker, the fastest gun in the middle of a raucous room, who could structure an economic and legal argument as well as any lawyer or economist I have ever met but always with his heart unabashedly on his sleeve. In the middle of every debate, he would always remind us, "This is about people."

And it is those same ordinary people who are the central concern of Mike Moore's plan for "Saving Globalization." We now know that in the past half-century the world has experienced more economic growth than it had during the previous 2,000 years. Central to that global success, he argues, is the fact that some 500 million people have been lifted out of poverty and turned into consumers of goods from all over the world. "The challenge in the next decade," he argues, "is to do this again by widening the global economic base." It's pure Mike Moore: economic development and prosperity for all people. Globalization *and* poverty reduction.

At the moment, however, globalization is not really working, as the title of this book implies: four billion people of the developing world—two-thirds of the world's population—are currently on the outside looking in, getting angrier every day. As a Third Worlder with 25 years of experience exploring the shadow economies of the developing countries, let me give you a sense of international trade from the perspective of small businesses in a shanty town in Latin America or Africa. First of all, globalization is not even on their radar screen. In a study of the informal economies of 12 countries in Latin America and the Caribbean, conducted for the Inter-American Development Bank by my colleagues at the Institute for Liberty and Democracy (ILD) in 2007, they found that an average of only about 8 percent of the businesses in those countries had the legal tools to participate in international trade. The ILD has also analyzed the business and property sectors in the Philippines, Egypt, Tanzania and Albania and found their economies to be largely informal: in Tanzania, one of Africa's most impressive economic success stories, 98 percent of the entrepreneurs were operating outside the law. The economic picture across the rest of the developing world is the same: one of massive informality.

Why? The existing laws and institutions governing property and business in those countries are too burdensome, costly, discriminatory and often just plain bad, making it virtually impossible for ordinary people to gain access to the legal tools that even small entrepreneurs in rich countries take for granted. This is especially true of property rights, forms of business to divide labor productively and identity devices to expand their markets beyond the confines of family and neighbors. Most Third World entrepreneurs cannot even trade securely with someone across the marketplace or bazaar, never mind internationally. So far, globalization has only globalized the westernized elites of the poor countries. Even developing countries with impressive economic growth in recent years, such as Peru and Chile in my part of the world or such African stars as Tanzania and Ethiopia, do not have real market economies.

There is a myth that "the real economy" is about natural resources, production and hard work. Yet in Latin America, we export gold, copper, soybeans, airplanes, cars, natural gas, and oil. Africa, too, is brimming with natural resources. What we Third Worlders are missing is what Europeans and North Americans take for granted: a trustworthy property system with the documentary tools that permit everyone to get connected to the rest of the world. What has bestowed prosperity to the West is the ability to trust and cooperate on an expanded scale, form credit and capital, and combine ingredients from a variety of sources into products of increasing complexity. That requires legal property paper, and therein stands the real economy. Currently, the developing world is full of valuable assets—some US$10 trillion worth, according to ILD estimates—that are languishing as "dead capital," unable to be leveraged through credit and investment for the lack of legal documentation.

The only globalization worth saving is one that includes the majority of the people of the globe. Up to now, the political leaders of the North Atlantic countries have largely treated globalization as a foreign-affairs issue; they have done little to see how trade works up close at a national level where the actual laws that make doing business possible (or impossible) actually operate. They have also ignored history, particularly the Industrial Revolution, where, as Mike Moore notes in this book, the West solved many of the problems we are facing today. There is also too much talk of the "clash of cultures," while ignoring the evidence that informal entrepreneurs in Christian Latin America and Muslim Africa operate similarly, creating their own spontaneous norms to do business and protect their assets, proving to the culture warriors that they are ready to take their place in a modern market economy.

Globalization is not about to go away. But we will have to work hard to make sure it proceeds justly and equitably. And that, I would propose, just might be the silver lining of the current recession, which has forced America and Europe to reconsider the international financial system. Those of us who care about poor people and market economics have a responsibility to ensure that whatever "new paradigm" emerges for the 21st-century global economy, the world's four billion poor people must have a stake in it.

How specifically to address this tragic imbalance? I would advise you to keep reading Mike Moore's book for some very good answers.

Hernando de Soto
Author of *The Mystery of Capital* and *The Other Path*
President, Instituto Libertad y Democracia

Preface

When I was first active in politics, I devoured books and quizzed people to discover how to do things. As I've got older the emphasis has shifted somewhat, and I've become fascinated to discover why we do things, and where these beliefs and ideas come from. We are what we have learned, a fact graciously acknowledged by the former British Labor leader Michael Foot, whose book *Debts of Honor* is an elegant tribute to all those who influenced him—family, writers and thinkers, people he met, figures and events from history.

In this book I've set out to praise the people, principles and institutions that have helped shape my belief that we can make this world a better place, and to explain some of historical follies that continue to impede progress towards that goal.

While writing my earlier book *A World Without Walls*, which dealt with the economic and social consequences of globalization, I was struck by the overwhelming evidence that open democratic societies, run by the rule of law, with accountable leaders, honest public servants and an engaged civil society, produced the best results. Human rights, labor standards and environmental outcomes all improved under such conditions. The Kuznets curve famously shows that environmental outcomes improve as living and educational standards are lifted. Just as a free market corrects economic imbalances and provides more effective and prudent use of resources, so a free political market corrects injustices because an engaged civil society and leaders accountable to the people respond to problems. The environmental movement, the women's movement and the civil rights movement all mobilized opinions that shaped the agenda to which legislators and businesses respond.

How have the rules, customs and habits that govern successful countries evolved? The big ideas of history—democracy, the separation of church and state, property rights, independent courts, a professional civil service, and the civil engagement which drove reform to widen the franchise, promote social mobility, the civil rights movement, the women's and environmental movements—have all played their part in the creation of our successful modern societies. Far from being pessimistic about the state of the world, I am always recklessly, even dangerously, optimistic. In most areas of human existence things have improved. Life expectancy is up, literacy is up, and human rights have improved dramatically in most places.

Globalization has lifted hundreds of millions out of extreme poverty. This should be a time of hope born of our historic experience. Yet the enemies of reason, with their dark destructive messages of doom and hate, still have a constituency and gain much media coverage by selling the old-time religion of protectionism and anti-enlightenment—anti-modernity. In this book I have tried to put all this into perspective; to examine and explain how it has all happened; to explore some of the great ideas and personalities that have shaped our world; and to offer some ideas for a future that should be faced, not feared.

A world without walls cannot function peacefully if it is a world without rules, standards or values. I write at length of the re-integration of China and India into the global economy because this will change everything. It already has. I have had a grandstand view—from domestic politics to international politics, in business, on the factory floor, at universities and in working men's clubs—and I have tried to weave those experiences and lessons into this story.

We have seen much progress over the past 30 years that is breathtaking in its magnitude and scope. Thirty years ago half of Europe, most of Latin America, South Korea, the Philippines, and Indonesia were all under the jackboot of command economics of the left or right. Nelson Mandela, Václav Havel and Kim Dae-Jung—individuals I have been honored to meet and admire—were in prison or in exile. The artificial and historic detour that was the Cold War, which had frozen freedom and propped up authoritarian dictatorships, collapsed when the Soviet Empire imploded. People power from Poland to the Philippines changed regimes, as it is hoped will happen in Myanmar too. Myanmar 50 years ago was the richest country in Southeast Asia, but is now the poorest because it is the most closed. The military government has a 400,000-strong army, the largest in the region, and is not reluctant to murder and make more martyrs out of those who seek freedom. Note the difference between open and closed societies as they respond to natural disaster. China, a society in transition, gave open coverage and welcomed foreign aid teams after the tragic earthquake in Sichuan province in May 2008. By contrast, Myanmar closed its borders and let its people despair and die after Cyclone Nargis devastated coastal areas along the Irrawaddy Delta.

Yet what is this common denominator, the big idea across cultures and continents that drives men and women to heroic acts in the human impulse to be free? It is a Western conceit to believe that this is a sudden, triumphant endorsement of the values and systems that have made the West the most successful model in history. Years before Christ, from Mesopotamia to tribal villages in India, Africa and China, people organized themselves along consultative, sometimes democratic, lines, often responding to the will of the people.

In helping to navigate new members into the World Trade Organization (WTO) from the Baltic States to the Balkans, China, Jordan, and Oman, I experienced first-hand the desire of politicians, officials and their public to be in a rules-based system. Theirs was an enthusiasm for more open society and the rule of law, sometimes democracy. Many are cautious, some fearful—they talk of social disruption, public resentment and the privileged fighting back—but the overwhelming direction is clear.

When launching the Doha Development Round as Director-General of the WTO, I was driven by the understanding that we had to speed the virtues and success of globalization to the most marginalized nations on earth. This could be an important factor in lifting hundreds of millions more people out of poverty, creating many more consumers to sustain the world economy. We need to remind ourselves that even in the greatest exporting nations, 80 percent of economic activity is still local. I have worked with the most venal, idealistic, corrupt and honorable of politicians, bureaucrats and businesspeople during my life. Among the best and most decent of leaders, a pattern of private and public behavior becomes clear. Tolerance, respect for differences, accountability, and freedom are good in themselves but are also an economic good. There will be setbacks. History will still throw up future Stalins, Hitlers, bin Ladens and Saddam Husseins. But they rise to fall.

All this got me thinking about the history of freedom, and the personalities, ideas and structures that have created our modern world and its values. It is a remarkable history, from the Greeks to the Geeks,

encompassing important technological progress such as the alphabet, the clock, the printing press and the internet, and also the corrections and contradictions between liberty and equality, technology,
growth and the environment. Working with economies in transition,
those which are emerging from the shadows of political oppression,
I was always struck by their idealism, courage, optimism and hope.
Heartbroken by working with failed and failing states, seeing dishon-
est leaders and corrupt officials and businesspeople exploit their own
citizens, I wondered just how we could advance a common system and
values that could deliver better results knowing that, given a chance,
people collectively would fix and improve things.

There have been memorable moments of inspiration. The faces
of the German people when the Berlin Wall came down; the girls in
Afghanistan smiling when they went to school for the first time; Nelson
Mandela's smile and dance when he was free at last.

I have stood in queues in Timor Leste as over 80 percent of the
people lined up to vote for the third time in as many months. In a village far from Dili, I spent time with a Catholic priest who was encouraging reconciliation through the ballot box. "Democracy is the voice
of God," he told me. After the election in 2007, dozens of homes were
burned and people beaten by supporters of the party that had won
the biggest number of votes but was unable to put a coalition together
with minor parties to form the government, and I wondered how my
priest was faring.

Under the umbrella of the National Democratic Institute, I visited
Bangladesh as part of a delegation meeting with political leaders, one
whose husband had been assassinated by the other side's political activists, and one whose father had been murdered by the first side's activists. Both had passed their hurt and hatred down to their children,
who have become political princes. None had a basic understanding
of the principle of loyal opposition—to accept the will of the people,
be in loyal opposition and organize for the next election. Each darkly
threatened that their supporters and the public would organize general strikes and mass rallies if they lost. Our advice was not taken; they
had already ignored the same advice from Nelson Mandela and former
United States President Jimmy Carter. The military moved in. At the
time of writing, I was preparing to return to Bangladesh to advise on
their transition back to democracy and how to manage a free and fair
election. Happily, an election was held, it was managed well, and the
result was decisive.

We have all witnessed those queuing in the snow of Afghanistan, risking bombs in Iraq or police batons in Zimbabwe in order to vote, and know of heroes who have been imprisoned, tortured, and exiled from South Africa, Russia, Indonesia and Korea to Cuba, the Ukraine and Chile. What makes them tick? It is not rational, as economists would say, to risk and "waste" your life for an idea, the promise of freedom and independence for others some time in the future. These people represent the best of the human spirit, standing up for rights and freedoms many of us take for granted. The beauty of our new information age is that no-one can now hide despotic leaders or corrupt officials and businesspeople.

Challenges like those of the dark days after 9/11, the Bali bombings of 2002, the war on terror (notwithstanding its many errors) and climate change are not reasons to retreat from the promise of freedom. Rather, they are reasons to advance toward it. But how should we respond to these new challenges? How can peace-keeping, peace-making and nation-building work on the ground to create laws, institutions, systems and opportunities that are owned by the people and responsive to them, to liberate people and attack poverty?

The lessons and models from history to the present provide us with a road map, a compass to address these challenges. That's what this book is about—a small book about big ideas. Isn't it good that leaders should have to persuade us first, or that businesspeople, through competition and choice, have to convince us to be customers? Global consumer democracy will quickly punish companies and countries that do not behave ethically. The young have more information, choice and taste, and these consumers will use it in the marketplace, at voting booths, and public spaces.

The first 50 years of the last century were the most violent in human history; the next 50 years gave us the greatest lift in living standards ever. Can the first 50 years of this new century continue this progress, and can we create the conditions everywhere and build the institutions to make it sustainable, or will the "dark" side prevail?

With unabashed glee, many commentators over the past year have again predicted the end of capitalism, some even suggesting a worldwide depression due to the global economic meltdown. Anti-Americanism is still strong, with some commentators and politicians gloating about the collapse of the Anglo-American economic model.

In 2008, billions of dollars were written off as many of the financial instruments in the US, and elsewhere, were caught out; overstretched bad loans and reckless lending had been exposed. Trillions have been pledged to rebuild confidence and keep the system afloat. I understand some of this and the choices politicians face. When I was briefly Prime Minister, we prepared a strategy to bail out the Bank of New Zealand. Critics suggested this would reward bad managers and that we should let the show fall over as a lesson. In the meantime, hundreds of thousands of "mom and dad" accounts, football clubs, school committees, and businesses would also fall over. We lent the BNZ the money, charged commercial interest, and did get all the money back: a success. However, that was not the perception. An incoming government implemented our plan and was able to paint us as helping the rich and being irresponsible. Alas, none of this is new. To understand this, we need to consult the history books as much as the textbooks and a crystal ball.

This current crisis will not be like the Great Depression because of what policy-makers have learnt in the interim. Trillions have already been spent worldwide to hold the system together. At the time of the Great Depression, there were few effective government-owned central banks and there was little global economic coordination. Indeed, international trade collapsed by 70 percent within the space of a few years as governments put up tariffs to try and insulate themselves, and indulged in a destructive cycle of competitive devaluations in an attempt to control global market share. This deepened and prolonged the Great Depression from which the twin tyrannies of the last century emerged: fascism and Communism.

No nation is talking of jettisoning its trade obligations under the World Trade Organization; the system is holding firm. Democracy responds; it is that flexibility that is its genius. In the 1930s Franklin Roosevelt emerged with a new deal: a powerful central bank, a new organization to pick up mortgages. (The fact that Freddie Mac and Fannie Mae, the twin mortgage giants, had to be rescued recently from a mess of their own making does not gainsay this point.) Central banks everywhere have pumped more money, liquidity, into the system to prevent panic. As Roosevelt famously said in the US's darkest economic times, "All we have to fear is fear itself." It is about confidence. The word "credit" comes from the Latin word for "trust."

The Bush Administration was guilty of inactivity, despite warnings that there was a fault line in the financial sector. Talk of transparency sounds glib and a cliché. But it's real. Out of this destructive chaos will come creative chaos as new entities emerge, picking up some good, low-cost, high-value assets, though this is cold comfort for the thousands who are losing their homes and jobs.

The last 10 years have been the most successful in economic history, lifting millions out of extreme poverty worldwide. Economic gains made from liberalized capital flows now equal or exceed those from liberalized trade. Few jobs are lost and many gained because of open trade and financial markets, yet even in the US more people think trade costs jobs, despite all the evidence to the contrary. The lesson of the Great Depression was that governments needed to intervene to protect the virtues of the market; to ensure there was prudent disclosure and proper competition; and to ensure that global markets were regulated through agreements, procedures, and the WTO. Central banks were necessary to even economic cycles and police adventurers who, as they always will, take advantage of existing conditions. Government has a role to ensure social security in times of stress and uncertainty, and to invest in common goods such as skills and infrastructure. Rebuilding must be done in a way that produces both economic and social confidence. There has to be a sense of fairness, of equality of sacrifice.

If the stunning greed and bad judgment of some of the CEOs and corporations results in those most responsible walking away with very few scars and big payouts, workers who lose homes and jobs will be enraged, creating a populist opportunity for politicians to feast off.

Since its beginnings in late 2008, the financial crisis has dominated newspaper headlines, board meetings and everyday conversation. Reputations—even that of former Federal Reserve Chairman Alan Greenspan—have been left in tatters, as the markets indulged in selling debt without regard to their own long-term interests. In this they behaved like those people on very modest incomes who took out 100 percent mortgages to get on the prosperity ladder (in Britain a few years ago, people were offered 120 percent mortgages and a trip to Spain) or like the small investors who, for an extra 2 percent, took risks with dodgy finance houses. Greed is powerful, nasty, classless and, alas, universal.

Bear Sterns had $33 debt for every dollar it owned. Stock markets have crashed, with billions of dollars written off. Governments have acted swiftly, committing trillions to back up banks and to build confidence. Bank failures are not like other bankruptcies; they can bring down healthy companies that have done everything right. Lord Keynes observed that when you owe the bank $100,000, the bank's got you; when you owe the bank a million dollars, you've got the bank.

Bankruptcy is an important part of a functioning private enterprise system because it allows companies to restructure, reform and get going again, often at a lower cost because the company has been sold at a much lower asset price. It's rough but a necessary part of the genius that keeps business moving. Later, we look at the genius of the idea of the limited liability company and bankruptcy laws that have given such a dynamic boost to enterprise. When this is removed, a moral hazard exists which can encourage, even reward, bad behavior. Alas, in the end, pragmatic policies mean that some institutions, such as banks with investments everywhere, can't be allowed to fail. This is what Marx would call the "contradiction of capitalism." The small businessman falls over; the big one gets bailed out. It's hard to justify, but harder to ignore. It is the conditions, flexibility and fairness of such deals that test our economic leaders. Otherwise, the contagion creates even more unfairness.

With commodity prices collapsing (for a while) and food prices in crisis in many places, some commentators are writing about the demise of the West, just as the Marxists and fascists did in the 1930s. But it's not the demise of the West: it's the rise of the rest.

I am part of a group that is currently considering what should be the global response in terms of trading and economic rules and institutions. It is just laughable that Belgium has more power at the International Monetary Fund (IMF) than China. The IMF, in its present configuration, cannot do much, since its resources are only about $300 billion. Compare this with Japan's household savings and investments of $15,000 billion. China and Abu Dhabi have more reserves than Japan. Russia is a creditor nation now. The world has changed and now needs standard rules that govern the transparency of banks, their write-offs, common accounting rules and disclosure. National rules don't work when so much business is done beyond domestic law, and financial institutions lend and swap with each other. The chilling truth is that no-one really knows how much is involved, such is the complexity of many global, cross-border deals and the real influence of dodgy financial instruments. Corrective political action is being taken after the event but no-one knows how much will be enough. Mistakes will be made but democracy, the economic and political marketplace, drives up different answers. In the main, our species learns, adapts, improves, and moves forward.

Over the years, I have come to realize that productivity is just about everything in an economy, and competition and choice are its key drivers and innovators. Inefficiencies in these areas are a tax, a tollgate on progress and growth.

In my view, government has a role to provide the legal, physical, intellectual, social and natural infrastructure for growth. It should give people confidence through a system of social security that enables them to raise and better themselves; a basic platform below which no citizen should fall—a hand up, not a hand-out. It should also cooperate internationally to achieve peace and free trade, to handle issues of a global concern beyond the reach of individual governments, and be a useful partner to this end.

Through my years in government I learned much, too often by making the mistakes others had already made. There is a cruel and iron economic reality that cannot be avoided but can be postponed at even greater cost by government subsidies, borrowing or deficit budgeting. Subsidies, protectionism, government borrowing or deficit budgeting are cowardly ways of governments pulling the blanket over our heads, assuming the fetal position or hoping the bogeyman of reality will go away. You can protect old jobs for a while but always at the expense of new jobs, and in the end you have neither. This is hard to explain to those at the bottom who see their lives disrupted and feel victimized by change. Change: the most frightening word in the English language.

Patience has a limit, however. It is important that growth does not falter, and that the rise in incomes is spread sufficiently widely across a country's population. As we shall see, inequalities sometimes worsen in the early stages of industrialization and economic change. What then matters is that people who have not yet benefited from this growth have a reasonable expectation that their turn will come.

The countries that made reforms are now doing the best. Ireland needs to be mentioned as an example, as the Irish too took the hard decisions. From being almost the poorest country in Western Europe, Ireland became one of the richest in the space of a few decades. Since 1996, the poorest class in Ireland shrank by 29 percent and the number of people in the very top social class increased by 22.34 percent in the five years to 2002.

Yes, Ireland has location and enjoyed European agricultural subsidies, but sound economic policies to welcome investment, to lower taxes, and to join the European currency were political decisions of great moment and controversy. Ireland has a demographic advantage: the youngest population in Europe, so the lowest payments for pensioners. Contraception was banned there until the 1970s, so Ireland's baby boom was later than in most Western countries. These late baby-boomers, 620,000 of them, moved into a frenzy of purchasing the good life.

However, Ireland, the Celtic tiger, has taken a savage hit because of the global economic crisis; it's predicted that the economy will shrink by 4 percent in 2008 and unemployment will more than double. Like other successful economies, it's paying for the indulgences of the past decade. Wages spiraled updward; the property boom gave investors too much confidence. Living beyond your means is not sustainable, our mothers told us.

Banks were once like the family lawyer or family doctor: trusted advisors. These relationship banks became sellers of financial products. Ireland's property bust has seen some corrective action with the government's deficit reaching 10 percent. The people are not amused, with more than 100,000 taking to the streets in protest. But it's a dangerous fantasy to suggest that the progress of the past 20 years should lead to policies that would make matters worse. Just as good global times lift all boats, when the tide goes out it affects all boats, and some will be stranded for a time. As the old Wall Street joke goes, when the tide goes out, you find out who's not wearing swimming trunks.

As my own experience has shown, it is one of the ironies of democracy that responsible governments who take firm corrective action to create sustainable growth and impose financial discipline create a climate for an opposition party to take power. Building durable, trusted instruments and institutions of democracy, civil and commercial law with a free and active civil society takes time. The core objectives of our reform remain relevant; it's how you ease and navigate them through that is the question of politics and local conditions. Despite its worthy and proper objectives, the model cannot be directly exported to countries that are socially and politically vulnerable, where corruption, public looting and violence will erupt. This takes political leadership and courage but if we live by evidence then we know what works best.

I am reminded here of the story of the god-fearing person who prayed a dozen times a day, imploring God to let him win the Lotto. After many years, even God grew weary and demanded of the petitioner, "Help me out here—buy a ticket!"

If we want to take the journey to progress, peace and security, we have to buy the ticket. For too many politicians, the short-term cost of the ticket is too expensive and difficult. I hope this book encourages people to make that investment and not to lose their nerve just when the evidence says that, in the main, globalization is a good thing and worth saving by permanent improvement and adjustment.

Acknowledgments

I'm indebted to many for this work, particularly staff and reports from the WTO, World Bank, United Nations agencies, Brookings Institution, Policy Network, New Policy Institute, Centre for American Progress, Foundation on Economic Trends in the US, The Work Foundation (UK), Enterprise Institute and La Trobe University in Melbourne.

The *Australian Financial Review, South China Morning Post, Gulf News* (Dubai), New Zealand *Dominion Post* and *New Zealand Herald* have published my articles over the years, some of which I have built on here. Thanks also go to Cambridge University Press, Canterbury University Press and Shoal Bay Press because I have expanded on previous books of mine published by them. I have drawn liberally on those publications, especially in the Preface and Introduction.

Graeme Colman, David Porter, Scott Bates, Mike Rann, John O'Leary, Philippe Legrain, Matt Browne, N. K. Singh, Peter Watson and Paul Goldsmith are some of the many researchers, advisors and friends who have encouraged and advised me. Many, such as Bill Jeffries and Michael Bassett, assisted without knowing so, in many arguments and discussions. Google, Wikipedia, the *Financial Times, The Guardian, The Economist,* the *Wall Street Journal,* and the research of many NGOs have been liberally consulted, appreciated, and occasionally acknowledged.

It goes without saying I owe a debt to the many personalities who appear in these pages as colleagues, and to the historic heroes and thinkers who have led in this drama. Thanks are also due to Lisa Barraclough and Robin Morton-Smith, who tried to make sense and order out of my handwriting and papers; to Peter Dowling for editorial advice; the tolerant team at John Wiley (Asia) led by Nick Wallwork; and John Owen and Joel Balbin who took this monstrosity down by one-third—to my horror cut out all of my stuff on New Zealand! Thanks to John O'Leary whose research on the ancient Greeks and Romans was invaluable because I've met very few of them. None should in any way be held responsible for this book's shortcomings. The many simplifications are my responsibility alone.

Introduction

The iron reality is that no nation, any more than any individual, can hope to prosper isolated and cut off from others. History has shown that isolation is no defense from the drama of international events, even for an isolated country like New Zealand. Just as the world's economy has globalized, so have its problems and solutions. From whaling to child labor, terrorism or climate change, no nation can hope to achieve peace and progress alone. It is of no use if one nation cleans up the air and water within its own territory but its neighbors do not. HIV/ AIDS cannot be cured or contained by any individual nation's actions. These days, no single economy can even run a tax system, fight drugs or run an airline without the cooperation of others. Nor can any domestic response get confidence back into global markets at a time of global economic crisis. No-one is isolationist or protectionist when their child is sick or wants to be educated—we seek the world's best for them.

Security, stability, sustainability and economic growth, the fight against terrorism, organized crime, and the struggle for human rights— all of these challenges need international solutions. No nation, grand or modest, can ever hope to assist with or be the beneficiary of the solution of the great issues of our age without the cooperation of others. We are all in the same boat, whether we like it or not. We need to cooperate as we are all each other's customers. It is good that an integrated global economy means that our neighbor's success determines our own.

The competitive advantage our species enjoys over other species is our ability to learn, enjoy, adapt and improve ideas from other cultures. We have progressed because of this cross-pollination. History shows that closed, chauvinistic cultures and societies decay and perish, while open economies and societies flourish.

Protectionism in all its forms retards progress by suffocating change and slowing down our ability to learn, adapt and improve. Essentially, it is a contest over which country has the most money to waste on subsidies to ignore and postpone the harsh realities of the world. We cannot avoid change by closing our eyes to it. Sweet dreams and fairytales are easier to sell to anxious voters, as is finding external enemies to blame.

All progress is originally hard won. Even the humble potato was opposed by the merchants and the church in its day. A church leader decried the potato as a dangerous narcotic, almost as bad as tea. Merchants and farmers wanted to protect the profits from their current crops. What if the people actually wanted potatoes? A campaign was duly launched. The direct intellectual descendants of these merchants are still at it: these days they oppose imports that threaten the privileged, or oppose immigration and offshore investment, the WTO, the World Bank, investors or multinational companies. Fear, self-interest, and a looming election are great motivators, as is a global meltdown or a global crisis such as climate change. These perils could well unite us.

There have been three great waves of change in world history. The first, agricultural revolution, took thousands of years to play itself out. The second wave, the industrial revolution, took a mere 300 years. The third wave, the information age, has taken just a few decades.

Economies that do not plan, or that try to suffocate change, are a bit like Iraq facing the information-age military response of the United States in the Gulf War. Saddam Hussein's industrial-age military machine did not stand a chance against a military machine based on the skills of the information age. Similarly, the massacre of the Mahdi insurrection by Anglo-Egyptian forces in 1898 saw an agricultural-age army destroyed by an industrial-age force. The future will not be kind or say "please" it will crush old industries and destroy old jobs and bypass societies that fail to respond.

The new information age means that electronic-based grassroots pressure groups and the media have more power than most politicians to influence the people.

It's a talkback, telecratic democracy. How we learn, what we eat, our values, our vote and our ethics are increasingly influenced by forces outside our homes, our workplaces, and our country. History is a great teacher, and it is by examining history that we will gain clues about how to handle the future.

What is it about our species that has driven us to this point? How did the nation-state develop? How did we evolve from civilizations in which kings were seen to have a God-given mandate to a more egalitarian, democratic age? What are these big ideas?

Why is it that some tribes, nations and civilizations prosper and others do not? Did economic freedoms create or follow political freedoms? What does globalization mean? Is it a danger to sovereignty, or the guarantor of it?

As we look back, we will see that all the great historic waves of change have one thing in common: all have been accompanied by violent resistance, unemployment, and great distrust and hatred of leaders. Change is inevitable, but that has never stopped us blaming its agents.

Just as the invention of steam and then its application to railways and shipping changed the power structures of the world, the new highways of the future—the information highways—are changing the way we talk to each other and do business. How does a progressive government prepare for this, and advance the interests of its people while protecting its most vulnerable citizens in such a time of historic readjustment?

This book makes the case for development and progress, widening the economic base by bringing more people out of the shadows into the formal, democratic market economy. Perhaps the present economic crisis will mean business will look at the new customers of the future, the 3.7 billion people at the bottom of the pyramid who are largely excluded at present. They have, in purchasing power parity, an annual income of US$2.3 trillion. Ninety percent of the world's new products are targeted at the top 10 percent of income earners. History must be our guide. Much of the world's success has been the half-a-billion new citizens and consumers who have been brought into the global mainstream, as they have been lifted out of extreme poverty. The challenge in the next decade is to do this again by widening the global economic base. The new consuming poor can rescue the rest. This is not new in history.

The case for economic internationalism

In today's economy the traditional Keynesian and monetarist remedies do not work well. To cope with the Great Depression, John Maynard Keynes urged deficit spending by government to put money into consumers' pockets. Once consumers had the money, they would rush out and buy things. This in turn would lead manufacturers to expand their plants and hire more workers. Monetarists urged manipulation of interest rates or the money supply, to increase or decrease purchasing power as needed.

These days, pumping money into the consumer's pocket may simply send it flowing overseas without doing anything to help the domestic economy. An American buying a new TV set or CD player may well be sending dollars to China, South Korea, Malaysia or India. It's dumb to be a Keynesian and pump out money, and deficit-spend when the economic cycle is at its peak, and it's equally dumb to be a monetarist when the economic cycle is at its bottom and things are tight. Keynes spoke of the savings paradox. Savings have to be good, yet in a downturn we need spending. Evening out the economic cycle is the objective but economic history cannot be banned; cycles are inevitable—they can be softened but not abolished. Boom-and-bust economic outcomes come from lax management, but then we can have abrupt corrections. Putting the brakes on too hard or swerving savagely to the right or left can cause a collision.

A fresh solution based on sound domestic policies is required. That solution also lies in economic internationalism, based on trading rules and prudent global financial instruments decided upon by sovereign governments. This is now made more urgent and real by the global economic crisis. This idea is not so very radical. It simply builds on the ideals and institutions developed at Bretton Woods, dreamed of by Kant, advanced by Woodrow Wilson and given practical meaning by Franklin D. Roosevelt and the great generation who created the United Nations, the WTO, the World Bank, and the International Monetary Fund. Unfortunately, the debate about how to best provide rules so that markets can function has been hijacked by tired slogans. The WTO, the World Bank and the IMF are often portrayed as complicit conspirators in a global capitalist plan to remove rules and civilization from our commercial, social and cultural life. These institutions can and should only do what governments allow and instruct them to do. A laissez-faire world is the absence of governance. Global trading rules are about governance. The idealized and demonized Adam Smith's much misquoted *Wealth of Nations* was about attacking the privileged and warning against a form of capitalism where monopolies, privilege, guilds and rules were used to block competition and reward insiders, those with the power and contacts.

Democracy and access to education liberate the skills and genius of all people regardless of race and gender. Equality is good economics. Social mobility, a by-product of the social democrats' thirst for equality, widens the economic base and is good public policy. If a nation's freedom can be measured by its level of democracy, surely this truth can be extended to the realm of international dealings and the management of domestic economics.

Totalitarian societies always go backward because they are not open to the freedom and competition of ideas, commerce and information (even humor—there are few joke books about Stalin, Hitler, Mao or bin Laden, but most know the melancholy humor of Abraham Lincoln and the inspirational wit of Winston Churchill).

This book argues for openness and the rule of international law abroad; and for economic freedom, social mobility and democracy at home. It is a plea that the current economic crisis is not used as an excuse to retreat, to go inward, and lose sight of the big ideas that have served us so well. De-globalization is the most dangerous threat our prosperity and security face. It has happened before, in August 1918, and with the savage advances of fascism and Marxism during the Great Depression. It invites us as citizens and governments of the new millennium to participate and thus build respect and trust in international institutions and the rule of law as a civilized arena in which we can conduct our affairs, resolve our differences and promote progress to ensure our economic, political and environmental security.

Such internationalism is not new. Like nationalism, it has been promoted by villains and saints alike. The Marxist ideal of a universal proletariat and the liberal dream of a big melting pot were also illusions. Archaeologists keep discovering ruins and monuments built to celebrate individuals and empires whose power was thought to be immortal. People are citizens, not subjects. But true individual liberty is impossible unless people have access to opportunity and the key to that door is skill, education and ownership. Tyrants always try to keep that door closed. Their power cannot withstand the scrutiny that freedom of expression and choice demand, or the fury unleashed when people and justice are denied.

For much of the last century international politics was dominated by the Cold War, which intellectually corrupted and distorted our vision and global institutions. It was a vital war to win, and it was won. Or, rather, Marxism failed. The West calculated that East Germany had a standard of living equal to 75 percent of that of West Germany, but it was closer to 30–40 percent. The Cold War perverted the decolonization process throughout the world, as emerging countries were courted, their economies, politics and cultures transformed into surrogate battlegrounds. These days we are returning to more ancient rivalries between cultures.

The clashes of the future may not be so much ideological as cultural and economic, if we classify the extremists in the Muslim world and the struggle within their civilization as a cultural battle between modernists and those who believe in a better past. While the world is regionalizing and globalizing, smaller and often quite ancient political units are seeking recognition and getting it. Since 1999, for the first time in 300 years, Scotland has had its own parliament. A party promoting an independent state for northern Italy was in the coalition government formed in 2006. Following elections in mid-2007, Belgium, a nation artificially established as a buffer between the great powers of Europe, went many months without a stable government.

Globalization does not mean the end of heroes either. Czechoslovakia was able to split peacefully into two countries, yet it took a bitter war and ethnic cleansing in Yugoslavia for that country to separate into new or very old nations. How would things have gone if Václav Havel had been in Yugoslavia, and Slobodan Milosevic in Czechoslovakia? Maybe everything would have been different.

The demand for recognition by the Kurds and the Scots, and by indigenous peoples in Canada, the United States, Australia and New Zealand, is part of a profound historical movement. At first glance these twin movements of globalization and localization, even tribalism, look like a clash of contradictions. Not so: they are opposite sides of the same coin. As people experience globalization, they increasingly want to assert their individuality, independence and cultures. That's a good thing. Nobody wants just one world football team. No one wants yesterday's medicine for their children. They want the best that the global economy can produce.

The principle of subsidiarity holds that decision-making power should be relayed to the lowest level of power consistent with the nature of the problem. Thus, in today's world, certain problems or issues have to be addressed at the supra-national level (for example, cross-border pollution), and the nation-state is too small to take all the decisions in this area. In short, the principle holds that the decision-making process moves up in scale. But equally, many decisions formerly taken at the nation-state level should be delegated to small aggregates of power, such as the local government level or, more importantly, to the individual. The centralized nation-state again has to cede power, but this time downward and sideways, not upward, and more to individual citizens, rather than the institutions created to serve them.

This trend poses complex issues for policy-makers. In the United Nations and elsewhere, worthy souls, egged on by a connected civil society, are working to thrash out issues of self-determination and sovereignty in regard to the role of the nation-state. It is in such international forums that our hope for the future lies, because what is happening there is not confined to one particular part of the world.

The big ideas developed in this book argue that freedom, both economic and political, works best when backed up by the rule of law. When I was serving on a United Nations Commission for the Legal Empowerment of the Poor, someone asked a simple question: "What is the law?" Commission member Justice Kennedy of the United States Supreme Court quickly came up with a simple, elegant and most profound explanation:

The Rule of Law requires fidelity to the following principles:

- The law is superior to, and thus binds, the government and all its officials.
- The law affirms and protects the equality of all persons. By way of example only, the law may not discriminate against persons by reason of race, color, religion, or gender.
- The law must respect the dignity and preserve the human rights of all persons.
- The law must establish and respect the constitutional structures necessary to secure a free and decent society and to give all citizens a meaningful voice in formulating and enacting the rules that govern them.
- The law must devise and maintain systems to advise all persons of their rights and just expectations, and to empower them to seek redress for grievances and fulfillment of just expectations without fear of penalty or retaliation.

I take these principles into a global context in regard to our noble international institutions. But the rule of law or a constitution is in itself no guarantee of prosperity and security, it simply—if truly implemented and real (after all, the Soviet republics had beautiful constitutions)—provides the platform of community values that allows the individual to grow freely. The United States Constitution does not guarantee the right to happiness but speaks of the right to *pursue* happiness. Free trade, open societies and open economies do not in themselves guarantee prosperity either; they do offer the gift of opportunity. What governments do with that opportunity is another matter. People and governments must spend wisely, though many don't. This reminds me of the person who won a big raffle and spent a third on whisky, a third on wild women, and frittered away the rest.

You can frequently judge a society by the attitude of its people to the police. On my visits to authoritarian societies I found it embarrassing to have police escorts and motorcycle outriders who hit the roofs of cars with rolled-up newspapers, and I noticed the scowls on people's faces. Visiting China I got used to large crowds cheering or waving badly printed flags. On my more recent visits, less official but still traveling in government cars, people have genuinely smiled and waved. It's a rough and quick superficial measurement, but has some truth in it. It speaks to the issue of trust and confidence in public institutions, the police being among the most important of these.

I also run a humor test over individuals and nations I visit. This is rougher still than analyzing attitudes to the police but just as instructive about how a society functions. If you are on the same humor wavelength as people you are negotiating with, then you can do business.

The themes I write of are, I hope, clear: freedom works, but democracy and the rule of law, free trade, and social mobility advanced by progressive domestic policies work best.

Big ideas

There are those who argue that it is conceited or foolish to suppose that the free society, taken for granted by Westerners, is appropriate for all people. In this world view, order is the primary good. The streets of North Korea are probably pretty well-ordered, but would we want to live there? And how do their living standards and freedoms compare? Freedom, equality, trust, tolerance, openness, reciprocity— none of these, with the partial exception of reciprocity, was obvious at the outset. That a king or the person with the biggest guns should be answerable to a set of laws was not obvious either. That all people—the strong and the weak, male and female, black and white—were created equal and should share equal rights and protections was not obvious, and still isn't in some places. Here's where religion has played a positive role: if we are all God's children, equal in his eyes, then surely we must be equal before the law. That a community should accept, or indeed welcome, people with different beliefs was not obvious. That it makes sense to engage with strange people, meanwhile, is more natural to instinctive traders but it also runs against the grain of instinctive hostility to outsiders. These were all big ideas that took centuries to be accepted in some cultures and which remain rejected, or quietly ignored in practice, in large but diminishing parts of the globe.

Today these values, which we might loosely group under the terms "a free society" and "liberal democracy," are being embraced by more people and nations than ever before, for the very simple reason that they work. Decency and trust, as well as democracy, are big ideas!

Western societies have done better in terms of wealth, health and general well-being for the past two centuries, in the main because they have embraced the insights of the Enlightenment, out of which human rights, freedom of religion and freedom from religion, equal rights under the law, and, eventually, formal democracy evolved. This march to reason and freedom began much earlier, beyond any one culture. The earliest political expression of the will of the people was not in Europe, and can be traced back to well before the great figures of Greece and the Old Testament. Iceland's democracy, which began when warrior-priests gathered in AD 930 and declared, "Icelanders have no other king than the law!" is an early variant. The most rapid progress occurred in England, where the Magna Carta held that even kings should be subject to the law. Centuries later, the "Glorious Revolution" fully established the principle that the king should seek the people's consent (albeit of rich people, then) before taking their money.

These were big ideas that shaped the world for the better. Others, such as property rights and the genius of the "limited liability company," which gave life to the notion that a commercial entity existed beyond the life of its creators, protected families from the threat of imprisonment for commercial setbacks, changed the concept of inheritance, and fundamentally altered the way we managed risk. Fancy being able to borrow against an asset codified by a piece of paper! These commercial developments gave the Dutch and then the English a trading and commercial edge. They worked in an environment where the rule of law could be trusted, and where the king or the man with the sharpest sword didn't win every argument.

Another set of big ideas, the rejection of tribalism and witchcraft, and the separation of church and state, destroyed the notion that people were born into a certain "fate." Earlier, it was accepted as being preordained that some should always be serfs, slaves or servants. This notion is captured in the splendid Anglican hymn which begins: "All things bright and beautiful, all creatures great and small... The Lord God made them all," before going on to outline how "The rich man in his castle, the poor man at his gate. God made them high and lowly and ordered their estate." Over the course of several centuries progress abolished "fate" and laid the foundation for the twentieth-century welfare state, which spread opportunities and extended freedoms.

All these ideas were contested vigorously during the past century, as they always have been. We thought the battle had been won against a dark foe when communism collapsed along with the Berlin Wall in 1989. In itself, communism was a new (but ultimately barren) set of big ideas that claimed to solve all the problems born out of the miseries and injustice of imperial privilege and corrupt regimes. During the Cold War there was a sordid consensus amongst the major Western powers on the benefits of the "authoritarian advantage"—that the development needs of newly independent colonies were best met by strong leaders. A squalid, but elegant, economic theory emerged to justify this proposition: that only strong men could be trusted to oppose communism, and if they crushed legitimate democratic opposition in the process, then that was an acceptable cost of victory for Cold War warriors.

There was no moral equivalency between the systems, democratic and Marxist. What is surprising is that there was ever such a debate. No freedom-loving people ever sailed from Florida to Cuba or tunneled from West to East Berlin or from South to North Korea. No-one is escaping South Africa to go to Zimbabwe, as I pointed out at a hearing of a United Nations commission into migration after listening yet again to a litany of anti-American tirades. Communism was not only a method for wielding political authority and a set of principles for organizing economic activity: it was also a system for mass murder. The Soviet and Chinese regimes practiced terror on a scale similar to their fascist rivals. These regimes also provoked, and presided over, the two worst famines of the twentieth century. Stalin's victims, by one estimate, numbered 30–40 million; Mao's 35 million; while the Communist Khmer Rouge, which ruled Cambodia between 1975 and 1979, managed to put to death two million of its seven million people.[1] A million people fled Vietnam at the end of its war for independence and liberation. Many are returning now that Vietnam is adopting more open economic policies and joining the WTO. Living standards have trebled in 15 years, and extreme poverty has dropped from 70 percent to 20 percent over this time. Vietnam now welcomes investment and trade. But many in the 1930s saw fascism as a bigger threat to them, their values and institutions than communism. It was attractive to my parents' generation and I can understand why so many took that fatal road.

The world has moved on. The number of democracies is increasing—in 1988, two-thirds of states were undemocratic; now the proportion has been reversed. However, the defenders of "hard-man" rule have not gone away completely. The appropriate phasing of economic development, individual liberty and democracy is much debated in these uncomfortable years when fragile democratic experiments have begun in Iraq and Afghanistan, just as it was during the Cold War and in the messy aftermath of the post-Soviet period, which unleashed religious and ethnic hatreds in some fledgling democracies. The new threat of radical Islam has forced itself to the forefront of the minds of policy-makers and concerned citizens throughout the world. Meanwhile, the old enemy—poverty and hopelessness—refuses to step aside, particularly in Africa. Some observers remain willing to tolerate corruption, a lack of transparency, and the absence of freedom on the grounds that the people of many failed or authoritarian states are not yet ready for democracy.

The argument is perhaps loudest in Africa. At the Commonwealth Leaders Conference in Malta in 2005, it was suggested that there should be a trade-off between trade and democracy, the argument being that democracy did not put meals on the table. But this is wrong. There has never been a famine in a democracy. However, this argument is one that many believe. And it's right, if it's simply saying that voting in itself is not enough.

Every great falsehood has to have a little truth behind it to make it credible. In Latin America the wave of democracy in the 1980s and ensuing pro-market policies have not produced the desired results for the very poor, except in Chile, which has been progressively governed by solid social democratic administrations. Voting in Afghanistan, Iraq and Palestine has not miraculously solved those societies' problems.

Most experts who think authoritarian governments can do better in a country's development phase are also strong believers in democracy. They assert that they are simply being realistic about how best to achieve that state. They worry that electoral cycles and populist politicians can put impossible pressures on resources to fund health education and create jobs, imposing economic constraints that can be counterproductive for an emerging democracy. They also note that appealing to mob rule can incite ethnic hatred.

That being the case, they suggest that the answer is to focus on building a middle class before expanding or establishing the electoral franchise. It has been suggested that countries need to lift per-capita income levels to $6,000 per annum before democracy can take hold. Once societies have achieved this income level, civil society and the middle class ensure that democracy becomes embedded and works. No country that has reached this income level has ever rejected democracy and reverted. The initial strategy of the major powers, according to this theory, should be to support "liberal autocracies." There can be negative consequences when countries elect what can be described as "illiberal democracies."[2]

This is a well-reasoned argument, but we have to ask how long support for authoritarian rule should be extended as the people wait for this middle class to arise. Is it true that only strong men and liberal use of force are successful in stamping out extremists who can exploit ethnic and religious differences?

No-one suggests these issues are easy. Here's an interesting test of democratic credentials: how do you handle a political party whose avowed aim is to stop any more elections? Many of those who were so loud about the violent military reversal of an election result in Myanmar had a different view when the matter was closer to home. In Algeria the military, with the acquiescence of the West, took control and prevented the result of an election being implemented. Having another fundamentalist Islamic state on Europe's doorstep was a terrifying prospect.

We are learning painfully in Iraq that no power, not even the most powerful nation on earth, can simply flick a switch and introduce democracy in the absence of trust, good governance, a functioning civil society and traditions of freedom and openness. The results can be catastrophic. There has to be a wide consensus to support freedom and its systems, as there was in post-war Japan and Germany, and in most of post-communist Eastern and Central Europe, and post-fascist Latin America. In these places, instincts and institutions that had been dormant flourished when given the opportunity.

However, people are born and yearn to be free. While under house arrest in Indonesia, Timor Leste independence leader Xanana Gusmao received a phone call from a priest whose church was under siege from the Indonesia-backed militia. The priest said to Gusmao:

"Don't give up the struggle; we will die as free men and women." All inside the church were butchered.

This is not the time for supporters of democracy, good governance and freedom to lose their nerve or self-belief, or to give in to the view that the freedoms we enjoy should always be subordinated to the maintenance of order. The Enlightenment values need their defenders as much as ever.

In recent years, a sustained attack on Enlightenment values and democracy has come from within Western societies. Too often, we have followed the politically correct principles of post-modernism and relativism. These deeply embedded theories claim that all truths are relative and thus there is no right or wrong, because at certain times in history, what was wrong became right (such as votes for women), and what was right (such as slavery) became wrong. While all cultures deserve respect because there is much joy and much to learn from diversity, these attitudes become dangerous when carried to extremes. All values are not equal. Political correctness takes one of the great cultural strengths of the West—self-criticism—then applies it selectively and negatively.

Democratic advance

This is not a pessimistic book. "Watchful optimism" best describes its tone. First, let's celebrate the past 30 years. The Soviet empire imploded and retreated without firing a shot. Most of Central America, all of South America and half of Europe, and South Africa have come out from under the jackboot of military and command economies. Within two decades of the Prague Spring, people power had exploded from South Africa to the Philippines, Indonesia, Peru, Chile and South Korea. Kim Dae-Jung, Václav Havel and Nelson Mandela all went from being persecuted opponents to freely elected presidents. Taiwan saw the peaceful installation of a multi-party democracy. Poland's Lech Walesa and the Soviet Union's Mikhail Gorbachev became presidents and Nobel Peace Prize winners. Perhaps even more startlingly, within a few years Walesa and Gorbachev were turfed out of office. Neither could muster 2 percent of the vote to be re-elected. Did that show democracy was flawed? Of course not, any more than Winston Churchill's defeat in 1945 at the peak of his power was a rejection of democracy. The people demand different things of their leaders at different times.

Perhaps we have become a little weary of good news followed by disappointment. The gap between expectation and delivery can often lead to cynicism, a backlash against all politicians and a general indifference to the political process in older democracies, though not in new democracies. After all, we have seen Indonesians go through a succession of increasingly open direct elections since Suharto was overthrown in 1998. In the Philippines, another corrupt president was ousted and his replacement was re-elected by popular vote. In the Ukraine, a battle-scarred reformer, Viktor Yushchenko, after mobilizing the people to protest a rigged election, became president of a free Ukraine. A similar process in nearby Georgia resulted in a new president. Both democracies are now under severe political stress. But so what? That's natural. What is unnatural is when an iron lid of repression is forced down on differences in order to mask and suppress those differences and difficulties.

We have witnessed the courage of thousands of people standing in the snow waiting to vote in Afghanistan in their first real election. We read how "At polling centers hit by explosions, survivors refused to go home, steadfastly waiting to cast their votes as policemen swept away bits of flesh."[3] In Iraq, the vote on the constitution in October 2005 saw millions turn out despite the threat of bombs, proudly displaying the purple-stained finger showing they had cast their vote and expressing their hope for a better life.

A pattern is emerging, a pattern of hope. Extremists threaten, bomb and maim, but continually fail to extinguish this wave of optimism. Democracy is on the march in Africa: South Africa and Nigeria stand out. In Togo, a military coup put a deceased president's son in power. That's not unusual, but what's new is that the African Union's leadership, which was once silent, even complicit, over such affairs, now has a public policy of condemnation.

Curious paradoxes are emerging. Once, a hereditary king was seen as the antithesis of democracy, but not necessarily any more. Good kings, operating within constitutional limits, have often in recent history preserved the constitution and democracy in Spain and Morocco, and sometimes in Thailand. The value of a constitutional monarchy is not the power it enjoys but the power it denies others. In Malaysia, the job of king rotates around Malaysia's many diverse regions. In the small kingdoms of the Middle East, the Gulf States are becoming laboratories for change, with royals in small states like Qatar and Kuwait leading the way. Kuwait has enjoyed elections, and has its first-ever woman minister. Constitutions are being written and elections are being introduced that should see constitutional monarchies evolve.

Despite threats of violence by rebels and the assassination of a top mayoral contender in the biggest city in the Kashmir region, queues of people stood in line to vote. Kashmir's most powerful woman politician, a member of the Indian parliament, made headlines by saying that Kashmir needed two things—peace, and its first McDonald's restaurant.

In 2005, Saudi Arabia had its first municipal election to fill half of its 14-seat council, with 1,818 candidates running in the first round, 646 of them in Riyadh. Women were denied the vote, a decision that was condemned publicly by many candidates and respected public figures. It will be different next time, they promise.

Those of us who have democracy take it for granted. It's hard to get people to vote in mature democracies. Those who do not have these freedoms stand in queues, braving sun and police batons in Zimbabwe, snow in the Ukraine and Afghanistan, and suicide bombers in Iraq. This must tell us—and extremists everywhere—something. Democracy is now the only legitimate revolutionary force, and it's coming to a place near you.

At the turn of the last century, only a handful of countries had what we would recognize as a democratic form of government. Today, 119 do, comprising 62 percent of the world's countries. For the first time in human history, a majority of people (58 percent) are living under a democratic system of government.[4] Many millions more now live in authoritarian societies that were once vicious totalitarian societies, and some authoritarian societies seem to be evolving into paternalistic societies with greater liberties.

Of the worst economic performances of the past 40 years, 95 percent were under non-democratic governments. Of all interstate conflicts, 80 percent are instigated by autocracies and virtually all refugee crises have been wrought by autocratic governments, which are more vulnerable to civil war.

Poor democracies and countries in transition to democracy have nearly always outperformed authoritarian countries. Consider what is important: life expectancy, literacy, infant mortality, agricultural productivity and clean water. Democracies rate 20–40 percent higher on these essentials than their authoritarian counterparts.[5] There is a popular misconception that democracies have greater debts and bigger deficits, but this is not backed up by the evidence. Democracies are less corrupt and more efficient because their leaders and public services are more accountable, and an active civil society, trade unions, and free media are irreplaceable watchdogs. This cleansing air of transparency and the adaptability of democratic forces make for better results. There is such a thing as a democratic peace; true democracies do not go to war with each other. As the number of democracies has increased, the number of wars has dropped.

Readers who are unconvinced will be asking: "What about Singapore? What about China?" Singapore is unique: it is highly advanced and free in regard to property rights, education, clean courts, honest, competent civil service and police. Its politicians are honest and extremely sensitive to public opinion. Singapore is more paternalistic than authoritarian, and no-one doubts that its leadership would be overwhelmingly elected.

The greatest expansion in China's history has occurred in recent years because it has embraced property rights, allowing farmers to manage and own their products. The more China has moved from a totalitarian regime to a market economy, emulating the success of Japan and the Asian "tigers," the better have been the results. China is a society in transition, moving toward a more inclusive system.

Meanwhile, as liberty and freedom spread like wildfire around the globe, the world economy enjoyed its greatest, most sustained economic expansion ever. The two things are connected. While most of this past decade has brought better times, it has been easy to take for granted the global framework that has enabled this success. This has been a time of stunning economic and social advances, which has delivered the most sustained period of global expansion since the 1950s and '60s. But at the time of writing, the global economy is in a downturn that is creating fear and doubt and threatening to undermine some of the recent advances.

We have learned what works and what does not in the struggle against global poverty. The countries that respect property rights, have independent courts, a professional public service, accountable, replaceable politicians, openness to trade, migrants, new ideas, democracy and a concept of human rights, have done the best.

These attributes have proven infectious, fed in large part by the globalization of information, not only because they are morally right and have in themselves an intrinsic value, but because they work by responding to the needs of the people and producing better social and economic outcomes. If individuals feel they have a part in making a decision, they are more likely to respect and abide by it.

The overall picture is highly encouraging. However, in some places economic and social progress has stalled, or actually gone into reverse. Thirty years ago, Ghana's income equaled that of South Korea. Now, South Korea's income is equal to that of Portugal. Myanmar and Thailand had equal incomes in 1945. Recent progress has been decidedly uneven. But we need to examine why some countries have prospered while others have gone back, defying expectations. (In the 1950s, experts predicted that in Asia, Myanmar and the Philippines had the best chance of success.)

In 2000 at the United Nations Headquarters in New York, more than a hundred leaders solemnly agreed to what were grandly called "the Millennium Goals." Their noble ambition was the halving of world poverty within 15 years. Over the past quarter-century, Africa is the only continent that has become poorer in many places. Sub-Saharan Africa represents 10 percent of the world's population, but has two-thirds of all people with HIV/AIDS. Corruption costs Africa nearly $160 billion a year. Africa's debt has tripled over the past 25 years. Who is to blame? What should be done?

If a democratic country has a per-capita income of less than $1,500, its government has an average life expectancy of only eight years. Increase this to between $1,500 and $3,000, and the life of the government increases to around 18 years. Political scientists recognize that once income reaches $6,000, democratic governments become highly resilient. Or, as some see it, "Once rich, democracies become immortal."[6]

Does this mean that only rich countries can enjoy democracy? And what comes first: liberty and democracy, or wealth and democracy? Why, then, are some oil- and resource-rich countries not democratic? One study by Harvard economists Jeffrey Sachs and Andrew Warner found that nearly 100 developing countries discovered that being resource-rich was strongly linked to economic failure.

Studies into seven civil wars between 1965 and 1999 have explained that once an economy hits a threshold where one-quarter of its GDP originates from a commodity like oil, there is an irresistible tendency for rival groups to fight for control of the spoils. Another study found that each doubling of per-capita income reduces the probability that a country will experience a successful coup by between 40 percent and 70 percent. The richer a country is in resources, the slower its economy and freedoms grow. Saudi Arabia, Nigeria and other countries living off "rents" for oil and raw resources actually did worse than other countries. Why?

xliv   **Introduction**

As one commentator put it: "Easy money means a government does not need to tax its citizens."[7] When a government taxes people it has to provide benefits in return, beginning with services, accountability and good governance, but ending up with liberty and representation. The success of the West has been about protecting the rights of the people against the state and the powerful.

A study conducted by the World Bank's environmental department,[8] began by defining natural capital as the sum of non-renewable resources (including oil, natural gas, coal and mineral resources), cropland, pasture land, forested areas and protected areas. Many of us think of capital, produced or built, as the sum of machinery, equipment, and structures (including infrastructure) and urban land. The study concluded that "Human capital and the value of institutions (as measured by rule of law) constitute the largest share of wealth in virtually all countries." The rule of law explains 57 percent of a country's intangible capital. Education accounts for 36 percent.

"Rich countries are largely rich," the report said, "because of the skills of their populations and the quality of the institutions supporting economic activity." Taking into account all the world's natural resources and produced capital, 60 percent of the wealth of poor nations and 80 percent of the wealth of rich countries can be classified as "intangible wealth." What was particularly new in this World Bank report was the inclusion of a rule-of-law index, devised using several hundred individual variables measuring perceptions of governance, drawn from 25 separate data sources constructed by 18 different organizations that included civil society groups, political and business risk-rating agencies, and think-tanks.

Switzerland scores 99.5 out of 100 on the rule-of-law index and the United States hits 91.8. Contrast these figures with Burundi's 4.3 and Ethiopia's 16.4. The 30 wealthy developed nations comprising the Organization for Economic Cooperation and Development (OECD) have an average score of 90, while sub-Saharan Africa's is just 28.

The natural wealth in rich countries like the United States is a tiny proportion of their overall wealth—typically 1–3 percent—yet they derive more value from what they have. Cropland, pastures and forests are more valuable in rich countries because they can be combined with other capital, such as machinery and strong property rights, to produce more value. Machinery, buildings, roads and so forth account for 17 percent of the total wealth of rich countries.

Overall, the average per-capita wealth in the OECD countries is $440,000, comprising $10,000 in natural capital, $76,000 in produced capital, and $354,000 in intangible capital. (Switzerland has the highest per-capita wealth, at $648,000. The United States is fourth, at $513,000.)

By comparison, the World Bank study found that total wealth for the low-income countries averages $7,216 per person—$2,075 in natural capital, $1,150 in produced capital and $3,991 in intangible capital.

Proving once again the value of good governance, the study pointed to some countries which, because of civil strife, corruption and kleptomaniac regimes, have a declining, even negative, "intangible capital."

In the United States, natural capital is $15,000 per person, produced capital is $80,000 and intangible capital is $418,000. Its annual purchasing power parity GDP per capita is $43,800. Mexico's total natural capital per person is $8,500 ($6,000 due to oil), produced capital is $19,000 and intangible capital is $34,500—a total of $62,000 per person. Yet its GDP per capita is $10,700.[9]

Given these disparities, migration makes even more sense for desperate people or those with marketable skills. Any legal migrant who arrives in an OECD country has automatic access to about $440,000 of assets of this intangible wealth.

A country's resources and luck, therefore, are not decisive. Indeed too much of a good thing may be a hindrance in certain circumstances. It is the rule of law, democracy, the quality and ethics of government that give the advantage. And democracy, in its deepest and broadest sense, takes time to develop. It draws on the big ideas of centuries: good governance, strong, predicable institutions and the rule of law; openness to trade, competition and new ideas; and a functioning civil society. These are the important things; all the oil or jewels in the world can't replace them. Even in mature democracies we find that governments in power too long become arrogant and lose momentum. Governments, like babies' diapers, need changing—often for the same reason.

Most of these values need to be embraced at a local level. But, there's also an international dimension. The efforts of each country can and must be reinforced by international institutions. This is especially so with free trade. Market access for exports is a big factor in development and input to force up competition and expose local crony capitalists, making people freer and richer.

Collective responsibility

We need to persuade voters in rich democracies to think beyond their short-term interests. This is no easy task: the short-term protectionist's view is politically potent and still has many adherents, regardless of the overwhelming economic case to the contrary.

Leaving aside the economic merits, which a diminishing number of people will never accept, and the moral imperative implied by the equal value of all human life, which many quietly ignore, why should voters in rich countries worry about those on the outside? Why does it matter if those states that are not free, open or democratic do not progress, and if Western democracies do not help them? The reality is that failure can no longer so easily be quarantined in a modern world integrated as never before by technology and access to information. We walk away from failed states at our peril. The destruction of September 11, 2001 made it clear that no state, no matter where, should be allowed to fail. From this reality has come the doctrine of the responsibility to protect, which we will discuss later.

Failed states also function as breeding grounds for disease when millions of people cross natural borders every day. As we saw from the Severe Acute Respiratory Syndrome (SARS) scare, health problems can travel very quickly. A cough in Hong Kong can close down Toronto. One sick person can endanger the entire world. Two million children die every year from diarrhea alone. Only when every child is vaccinated will polio be eradicated. Diseases can be banished (as was shown with smallpox), and the sums of money required are not impossible to raise. It is the management and delivery of the funds that cause questions and problems.

Our borderless world has given terrorist groups a greater ability to raise resources globally. The command structures, discipline and organization of political groups as diverse as the IRA, FARC, ETA and Shining Path, who raised funds through bank robberies and extortion, have enabled them to go into even more fertile and imaginative ways of financing their "cause." Money-laundering and drug-running are now multi-billion-dollar enterprises. Many of these groups are now simply sordid gangs and warlords, their original cause having been subsumed in this evil industry. Indeed, some rogue states, and rogue elements within some failing states, see profit in such enterprises. The military in Myanmar and former KGB officials, for example, have turned to activities ranging from people smuggling and prostitution to illegal timber sales and the global drug trade. The North Koreans have been accused of filtering methamphetamines and other drugs into Japan, possibly through a North Korean government agency. Such behavior happens mainly in closed societies, not societies open to scrutiny, where the public demands action against such evils.

Surely the key message of our time is that we are all in this together. The issue of global climate change has removed any doubts on this. No country can solve that problem on its own, just as no country can isolate itself from the risks of inaction. That lesson is sinking in with regard to other global problems, too. Like it or not, the peoples of the world are tied closer together than ever.

History tells us that we can win: that in the main, the story of civilization is one of progress. That change is possible is attested to by the example of the IRA, which has become a positive force in a peaceful Ireland, and the fact that factional leaders are now making a positive contribution to the beleaguered government of Iraq.

All that's different now is that the speed of change has accelerated. How do we ensure we move peacefully into a new age, without the violence, pain, unemployment and poverty that have accompanied other major historic global changes? It will take bold internationalist policies as well as solid domestic policies in each country.

The best starting place is the concept of freedom. Liberal democracy holds the greatest promise for peace, development and general well-being. Genuine freedom relies on a broad range of factors beyond the simple right to vote, but it offers the best prospect for success nationally and internationally.

The purpose of this book, then, is to champion, unashamedly and unapologetically, the essential ingredients of freedom. Part 1 surveys some of the current issues surrounding globalization, development, the rise of China and India, the position of the Islamic world, and how the world is getting better. Part 2 then goes back in time to trace the origins of our current situation, through the history of the big ideas that drove progress (and the future shape of international architecture). Part 3 explores the pillars of freedom—good governance, openness, choice, civil society, and democracy. It also examines how technology can advance ownership and accountability and suggests how we can improve on the Western model of the welfare state by enhanced social mobility to build a more decent society. Part 4 examines and attempts to explain the new enemies of the open society, the enemies of reason, science and progress. In the final section, I bundle together various ideas, optimistic fears, possibilities and problems, and warn of historic follies under way at the moment.

A Note About Terminology

The word "liberal" has different meanings wherever you go. In Australia the conservative party formally calls itself "Liberal." In the United States, for many, "liberal" means "left;" for some, "very left." In the United Kingdom, it normally means open in social policy, tolerant and egalitarian, although the successor to the Liberal Party, the Liberal Democratic Party, would be seen now as "center left" and "greenish." European liberals are very pro-business, liberal in economic policy and strong free-traders, as was the original British party of that name. In the United States, Social Democrats are often confused with socialists or even communists. In New Zealand, Social Democratic (although the term is seldom used) means labor, center left, egalitarian, in favor of the welfare state.

If I were an American I'd describe myself as a Jackson or Moynihan Democrat; if British, New Labour. But I'm a New Zealander, so I'm just plain skeptical Labour.

PART 1

THE WORLD TODAY

This is not another book that surveys only contemporary issues and offers contemporary solutions. My thesis is, in fact, that challenges faced today by the global body politic are a progression of the debates and conflicts that have marked human development since the rise of the first civilizations. But let us first consider some of the most important trends in the world at the start of the twenty-first century. For while the issues may be variations on long-standing themes, we confront them within a context of faster, more widespread change than has been experienced by any society before us—and the pace of technological, social and political change is only going to accelerate over the next decade. How individual societies respond to that acceleration will determine their relevance in the coming world order—whether as open, emerging heavyweights such as fast-developing China and India, or the Islamic world, where those who wish to look forward are locked in battle with those who would drag us back to the Dark Ages.

I hope I offer some practical insights from the standpoint of a political practitioner-turned-theoretician.

CHAPTER 1

Accelerating Change and the Threat of De-Globalization

In his 1760 masterpiece *The Theory of Moral Sentiments,* Adam Smith noted that: "If [a citizen] were to lose his finger tomorrow, he would not sleep tonight, but provided he never saw them, he would snore with profound security over the ruin of hundreds of millions of his brethren." Humans have always been adept at blacking out suffering that is around the corner, over the hill, or in another country.

But it is becoming increasingly difficult to sleep the blessed sleep of the ignorant. Now, we know the pain of others—we see it on TV every night. The information revolution and globalization are destroying distance and knocking down walls with alarming speed. More than half the world's population now has access to a cell phone, with the numbers growing at a rate of millions a month. This has profound and positive implications for the advance of freedom. Governments and businesses in undemocratic or closed societies are losing their monopoly on information. This is leading steadily to the democratization, even privatization, of public and private policy-making. The growth of international trade is imposing the disciplines of the market—the demands and concerns of free consumers all around the world—on governments and regimes, from Beijing to Warsaw, that were previously resistant to change.

It is worth stepping back to marvel at the information revolution's transformative power. It is providing freedoms not previously imagined. The world's newspapers, radio stations and most sources of news are available to anyone, anywhere in the world, at any time, at the click of a mouse, either from the computer at home or at a cybercafé. People read, watch or listen only to what they want; choice is expanding. This is liberating. If I'm not happy with the local media's coverage of international news I can now safely ignore it and go direct to the *Financial Times, Guardian* or *Wall Street Journal* online. If I want a different "take" on a subject, I can watch Al Jazeera, China TV, FOX, BBC, French or German TV channels. Imagine how liberating this is for the millions who previously had no access to global opinion, or the ability to contribute and differ. Power continues to swing in favor of the consumer, whether in the realms of ideas, information or pop music. Consumers' choices have expanded as politicians' options have narrowed.

Technology costs relative to income have crashed. In my youth the dream of a working-class family was to own a set of the *Encyclopedia Britannica*. It cost a year's pay then; now it's an hour's pay to buy a DVD; less on the internet. Twenty-five years ago, phone connections carried fax messages over a copper wire at one page a second; now live videos can be streamed through mobile phones. Millions of pages of information can be moved in minutes.

Nobody can predict where all this will lead. Just how much of a shock does the future hold? Predictions throughout history have often been well wide off the mark. Thomas Edison thought the phonograph would be used mainly to record people's wills and perhaps some office dictation. The Mercedes motor company in 1903 envisaged that "there will never be more than a million cars worldwide. It's implausible that more than a million artisans would be trainable as chauffeurs." More embarrassing was the 1897 claim attributed, probably apocryphally, to United States Commissioner of Patents Charles H. Duell: "Everything that can be invented has been invented." In 1795 Immanuel Kant's essay *Perpetual Peace* suggested that the nation-state would ultimately become almost irrelevant, and, a few decades later, Karl Marx agreed. The state would wither, Marx heroically predicted.

In 1992, Francis Fukuyama's triumphant best-seller, *The End of History and The Last Man*, explained the victory of democratic capitalist ideals: we win, you lose. Then came 9/11. The short period from the collapse of the Berlin Wall to 9/11 was, perhaps, one of absolute hope and certainty. Then came another best-seller, given credibility by 9/11. In *The Clash of Civilizations*, Samuel P. Huntington warned of a fearful new war between civilizations in the wake of the collapse of the Soviet Union, causing a rise in nationalistic, tribal and religious impulses—a struggle along religious fault lines, he argued. D. K. Matai, founder of the Asymmetric Threats Contingency Alliance, writes of the convergence of a bio, info, nano revolution and how humanity faces the unknown of a future dominated by mass robotics and climate change, which could change everything. "The stock market," he said, "is an indication of instability from a geo-political standpoint, and from a financial standpoint. We are encountering the instability inherent in not being able to plan for the future." In his book *Black Swan*, Nassim Nicholas Taleb points to challenges beyond our comprehension: "A black swan event is [one] outside the realm of our expectations, because nothing in the past can convincingly point to its possibility." Everyone thought swans were white, until black swans were discovered in Australia. Risk management becomes even riskier given the pace of change, and the black swans will arrive in flocks in the twenty-first century. The are no simple answers: the world of uncertainty is here.

The truth is we don't know exactly what will happen. We can only do our best, make decisions based on rational research and adjust when necessary. We can confidently predict that the present system will change, that new players, products, threats and opportunities will arise. How to adapt, keeping and advancing the best of what we have achieved, is the issue.

This book explains that the system is worth saving, and will succeed so long as it evolves and corrects itself when it over-reaches. That's the pattern of progress. It's an ironic fact of history that it's frequently up to the liberal and left-leaning social democrats to rescue capitalism when it runs out of control. After rescuing capitalism in the 1930s and receiving abuse from business, FDR famously commented that those he'd saved from drowning complained that he had mislaid their top hats.

Disruptive change: The information age

The ability of people anywhere on the planet to move capital and information across the world at light speed is transforming the old economy and creating unbelievable wealth—both for the masters of this new world and for the millions who benefit from the advances in productivity.

The information economy reinforces economist Paul Krugman's Nobel Prize-winning argument that extended David Ricardo's nineteenth-century theory of competitive advantage. The downside of this causes political problems in developed countries that politicians struggle to answer. "But, China, India and Chile can produce everything we can at a fraction of the price," we are told. The knee-jerk response to this is protectionism. Krugman points out that most trade and investment is still between economies of a similar nature—Canada, the US, the EU, and Japan. This brings into play an explanation of economics of scale, agglomeration. Clusters of skills and innovation are important for development and new, creative industries. Nations with similar endowments and labor costs do trade more extensively with each other because, as Krugman explained, there is such a thing as product differentiation. Even though they might live in Detroit, some people are attracted to Peugeot or VW cars. What is changing is the supply chain where various components and parts are sourced, where supply is most price- and quality-effective. Innovation is still the key to sustained creative growth.

Wars always drive new technologies and methods to kill and produce more because in times of crisis old habits are swept away. Women entered the workforce during the First World War, sweeping away old protectionist procedures. The Space Race and the Cold War gave us new technologies and the internet. The Iraq war has seen far fewer deaths because previously deadly catastrophic wounds can now be treated. These life-saving technologies will migrate to health systems. Remote doctors, far from the field, can operate via robots. This will affect small local hospitals; ambulances will one day be outfitted so that surgeons far from the scene of an accident can save lives. Specialists in Mumbai and Boston may be able to operate on patients anywhere. It is sad that it takes a war to provide the impetus to sweep away old bureaucracies and procedures, but war has always produced fresh research resources. In our parents' day, heart-attack patients were advised to stay in bed for weeks; now we insist they get up and out quickly. Pregnant mothers once spent weeks in hospital; now they go home as soon as possible. All this changes the way we run hospitals but not the way we judge them.

Who knows what effect the massive advances in genomics, proteomics, nanotechnology or any of the other new fields of scientific endeavor will have on the way we live in five years' time, let alone 20 years. All we can say is that some things that we think will be revolutionary won't be, and some technologies yet to be invented will yield great benefits.

Now, in theory at least, whole populations will have direct access to information without waiting for it to be filtered through a government or the media—or, indeed, filtered at all. This raises all sorts of issues for the way leaders deal with their people. As Kofi Annan commented, "If you are into control, it's frightening. This thing [globalization] cannot stop."

Rapidly advancing countries, such as China, haven't entirely been able to shun the anarchic power of the internet. They cannot escape the texting communications revolution that sees messages, and ideas, spreading through communities faster than any army of bureaucrats can monitor. Governments which have opened their economies fully to the outside world are feeling the full force of the change. Democracy and freedom will only advance with the internet and globalization. Open economies eventually force open political systems and hold the powerful accountable. That is why tyrants fear information. They fear the people, because knowledge is power.

New technologies can liberate ordinary people. E-governance can allow governments in underdeveloped places to leapfrog over incompetent, corrupt agencies and civil services, as evidenced in the Indian state of Andhra Pradesh, which has 1 million public servants to service a population of 75 million. The fact that the government has had a monopoly on all sorts of services—issuance of drivers' licenses, admission to schools, payment of utility bills, registration of property— over many decades has helped sustain a vast, corrupt system of favors. Since 2002, the state has put a complex variety of services online and set up public kiosks to service the system. Land title searches that previously took many days now take only minutes. Copies of documents that once took weeks to obtain are now available on call. In Hyderabad alone it was estimated that queuing to pay power bills cost people $45 million a month in lost wages. Now an e-service system allows citizens to pay bills online at a kiosk, without having to queue or pay the "speed-up" money that so corrupted the system.

Technological advance has accelerated the recent bout of globalization. Few words excite such passion as "globalization." It is a process not a policy, and should be neither demonized nor idealized. In fact, there are those who argue that there is less trade now as a percentage of GNP than there was a hundred years ago. The proportion of people migrating permanently is certainly lower than it was a hundred years ago. In the main, the renewed globalization of the past few decades has been a good thing.

Globalization and the information revolution increase sympathy and solidarity across nations. Markets punish countries and companies that indulge in bad practices. A global market has greater power and reach than an isolated and closed one. Now everyone is everyone else's neighbor and potential customer, and outraged public opinion at home or on the other side of the world can force governments to act.

Many people still fear the Orwellian Big Brother state. They worry that technology brings more power, greater opportunities and more temptation to those in charge of the state. There are now few places you can wander in London without being watched by a CCTV camera. Technologies to tax the movements of your car will enable the state to know where you are at any given time. But, in reality, the opposite is actually happening: we are watching Big Brother, exposing its propensity for corruption, arrogance and stupidity.

The global economy

The continued integration of economies and the increase in world trade is allowing more and more countries to hop on the elevator to rapid economic and social progress. Some, sadly, stubbornly persist with waiting on the sidelines, notwithstanding the obvious differences between Myanmar and Thailand, North and South Korea and other neighboring countries that have taken different paths in the past 50 years.

There has never been a period in the history of our species where we've seen freedoms and living standards rise so consistently for most people. Property rights and ownership have also been vital. Globalization cannot be stopped, and nor should it be. The question is how we should manage it; how we can insist that more people in more countries share in the opportunities it offers.

We have the levers, but in many countries leaders just refuse to pull them. To ignore economic reality and reject good governance principles is a bit like an overweight chain-smoker saying, "I'll give up and go on a diet in five years." Nations that do not understand this will be punished. The future will not be gentle. New ideas and technology wait for no-one; they crash through, making old industries, procedures and ideas redundant.

We live in an interdependent world which is not yet fully politically integrated. Science, commerce and technology are advancing faster than our political, ethical or legal capacity to cope. Some computer nerd in the Ukraine flicks out a virus and ruins my day in Auckland. Yet we know that no nation, mighty or modest, can prosper, be free from terrorism, enjoy clean air, manage a tax system, or even run an airline, without the cooperation of others.

It seems to be a world of limitless opportunity. Within the space of 20 years, we've seen most of Central and Eastern Europe break free of bondage; 30 years ago, Spain and Portugal were under fascist control and all of Spanish-speaking America was under some form of military rule. Now Cuba alone is a one-party state. In Asia, people power has produced more democratic regimes, from South Korea to the Philippines to Indonesia. In China, people have never been freer, and those freedoms are growing.

Globalization has not meant the end of democracy, nor has it meant, as some have suggested, the end of the nation-state. On the contrary; three-quarters of the national currencies, flags and anthems at the United Nations did not exist 50 years ago.

Then there is the argument that globalization is a plot by big business. Read the *Fortune 500*—the list has changed fundamentally from 10 or 20 years ago. If globalization is a plot, it has been a spectacular failure. The world is littered with chief executives and businesses that have gone belly-up; great companies have disappeared or been reconfigured to survive. For example, the iconic US company Western Union almost collapsed when telegrams were replaced by better technology. The company now earns $1 billion a year through migrant remittances and transfers, and is reported to have five-times more locations worldwide than McDonald's, Wal-Mart, Burger King, and Starbucks combined. Within a decade, a stamp with a computer chip in it to trace mailed letters will be cheaper than the cost of the envelope. How many trees and how much pollution has been prevented by the email and internet revolution?

Through my work with the WTO, it became clear that the organization was widely seen to be an "American Wall Street plot;" yet according to Thompson Financial in 2006, the fast-growing BRIC economies (Brazil, Russia, India and China) were producing the best results of major stock markets.

Has globalization led to a world run by logos? Is this dangerous? What is a brand but a reputation? All a brand represents is the goodwill and trust stored up over years of success. After the crooked dealings of Enron, former chairman of the United States Federal Reserve, Alan Greenspan, reminded us, "In virtually all transactions, we rely on the word of those with whom we do business. There was a time before commercial law and courts when all people had was their reputation. It's still important."

A reputation is vulnerable. It's hard to win, and easy to lose. Corporates live in a world of free information, populated by investigative journalists, NGOs, and opportunist politicians on the prowl for a headline. Business and government must conduct themselves in a more ethical and transparent manner. Virtue will be prized and rewarded. Companies will have to explain themselves.

To those activists who fear the worst I'd say, we need to get a little real from time to time and base our arguments on facts and evidence. For example, Nike has been attacked for ripping off workers in Vietnam. However, officials in Vietnam have told me that Nike pays five times the average wage, and this is causing enormous problems because even doctors and professors are clamoring to get onto the factory floor to get a higher income.

Perhaps it's little different from Victorian England. The rich had their flash, huge mansions, and thought things were great. But it was no good being the richest person in Manchester, with the biggest house, if the cleaner and cook came in and brought influenza or some other disease to you. The Victorians responded by inventing municipal socialism, public goods, clean water and public sewerage. We have to do this on a global basis because we cannot live in isolation from the influences, good and bad, of others.

If you're digging up gold in Africa, you've got to price into the cost of each ounce of gold the cost of AIDS. If you're employing someone in Zimbabwe, you've got to employ three people, because two of them will die. Companies are waking up to this and are putting together health programs for their workers. They know that if they don't do it, some governments will tax and steal from them.

It is good business to be a good citizen. Increasingly, we hear of how investment funds are insisting on ethical behavior. This blowtorch of transparency is a cleansing agent for the business and political world. None of this should replace the solemn duty of the state, but when the state does not function, other players must move in.

We get improvements in society and politics because people in free societies demand better outcomes. Thirty years ago, no country had a Minister of the Environment. Now every country has one. Twenty years ago, very few political parties had manifestos on gay rights or gender rights. Now every political party has to make a case. That's responding to the political market. The political market will correct itself, given the opportunity. People will make wise decisions, given the opportunity.

If people worry about corporate power, I say they should pray for globalization. Freeing trade curbs domestic giants by exposing them to competition. Closed domestic markets, where national champions cozy up to governments, are more likely to harbor monopolies than open ones. Even though many global companies are getting bigger, this does not necessarily give them more clout. It's the absence of competitors, not their own size, that gives companies power. Open markets make life difficult for crony capitalists looking to purchase privileges from politicians against the interests of workers and consumers.

Globalism is seen as a gigantic invisible hand crushing the world. Most trade is still local: exports account for less than 10 percent of the United States' GDP and less than 20 percent of Britain's. About 25 percent of world trade takes place between countries sharing a common border, and about half still takes place between partners that are less than 3,000 kilometers apart.

In the poorest countries, it's not globalization they fear; it's marginalization. We get the impression from the media that everyone in developing countries is chanting, "Yankee, go home," when the reality is closer to "Yankee, come here," and, more recently, "China, come here, too, please." The poorer, most marginalized countries want access to global market investments, as well as the latest technology and the latest ideas and medicine.

That's why protectionist policies from rich countries that spend a billion dollars a day on agricultural subsidies, while locking out producers of sugar, cotton and coffee from poorer countries, are such a disgrace.

Open trade and good governance are all about attacking poverty and privilege. Given proper rules and opportunity, the market does both. From time to time, we need to draw breath and revisit the ideas of the founders of modern economics, and the Enlightenment, upon which our civilization is based. More than 200 years ago, Immanuel Kant wrote that durable peace could be built upon the tripod of representative democracy, international organizations and economic dependence. It was he who first coined the phrase "a League of Nations." And in 1776 Adam Smith wrote, "Commerce and manufacturing can seldom flourish in any state in which there's not a certain degree of confidence in the justice of the government." Investment, and thus jobs, will go where it can get the best and most secure results.

Change is always unsettling. In the West, "outsourcing" has become the focus of political attention. Essentially, the internet and the communications revolution have abolished time and distance. Any job that is not "shop front" can be moved anywhere. There's no difference between sending information upstairs and sending it a continent away. In the 1980s, heavy industry and manufacturing jobs moved to developing countries, creating restructuring and rust belts in OECD countries. Now the same is happening to white-collar jobs—call-centers being the most obvious beneficiary of this, with India alone gaining 500 new jobs every day in the middle of this decade and countries like the Philippines entering the market strongly. Whether the US economic slowdown will accelerate the cost-driven outsourcing trend or lead to cutbacks globally will be a matter of great interest. However, increased transport costs are giving local producers an extra competitive edge.

To the consternation of many Western families, the service sector in developed countries, long insulated from international competition, is now outsourcing to highly educated, motivated competitors in India and China. Doctors in the United States and Europe are sending blood samples and x-rays to India for diagnostic testing. Legal and accounting firms, researchers and software developers are also moving non face-to-face services offshore. Management consultants McKinsey report that while around 90 percent of services are now carried out in-house, within 10 years this will decline to 60 percent. For every $1 that is offshored, a company gains 58 cents in cost savings, with no drop in quality. Sierra Atlantic, a US software company, claims that a majority of venture capitalists in Silicon Valley require start-up companies to subcontract some work offshore. India's share of this work has grown at 60 percent a year since 2000.

Economic history and the laws of competitive advantage have not been abolished. IT, biotech, nanotech, or pharmaceutical research companies cannot afford to lose their competitive edge or they will miss out and disappear. Protectionism can save jobs in the short term, but that's at the expense of better new jobs; long term, you will end up with neither. Jobs are already moving from China to Africa to take advantage of lower wages there. That's the system working; wealth spreading from country to country, from the developed to the developing. Consumers gain because of cheaper prices, companies gain from lower input costs, and developing countries gain new jobs and new wealth; and their middle class become our customers of the future.

A study by Britain's Centre for Economic and Business Research concluded that outsourcing will have a net positive impact on the British economy by reducing costs and creating higher-skilled and better-paid jobs. Aviva, HSBC, and Lloyds TSB announced in 2006 that 7,000 jobs were going to Asia, and it was predicted that 200,000 UK jobs would migrate there over the next five years:

> Outsourcing will boost the United Kingdom economy by $16 billion in that same period, and narrow the productivity gap the United Kingdom faces... Even if the only result of outsourcing is to cut costs, this gets passed on through lower prices and gives consumers more purchasing power. And if inflation is lower, this creates a lower interest rate environment which will also benefit consumers.[1]

The same study found that nearly all people who lost jobs to outsourcing were re-employed, with 388 in every 500 going on to higher-paid and higher-skilled jobs. In this new world, middle-class families in the West can now afford qualified, specialist tuition for their children—so long as the teachers work out of India.

Politics is perception, not reality. As a politician who knows the language of the street-corner meeting and door-to-door canvassing, I am haunted by one "TV grab" I saw during the 2004 US election campaign. A middle-aged South Carolina voter explained how, having lost his textile job to China, he had then retrained himself in information technology only to lose that job to India. Now, he explained, he was studying real estate because "that's the one job that can't go offshore." It's a big task trying to explain the theory of creative destruction, or how infrastructural inefficiencies are a tax on every other job, or how lower input costs make us more competitive, to an unemployed 50-year-old who likes to think of himself as more than an input.

I went to Cambodia to help get the country into the WTO. Twentieth-century history does not get worse than in Cambodia—millions murdered; the population of Phnom Penh reduced from a million to just 30 people; fewer than 100 graduates left alive in the country. When I flew into that ancient capital late at night there were only a few dozen lights showing. In an earlier era, they might have been bars and brothels. They were, however, cybercafés, with queues of young people waiting for their chance to be a part of another future, a wider world.

Property rights: Not glamorous but still the star

Much of the progress and success I've explained is based on property rights. They, too, are easily undermined even in the most mature of economies.

Piracy is a multi-billion-dollar business, far larger than in the now-romantic age, immortalized by Hollywood and Errol Flynn, when Queen Elizabeth I licensed and knighted privateers to finance her ambitions.

The right of passage for shipping was one of the first treaties of modern times. A coalition of the willing drew the United States military into the battle with the Barbary pirates in North Africa, a decisive action that broke with an isolationist foreign policy based on George Washington's warning to beware of foreign entanglements. The US doctrine of preventative attack was established and lives today: "Nothing is new but the history you have not read," as President Harry Truman once commented.

Some governments today, like Elizabeth I, reward privateers who steal from others. This is changing, and it must. Ordinary consumers may see piracy as a bit of a joke: buying rip-off CDs or a fake Rolex at the flea market seems harmless enough. It's theft, nevertheless. The US Chamber of Commerce suggests that the annual cost of piracy to the national economy is now $250 billion, at the expense of 750,000 jobs, as well as exposing consumers to potentially defective products.

Even counterfeit motorbikes and cars are in circulation. Perhaps the world will only take this issue seriously when an aircraft crashes because of counterfeit parts. Medicine is another area where callous crooks are prospering. Millions pray daily for a cure for AIDS and cancer. But when drugs are stolen and duplicated illegally, why should investors put their money, your savings and pension funds, into finding cures if they don't own the result? And the standards and quality of such drugs are suspect. Protestors claimed that WTO intellectual-property rules helped the spread of AIDS. However, they soon came to realize that the WTO rules do allow for parallel importing at a time of designated crisis. Brazil and other countries are now using the WTO exemption to make their own generic drugs, and NGOs are urging countries to protect WTO rules in regard to medicines.

Common customs-valuation agreements are central to keeping business clean and products moving. Cleaning up trade facilitation offers great benefits to business and governments at both ends.

APEC research shows that reforming trade facilitation brings greater economic gains for the Asia-Pacific region than abolishing tariffs. Inter-American Development Bank research explains that taking a container from Country A to Country C through Country B costs 200 hours: 100 hours is spent at the borders. Getting a container from North Africa to New York can take three times longer than getting a container from Hong Kong through the Panama Canal to New York. Where such inefficiencies exist, governments lose revenue, businesses incur costs, and investors stay away from countries that desperately need investment. Yet the technology and systems exist to clean up this costly mess.

There must be common international standards and binding, enforceable agreements between countries to make this work. That's where the WTO comes in. Intellectual property and trade facilitation are on the agenda of the Doha Development Round of trade negotiations.

Progress is complicated and difficult, especially when so many developing countries do not have the bureaucratic capacity, or sometimes the political will, to do the job. Why stamp out corruption if you are a beneficiary of it?

Development under threat?

On almost every useful measurement of the human condition, we have seen the greatest advances ever in the history of our species during the last half-century. Indeed, these advances are accelerating in most parts of the world. But there is always room for improvement. There is still much to protest about, and injustice is still rampant in far too many places where the enemies of reason continue to plot and plan.

However, there is much to celebrate. Never have more people lived in free, democratic societies and had choices in the marketplace. Even in the few remaining one-party states, freedoms are growing. To suggest that the world is becoming less free, or that we have not made remarkable progress over the past century, is simply not true.

Let's not forget that in 1900 male life expectancy in America was 49 years. In the 1920s, the majority of US farms didn't have electricity. In 1940, just 1 percent of African-American families were classified as middle class (that is, earning twice as much as the poverty line). Across the Atlantic, pollution in the River Thames contributed to cholera epidemics that killed over 35,000 people between 1831 and 1866. In 1952, smog killed 4,000 people in London in one week, and over the following three months 12,000 more died of smog-related complications. Cities such as London, Los Angeles and Pittsburgh, once heavily polluted, are now much cleaner. New Delhi and Beijing, while polluted, are about as filthy as London was 60 years ago. This is not to say that this is in any way acceptable. But this is an evolutionary process. Despite what the nay-sayers might claim, a greater proportion of the world's population today enjoys better living conditions than ever before. World GDP growth overall in 1993 was just 1.2 percent, and inflation was out of control across the developing world. Little more than a decade later, thanks to wider liberalization and competition, the average rate of real GDP growth was 3 percent and total growth over the period was 45 percent. These figures jump to 3.9 percent and 65 percent respectively when national GDPs are weighted to account for differences between countries (known as PPP, purchasing power parity). Inflation globally dropped to just 3.7 percent in 2005.

World population increased by 18 percent during this period but living standards rose, on a PPP basis, by 40 percent.[2] In 1993, the proportion of people living on $1 a day or less was 22 percent; by 2001 this had dropped to 17.8 percent. The World Bank estimates that by 2015 this will fall to about 9 percent. And that's without the completion of the Doha Trade Round, which could lift 300 million people out of extreme poverty.

More than 85 percent of the world's inhabitants can expect to live for at least 60 years—more than twice as long as a hundred years ago—while deaths from infectious diseases are expected to drop from 9.3 million to 6.5 million. In developing countries, life expectancy has risen from about 30 years at the beginning of the twentieth century to 65 in 1999. The trend is improving in most places, although the gap between rich and poor countries remains. Life expectancy is still much higher in OECD countries (where the average person born now can expect to reach 100 years) and much worse in sub-Saharan Africa. There are huge areas of concern about the impact of AIDS in Africa, as well as the recent decline in life expectancy in the former Soviet republics. However, many developing countries are now about where developed countries were a hundred years ago. When Queen Elizabeth II first came to the throne, she sent out 250 telegrams a year congratulating individuals achieving their hundredth birthday; now it's 3,000. For the first time in the history of humanity, people over the age of 60 will outnumber those under 15 by 2047. (This, of course, will bring a fresh set of challenges, not the least being health and retirement costs.)

Infant-mortality rates have also significantly improved. Worldwide, the under-five mortality rate went down from 123 to 78 per 1,000 between 1980 and 1999. In low-income countries, it dropped from 177 to 116 (the largest drop being in South Asia, from 121 to 89).

According to the World Bank, even in troubled Bangladesh per-capita income rose fourfold between 1972 and 2003; poverty dropped by a third; life expectancy increased by 40 percent; and primary school enrolment went up by 8 percent. More than half-a-billion people have been lifted out of extreme poverty in India and China over the past 30 years.

Thomas Robert Malthus was wrong. The Green Revolution has been victorious. We now have far more food per person than we used to, even though the world's population has doubled since 1961. Production in developing countries has tripled, and enlarged international trade has played a key role in enhancing food security. Globally, the proportion of people starving in the developing world fell from 45 percent in 1949 to 35 percent in 1970 and to 18 percent in 1997—and the United Nations expects that figure to fall to 12 percent by 2010. The global economy grew by 5.4 percent in 2006, outstripping population growth by 1 percent. At this rate, world poverty can be cut in half by 2015, meeting the United Nations Millennium Goals for poverty reduction, except in sub-Saharan Africa.[3]

Most predictions about the population explosion have been proven wrong, especially in countries that have become more open and progressive. The United Nations has revised its global fertility rate down from 2.1 to 1.85, and now predicts that the world population will peak and begin to decrease in 2050, earlier if the global economy continues to grow. It's a statistical fact that the biggest families occur in societies that have yet to learn the lessons of democracy and how to create and share wealth.

We are living longer and better because we have made important progress in obtaining better access to clean water, medicine, sanitation and food: the greatest boost to life expectancy in London's history was the invention of the public sewerage and water system. The percentage of doctors in poor countries has doubled, despite a massive migration of graduates to OECD countries. There is clear evidence of a link between democracy and better social and environmental outcomes. Totalitarian societies of the left or right always produce the worst results. The rise of petro-authoritarian societies and regimes from Venezuela to Iran, and ominous rumblings in Russia, has produced another pattern of political behavior born from resource wealth.

While we will never do enough to improve the lot of mankind globally (because no one will ever accept that the human journey is over), we have experienced the most stunning advances in the history of our species. For the first time, more people will die from obesity-related diseases than direct starvation.

Given this, it is remarkable how the sudden rise of food prices in 2007–2008 has raised insecurities about global food supply and threatened the advances made over the past 50 years. In the 12 months from mid-2007, corn and rice prices doubled, the wheat price tripled, and soy bean prices leapt by 87 percent. Global food reserves slipped to their lowest recorded levels. Already more than 100 million of the poorest have slipped further into desperate poverty. Riots, hoarding, and pilfering from farms have become commonplace from Egypt to the Philippines. In Thailand and Pakistan, troops have been deployed to stop the theft of food from farms and warehouses. Major producers such as Argentina and Vietnam have moved to restrict agricultural exports or increase export taxes on farm produce, leading to protests and political tensions. The World Food Program has described food insecurity as a threat to peace as well as to adequate nutrition. Most of the nations worst affected by spiraling world food prices are in Africa.

For the causes of this, we must look at a complex combination of global factors. China and India, whose low-cost exports were welcomed by consumers everywhere and helped keep global inflation down for a decade, are now exporting inflation because of their spiraling demands for energy and new types of food. China was self-sufficient in energy until the late 1980s, but is now the world's second-biggest importer of energy. The increase in its energy demand over the past five years has been equal to Japan's total energy consumption. Energy costs feed into agricultural prices through the increased cost of fertilizer and distribution.

In a bid to break its addiction to Middle East oil, the US has moved to a populist bio-fuel program that is really just another sordid subsidy to farmers in the Mid-West, since the ethanol program actually consumes more energy than it saves. The bio-fuel needed to fill the tank of an SUV represents the grain needed to feed an African family for a year. Up to a third of world food price increases can be traced to those programs, which have resulted in up to a third of some US crops being diverted to create automobile fuel. Meanwhile, a 30 percent tariff ensures that an efficient, non-subsidized Brazilian bio-fuel is kept off the US market.

Such was the crisis that the UN, World Bank, IMF, WTO and senior finance members pushed through a move to provide US$500 million in urgent food aid by May 1, 2008. This is a good short-term move to put food in the mouths of the world's poorest, but how can you encourage poor countries to grow food when surplus production from rich countries, whose farmers are subsidized to the tune of a billion dollars a day, can be dropped into the local market for as little as a third of the local price?

The medium- and long-term solution has to be the Doha Development Trade Round, because all of these subsidies are on the table. If the deal was done in agriculture alone, Africa would receive on an annual basis four to five times the total of all of its aid and debt relief put together. Access to international markets and the ability to compete on a level playing field would encourage investment in the inadequate infrastructure that currently means that half of all African agricultural production doesn't make it to market. If rich countries cannot summon up the political will to take on their cosseted farmers, a small percentage of whom consume over 80 percent of the subsidies that distort global food markets, then they must accept responsibility for global hunger. Politicians naturally think short-term—the next headline, the next election. Sadly, much of the world risks being reduced to even more short-term needs—finding the next meal.

Water: The new oil?

Water is the raw material of life. There is no substitute. But, of all the water on the planet, less than 3 percent is fresh. Of that, about 0.3 percent is contained in lakes and rivers, with the polar ice caps, glaciers, and permanent snow accounting for over 69 percent, and 0.9 percent is attributable to soil moisture, swamp water, and permafrost. The remainder comes from natural underground sources and ground water.

The world has seen a sixfold increase in water usage since 1900. The demand for fresh water is currently increasing at twice the population growth, and the world's population is predicted to increase from six billion to eight billion within 25 years. Each year, 23 million people worldwide die because of unsafe water, three million killed by diarrhea alone. Three-quarters of all diseases have to do with bad hygiene and unsafe water. Pesticide pollution carried by water increases the hazards and puts even more people in danger. The UN Food and Agriculture Organization (FAO) reports that in the 1990s South Africa's poor spent about three hours a day hauling water to their homes, while in a typical middle-class household in OECD countries people can pay for a day's worth of water in one or two minutes' work. The price of water in the poorest areas of South Africa is thus about 25 times the price of water in a modern, middle-class area.

Having said that, it should be noted that in developing countries access to good water has increased from 30 percent in 1970 to 80 percent in 2000. The World Watch Institute's studies report that 30–90 percent of water could be saved at no additional cost to industry.

Irrigation accounts for two-thirds of global use of fresh water, but less than half of that actually reaches the roots of plants. Drip irrigation systems have been shown to effect consistent reduction in waste water by 30–70 percent, while increasing yield by 20–90 percent.[4] Israel is now reusing 65 percent of its domestic water waste for crop production, freeing up fresh water for households and industry. Singapore recycles and proudly sells this as clean drinking water.

The European Commission reports that water consumption in Madrid fell by 29 percent between 1992 and 1994, saving 100 million cubic meters each year. Aged, inefficient water-distribution systems create losses estimated at 30 percent throughout Europe and, in certain urban networks, may reach 70–80 percent.

Efficiency is another word for conservation. Honest, transparent costing sends market signals that will be responded to by consumers. In Australia, you can buy a ton of water from the tap for less than a bottle of Perrier. Inefficient pricing stalls research and development. Only the rich have the resources to invest in new technologies and research such as genetic engineering to produce crops that are more salt-resistant and use fewer pesticides and less water. The arrogant indulgence of the rich environmentalists who resist such research is mind-numbingly short-sighted. Low-cost, targeted schemes are beginning to work in the most difficult places. The ANC government scored success in South Africa by bringing water to thousands of villages, and in Kenya 50,000 more people are drinking clean water as a result of low-scale projects funded by the United States-based Overseas Private Investment Corporation.

We know what works; we have the systems and the research. The capacity is there. What we can't seem to do is to organize the political will to unleash the creative capacity to do the job. The political, economic and military—even terrorist—potential arising from this crisis may force results. (Water as politics is by no means new. In 1503

Leonardo da Vinci and Machiavelli planned to divert the Arno River away from Pisa during its conflict with Florence.)

Authoritarian rulers, who are themselves rarely affected by famines or similar economic calamities tend to lack the incentive to take timely preventive measures. Democratic governments, in contrast, have to win elections and face public criticism, and thus have strong incentives to undertake measures to avert such catastrophes. It is not surprising that never in the history of the world has a famine ever taken place in a functioning democracy—be it economically rich (as in contemporary Western Europe or North America) or relatively poor (as in post-Independence India, or Botswana, or Bolivia).

Fishing for fair food management

Zimbabwe reported its first food shortages since independence following Robert Mugabe's political repression and protectionist policies. Famines have tended to occur in colonial regimes governed by overseas rulers (as in British India or in an Ireland administered by alienated English rulers), or in one-party states (as in the Ukraine in the 1930s, China during 1958–61, or Cambodia in the 1970s), or in military dictatorships (as in Ethiopia or Somalia, or some of the Sahel countries in the recent past).

There is much evidence to suggest that China's leaders were reassured by their own propaganda and by statistics based more on the desire of cadres not to disappoint than on reality, while 30 million people died of starvation during the Great Leap Forward. China finally rejected its previous policies, and is allowing farmers to own and trade their production, with stunning results.

We have reduced poverty more in the last 50 years than in the previous 500, and it has been reduced in practically every country that is free of war. Columbia University's Xavier Sala-i-Martin agreed with the UNDP view that inequality has probably increased, on average, within countries; but on inequality across countries, he had this to say:

> The increasing integration of the world's economies does not inevitably increase the inequality of incomes. The nineteenth century saw an explosion of inequality, but by the middle of the twentieth century it had stopped rising. The proportion of the world's population in absolute poverty is now lower than it has ever been.[5]

Indeed, although the total number of poor has remained about the same (1.2 billion), the proportion of poor people has been more than halved from around 50 percent in 1950. Thus, over the past 50 years, some 3.4 billion more people have risen out of poverty.

The Millennium Goals mentioned earlier were confirmed and given political momentum at what has become known as the Monterey Consensus, after a summit of leaders in Mexico. I was there, pushing for the Doha Development Round which the World Bank suggested would lift 300 million people out of extreme poverty in a decade and lift incomes in wealthy countries through more-effective use of resources. Those who say globalization and the world trading system are unfair management are correct, but that is reason to advance and widen global trading, not to reduce trade and opportunity. For most countries, it is the absence of trade that hurts.

To make things even better we need to move through the Doha Development Round on a number of areas. The most important of these is agriculture, which could return up to five times more to Africa than all the aid and loan write-offs put together. As we saw earlier, rich countries subsidize agriculture to the tune of a billion dollars a day: as always, a direct tax on the poor to subsidize the rich. United States cotton subsidies cost nearly $4 billion a year. In 2001, three times more went to United States cotton growers (equivalent to $156,000 per farmer) than all the US aid to sub-Saharan Africa.

The story of sugar is as bad, and coffee is even worse. Coffee is the major export of some of the poorest countries in the world. Yet when these countries try to add value, by processing and working locally, the United States and Europe escalate their tariffs accordingly, keeping jobs and profit from local, poor producers. This appalling story is true too of protectionist policies in the Nordic countries, Switzerland and Japan. It's the rich in poor countries who always do best out of these subsidies. India's elite and the agricultural elite in America, Japan and Europe have much in common and much to protect. The second-biggest item in New Delhi's agriculture budget is fertilizer subsidies.

In the words of the Indian Government, two-thirds of all subsidy-spending is non-merit: it goes to the "non-poor."[6] India's support systems were designed to reduce poverty. A small proportion of rich farmers harvest nearly all the subsidies.[7] But they are, as elsewhere, a potent, political force; not just because of their income but because the politicians and bureaucrats get their share of the action also. The coalition for reforming these policies must be the poor in rich countries and the poorest in poor countries, who suffer most from the ever-rising taxes.

On all levels, we have become more civilized and more aware. Poverty is a disease for which there is a cure. Millions of people in the West have been mobilized to put pressure on their leaders, and poverty in poor countries is increasingly on the agenda of domestic politics in rich countries. Votes are now involved and that has to be a good thing.

One trade issue on which (at last) environmentalists are supporting the Doha Development Round is fishing subsidies. It is known that some 2.6 billion people get at least 20 percent of their total animal protein from fish, and 1 billion people depend on fish as their primary source of protein. The FAO claims that 75 percent of the world's fish population is over-exploited, fully exploited, significantly depleted, or recovering from over-exploitation. A significant proportion of the world's big predator fish, such as marlin, tuna and swordfish, has simply gone. The global fishing fleet capacity is now 250 percent greater than the capacity required to catch what the world's oceans can sustainably produce. Fishing subsidies encourage inefficient, energy-costly over-fishing. The University of British Columbia suggests that annual fishing subsidies cost $30–34 billion a year, and support fishing fleets sucking up species in places that would not be profitable without such subsidies, which account for about 25 percent of worldwide fishing revenue. In May 2007, the *Financial Times* reported that the biggest subsidies were by Japan ($5.3 billion), the European Union ($3.3 billion), and China ($3.1 billion).

Other than the fish, the biggest losers are poor countries. Subsidies are always a battle about which country has the biggest treasury. All this money slopping around creates a terrible moral hazard: governments are offered millions of easy dollars for their fishing rights, so long as they don't ask questions. Richer countries have been known to use their continued "aid" money as bait to ensure that their fishing fleets (or other investments of interest to their governments) are not excluded by the poor.

Mauritania, where local fishermen are put out of business by the trading of fishing rights to the highest bidder, provides a good example of this evil.[8] Some 340 foreign vessels are licensed to fish in Mauritania's sovereign waters and local fishermen have to compete with Russian, Spanish and Chinese ships which have their fuel bills paid by their governments. This is a classic case of government subsidy being used ruthlessly to out-compete family fishermen, and of corrupting governments with easy money, much of which doesn't make it into the national treasury.

Worldwide action

Advances in technology have meant that information is now much more readily available to anyone with access to a computer. Wikipedia is a good example of this democratization of information and has become something of a treasure trove (in much the same way as the 500,000-book library in Alexandria was in the ancient world) for researchers. As consumers, lobby groups and NGOs get better organized we can expect their influence to be more extensive and more effective. The point is that a global movement on important issues such as poverty and the environment is gaining traction. Boycotts—still a potent weapon of civil society and governments when used wisely—of unethical behavior will be a major weapon of progress and reaction in the future. Such action begins at home in mature democracies, but will spread to their investments and manufacturing plants offshore. It's the next big idea for social activists.

Reputations will become a major vulnerability of great corporations, a key factor in future risk management, driving up a better appreciation of people's rights, working conditions and policies to preserve the environment.

If you have faith in human nature and progress, then this power is good and history proves it. Our attitude to minorities, even animal welfare, has improved, as Steven Pinker points out:

> Conventional history has long shown that, in many ways, we have been getting kinder and gentler. Cruelty as entertainment, human sacrifice to indulge superstition, slavery as a labor-saving device, conquest as the mission statement of government, genocide as a means of acquiring real estate, torture and mutilation as routine punishment, the death penalty for misdemeanors and differences of opinion, assassination as the mechanism of political succession, rape as the spoils of war, pogroms as outlets for frustration, homicide as the major form of conflict resolution—all were unexceptional features of life for most of human history. But, today, they are rare to non-existent in the West, and far less common elsewhere than they used to be, concealed when they do occur, and widely condemned when they are brought to light.[9]

Despite Iraq, Afghanistan and Darfur, the world is becoming a more peaceful place. In Africa, the number of conflicts fell from 16 in 2002 to five in 2005. Violence against women by men continues to cause more casualties today than wars do.[10]

We now have international institutions to deal with these dreadful excesses and are appalled when they fail. Global instant media can be our conscience and motivator in producing global solidarity and driving better results.

As Robert Putnam reminds us, social capital—that complex system of habits, laws, volunteerism and generosity that has made open societies healthy and richer—is in decline in many mature democracies. Natural capital—fertile soils, fisheries and forests—is under siege in many places and is in decline in others. Despite all this, many polls suggest that, even in some successful nations, many are skeptical. Apprehension and fear of a globalized future is, as ever, a powerful political motivator. In times of economic (and thus social) turmoil, reaction can set in.

There is some evidence that wages in rich countries have stalled or, for the unskilled, gone backward. If all you have to sell in a modern economy is your sweat and muscle, then a machine, or lower-cost wages elsewhere, can out-compete you. The answer here is not to ban machines or trade, although that's been tried. It's to re-skill and retool, and that means government intervention to make the labor market function by continuously upskilling the workforce. Handing out benefits to do nothing may have seemed humane some years ago, but it's not an answer anymore—if it ever was.

Rich countries urgently need to offer readjustment programs for displaced workers, or the backlash against globalization and modernity could make it unacceptable for leaders to promote change. This would have a deadly impact on the poor, in rich and poor countries alike. At the moment, workers see big business capitalizing on its profit and socializing its costs by allowing loyal workers to be laid off and become a cost to government and society. Times of change demand leadership that values the virtues and solidarity of equality of sacrifice, yet some CEOs are undermining that social cohesion by sheer greed while preaching the need to change and adjust. The typical CEO in the United States gets a pay package 170 times greater than the average worker; in the United Kingdom 22 times greater; and in Japan 11 times greater. Some commentators believe that there are signs that rising inequality is intensifying resistance to globalization and impairing social cohesion and could ultimately undermine American democracy. While the evidence proves this wrong, that's not the point: in public affairs, perception is reality.

In the United States, the top 1 percent of households now have more wealth than the bottom 90 percent, and the top 1 percent earn more pre-tax income than the entire 40 percent of American workers at the bottom.[11] It's little consolation to workers made redundant that they can buy cheaper CDs from China now, or that their Medicare costs will be reduced because of pharmaceuticals from India. The greatest threat to the poor in Africa, China and elsewhere is the perception of workers in OECD countries that they are losing out and their children will be worse off than them (polls in 2006 showed that 40 percent of Americans think the next generation will have a lower living standard).

The rich are indeed getting richer, but this is not automatically at the expense of the poor—they are also getting richer. Governments in OECD countries often define "poor" people as those living on about a third of the average wage. Thus, whatever happens, the poor are always with us. Fifty percent of those defined as "poor" in the United States have air-conditioning, 60 percent have microwave ovens, 70 percent have one or more cars, 72 percent have washing machines, 77 percent have telephones, 93 percent have at least one color TV, and 98 percent have a refrigerator.[12] Poor people in the West have a better standard of living now than the middle class did 50 years ago. This is good for them, and we can do better still, but figures like these expose the silliness of statistics that guarantees the poor are always a fixed percentage of the average wage.

Growth is not a zero-sum game; there is not a fixed amount of wealth in the world. If I do well, that does not necessarily make you poorer. In fact, the opposite is true. This is as true of nations as it is of individuals. Questions of economic and social progress are often based on the problem of how much grain to eat, store or plant today. Business and voters in the West are perilously close to demanding more corn today (not saving and investing in the future), and fear that imported corn is bad because it might force us to grow other plants (no matter that the returns will be higher). These pressures create enemies of reason, the enemies of the future.

Honest globalization

As we grapple with the implications of globalization and the new enemies of the open society, we need to remind ourselves that the success of the last 50 years should not be taken for granted. Globalization has been slowed, even stopped, before—most dramatically in August 1914 and during the Cold War. As I write, the Doha Development Round is still stalled. Protectionism and fear are lurking.

At the G20 meeting of the leading industrialized nations in Washington, D.C. in November 2008, presidents and prime ministers triumphantly agreed not to introduce any new protectionist measures, and to give added impetus to conclude the Doha Development Round. Mindful of how the Great Depression was prolonged and intensified by unilateral trade restrictions, leaders left this meeting basking in the glory of dynamic, collective, and corrective action. Once home, however, the opposite of what was said happened. China re-introduced tax breaks for exporters; India imposed caps on steel imports; duties on car imports into Russia have been raised; billion-dollar bailouts to US car manufacturers were announced; France pledged US$7 billion to protect its companies from foreign predators. From Indonesia to Ecuador and Argentina, countries have introduced protectionist policies. There is a rush for governments to spend to promote local enterprise.

Trade specialists and historians write that things can't spin out of control as they did in the 1930s now that we have the binding rules of the World Trade Organization in place. While this is certainly true to a degree, in many countries there's a big difference between what is in the agreements they're locked into and what the tariffs actually are. If all countries raised their tariffs to what is legally possible, even under the WTO, there would be savage trade falls. Nevertheless, congratulations are due to the WTO, which recently implemented a system to monitor and publicize protectionist measures.

Every day, we hear stories of how the current economic crisis is having an impact all around the globe. The Baltic Dry Index, which measures freight ratios of bulk commodities like grain and iron ore, has crashed by 97 percent (January 2008). Lloyd's reports miles of ships anchored off Singapore and elsewhere, with shipping companies offering to waive fees on containers and just charge broker costs to move half-full ships and maintain some cash flow. The Bank of England now has the lowest interest rates since records have been kept 400 years ago. Mexico's car production has dropped 51 percent. Brazil shed 650,000 jobs in February 2009... and the list goes on.

We don't know how long this crisis will continue or what will work. But we do know what won't work, because it's been tried. We do know that protectionism will make things worse. We know that global trade has increased quicker than domestic trade and growth. We do know we are all in this together. Our success is based on the success of others, and that is a healthy thing. Unlike in the 1930s, governments are cutting taxes, re-capitalizing banks and boosting public expenditure, which is smart. The world's economy will recover. Recessions are not unusual, depressions are.

Historians should write of the great follies of this decade: the unregulated, insane un-transparent lending and leverage practices of global financial companies; the reluctance of politicians to take a few local hits by concluding the Doha Trade Round; the slow acceptance of the importance of China, India, Brazil and Russia at the top table of decision-makers; and the historic stupidity of not negotiating Russia into the WTO and having binding rules for the export of energy.

The current crisis is not an argument to reject globalization or a rules-based global system. Opportunistic politicians and pressure groups will try to cash in on the public's natural unease at the failures of the economic system by bringing back policies that rewind and favor special interests. The great fear of the poor must be a period of de-globalization.

We have the right to be angry when banks fail, leaving governments to bail them out with taxpayers' money. Anger turns to outrage when the top executives responsible for this mess are then allowed to walk away with huge severance payments, seemingly rewarded for their sheer incompetence and, in some cases, negligence bordering on the criminal. But, unpopular though it may be to say it in such circumstances, there is a real danger of over-correction by politicians and populists, who can take advantage of people's fears. The reality is that globalization is worth saving, as is the democratic capitalist system. This crisis should make the system stronger, more accountable, and more transparent.

Recent history shows that the most recent financial crises—savings and loans in the US, the Japanese asset-bubble burst, and the Asian crisis—were years in the making and took years to correct. There will always be an over-correction when a problem is faced after the event. When a house is burning down, it is only right to call the fire brigade, though many complain about subsequent water damage to furniture and personal effects. However, if the fire brigade is not called, then there is absolute destruction.

As historian Niall Ferguson points out:

> The ascent of money has been essential to the ascent of man.
> Far from being the work of mere leeches, intent on sucking

the life's blood out of indebted families, or gambling with the savings of widows and orphans, financial innovation has been an indispensable factor in man's advance from wretched sustenance to giddy heights of material prosperity that so many people know now.[13]

Of course, we should acknowledge that there is more to life than commerce. Unbridled capitalism, unfettered, out of control, can destroy its very virtues. There are more internationally accepted rules to govern the export of beef than there are for global investment flows. (It is worth recalling that rules for meat products were driven by scandals over safety and hygiene, and that these are policed by both exporters and importers.) Capitalism without rules, accountability and values is anarchy. A world without borders is not a world without rules, standards or values. If global trade treaties are not reframed and made relevant by the Doha Trade Round there will be a dangerous backlash.

Unless power is diverse, unless the people see a better future for their children, unless there is social cohesion at home, as we have learned, reaction can set in, and progress can be rejected. It is reasonable in a domestic political situation that people need to be convinced and see in practice the costs and benefits of change shared fairly. Many people remain unconvinced and that number is growing in wealthy countries.

Globalization and trade always create losers. All change does; even *no* change does. The losers can be seen immediately, but it always takes time for the winners to emerge. That's why, despite record employment figures and record low unemployment figures in most OECD countries, polls are beginning to question whether this, the most expansionist decade in history, has been in the people's interests.

The very rich have done much better than low-income people in many wealthy countries. This is especially true in countries such as the United States where a worker who loses her job can lose her health cover and retirement schemes as well. Companies that go broke can take down with them pension funds and healthcare provisions that were fairly negotiated. In cases like this, of course, questions of equity arise. Even more bitter for workers' families is seeing top executives getting enormous financial rewards from the same companies that have failed them and broken their contracts. (The CEO of Home Depot, for example, got a $210 million "golden handshake" when his company did very badly and workers were sacked after investors lost out.)

United States bankruptcy laws, which allow companies and managers to start again, are important for restructuring business and the economy and are part of America's success. While this is useful in a time of transformational destruction or creative destruction, as some economists have explained, it's difficult to persuade a retired worker and his family, who cannot start again, who thought they had a contract, and paid into schemes during a lifetime's work, that this is so. Too often it's workers and investors who are not in the know who carry the cost. By 1995, United States pension funds held one-tenth of the equity capital in United States publicly owned companies, 40 percent of the common stock of the nation's large and medium businesses, and 40 percent of the medium and long-term debt of its bigger companies. If socialism is defined as workers' ownership of the means of production, then the United States is very socialized.

The United States is the world's most successful economy ever, and its success drives ours, whether we live in China or Uruguay. The über-rich Bill Gates, once the world's richest man, owned 1 percent of United States GDP but today's IT moguls face competition in the form of new ideas from another nerd in another garage somewhere, possibly Bangladesh.

We all must be aware of the mood and needs of America. Some of the very policies that have made America successful are now a dangerous cost to its success. Economists are almost unanimous in their view that labor market flexibility is a key to new jobs and growth. But if your employer also owns your healthcare and pension plan, that flexibility is obviously restricted. The United States has the very best of healthcare; that's why so many who can afford it from around the world flock there for care. Yet I still feel uncomfortable with the proposition that the rich can buy healthcare and the poor cannot. Access to healthcare is a true measurement of civilization. The best systems deliver on the basis of universal coverage, and both private and public delivery mechanisms should be available to provide choice and drive up efficiencies so we can measure results, the better to be accountable and to improve outcomes.

This is important because maintaining the public's support for open economies is vital to their success and sustainability. There must be strong domestic policies to share the costs of economic transition, which will be a permanent feature of progress. It's not a great leap, indeed it's an inevitable policy leap, to continue to work to ensure that our global institutions accept this and work together to ensure better coherence and common strategies to adjust and readjust to this dislocation. This will always be the primary responsibility of domestic governments with positive national policies.

A weakness in democracy is short-termism. When do we fix the roof—when the sun is shining or when it's raining? History shows that democracies are capable of quick corrections, sometimes even over-corrections, to policy when it's perceived to be failing. That's why we should protect individual workers rather than big business, because the latter always ends up with the subsidies and handouts that go with protectionism.

In surveys around the world, people have been asked whether they think that growing trade and business ties with other countries is good for their country. Nations in which more than 85 percent say "yes" include China, India, and Malaysia. The highest percentage is actually in the Ivory Coast and Senegal, countries marginalized from globalization. Of wealthy countries, Sweden and Germany have the highest percentage at 85 percent; the lowest were the United States and France. Among wealthy countries, Sweden has the lowest percentage of those who say their way of life needs to be protected from foreign influences.[14] Sweden's trade, as a percentage of its economy is 40 percent; in France the figure is 22.5 percent and the United States 7.8 percent. Swedes have the highest individual internet usage rate in the world, and generous social safety nets that protect individuals in times of economic change. Unemployed Swedes must find a job within 28 months or their benefit will stop, and they must accept retraining. Sweden spends seven times more, as a percentage of GDP, on retraining than the United States. The social confidence and trust that they have a future and will be looked after is why Swedish workers and unions have a positive view of globalization. All this creates a mobile and flexible workforce, something other capitalist economies talk of but can't achieve without great cost because they see no role for government. How very short-term!

CHAPTER 2

The Rise and Rise of China

There are only two types of people: those who are thinking about China and India, and those who are not. These two countries are not joining the world economy; they are rejoining it (their share of world trade is not quite where it was 500 years ago). It is no longer a case that China and India *will become* this or change that. They *are* changing the modern world order now.

China has taken a million people a month out of extreme poverty over the past 20 years, generating wealth, jobs and growth. Over a thousand new motor vehicles are registered every hour. The new Terminal 3 at Beijing Capital International Airport—the Earth's largest covered structure—will help the airport welcome more than a million passengers a week. The increase in its energy demands has had a significant impact on world prices, yet the Chinese themselves are increasingly able to pay: wages in coastal China exceed wages in the Philippines and Indonesia. Salaries in the Pearl River delta increased 13 percent in 2007. New labor laws have raised both wages and awareness among Chinese workers.

India has a tradition of robust democracy, regrettably matched for much of the post-Independence era by an ability to develop bureaucracy to a level unequalled even by many Warsaw Pact nations. Its very democracy ensures that economic progress has been uneven and the path to reform, begun in the early 1990s, has often been stymied by prickly nationalism and ideology. Yet a broadening consensus appears to have taken hold about the need to deepen reforms while ensuring benefits are shared with the vast ranks of the poor. Nationalistic pride in its economic achievements will help: since the 2006 acquisition of Arcelor by Mittal Steel, India how has the world's largest steel manufacturer. In mid-2008 India held foreign exchange reserves of over US$300 billion; it registered economic growth of 9.1 percent in fiscal 2007–08; and, measured by purchasing power parity, its GDP is now valued at $4.7 trillion, making it the world's fourth-largest economy. Warming relations with the United States and China come as the country projects more influence to the Middle East and Africa, confirming its position as a mammoth, nuclear-armed, global player.

China: No doubt about it

I admit to bias. When I became Director-General of the WTO, my top priority was to assist in navigating China into the organization and then launch a new trade round with development at its heart. Imagine how unpredictable and dangerous the world would be if China was not now a member of the WTO. Every year it would have to face the humiliation and uncertainty of having to seek approval from the US Congress to trade with America. At any time, politicians in Tokyo or Brussels could just stop business. Trade between Taiwan and China would become more political and uncertain. Give politicians levers and they will use them. Under the WTO, a rules-based system, we have legal, transparent, independent, rule-based, binding mechanisms to handle trade disputes and differences. Chinese officials were very cooperative and eager, and said this was the most important economic decision they had made in 50 years. Leaders said WTO membership locked in reforms they were making for their own good anyway. Five years after membership, Chinese TV ran a 15-hour documentary explaining their long march to membership.

Visiting China and being an honorary professor at several Chinese universities is fascinating. Several thousand students attend lectures. They are keen, asking serious questions about the role of central banks, state-owned enterprises, currency, and always wanting to know, "What should come first, economic liberty or political liberty? Are human and labor rights a cost to growth?"

Chinese students, unlike many of their counterparts in the West, have no problems with globalization. They know from their own experience how much better life is for them than it was for their parents and grandparents. Writing in the *China Daily*, researcher Qin Xiaoying talks of how the Chinese generation born after 1980 are "a unique generation," whose experience of the one-child policy and economic prosperity are leading them to value freedom from established rules and seek a humane, democratic society in which personal values matter more than mere material success.

Like the Indians, the Chinese (actually, parents everywhere) know that education is the way out and up. Today, 500,000 Chinese students study overseas. In 1985, a mere 3 percent returned home; now 25 percent come home. In 2004, 1.3 million engineers and scientists graduated from Chinese universities.

Only those who visited China before the opening up can understand how much it has improved on every level, except for the environment. It is unrecognizable from the place I first visited in 1984 as New Zealand's Trade Minister. (New Zealand recognized China before the famous Nixon visit, to the public dismay of our American friends, and was the first developed country to agree to the terms of China's accession to the WTO, the first to grant it market-economy status, and as of April 2008, the first to have a free (preferential) trade agreement with China.)

It is easy to forget that China remains a communist country with millions still in poverty and without many democratic or civil rights. The history of our region proves that economic liberalization leads eventually to individual and political liberalization. Serious Chinese officials have asked me about the sequence of reform, quoting how Russia had moved on political reform first before the introduction of economic and commercial reforms. The fact that property rights were not locked in place first caused massive dislocation and squalid theft of public resources during Russia's privatizations.

Stability, the cohesion of the nation, is still the most dominant, central concern of Chinese leaders. (Many say the Tiananmen Square student demonstration would have led to a civil war; a few confess that perhaps it was an overreaction.) China's years of humiliation before the revolution were marked by the occupation of the homeland by foreigners, civil war, warlords, anarchy—weaknesses that invited an invasion by the Japanese. Even those who say openly that Mao's policies failed in the end still praise him for unifying the nation and freeing it from foreign occupation—making him one of the great figures in Chinese history. Only 20 years ago the Pentagon's Office of

Assessments predicted that China would disintegrate. Japan's Kenichi Ohmae confidently suggested China would collapse into 11 republics and re-form into a "Federal Republic of China."

This all helps to explain China's obsession with the often-contradictory concepts of growth and stability. No country has moved to the front rank of industrialized nations without moving away from a peasant-based system of agriculture. For the West, it took hundreds of years; for China it will take a few difficult and dangerous decades. In a society where not so long ago an official pass was needed to travel internally, the greatest internal migration of people in history is under way, with tens of millions of people moving to the cities. How to handle this without serious political problems will be hard.

In China, up to 400 million people have been lifted from extreme poverty in 30 years. If China can maintain the growth of the past 25 years, in another 16 years its average income will equal that of Portugal and South Korea today; a further nine years will see it equal that of the United States today. These are heroic projections: growth from a low base, picking the low-hanging fruits of inefficiencies, is harder to maintain and sustain as society demands better social and environmental standards.

Even with their massive labor pools, neither China nor India can completely abolish theories of labor market elasticity. Wages in areas of labor shortages in southern and coastal China are equal to those of the Philippines and Indonesia now. Some 24,000 new cars, trucks and buses are registered every day in China. Where 20 years ago China was self-sufficient in oil, it will soon be the world's largest importer.

In the light of such projections, it was reported at the World Food Business Summit in 2007, by 2031 "China would consume two-thirds of the world's grain, and its paper consumption would double the world's output."[1] That's worth thinking through, but like all projections it is based on today's technologies, today's consumption, and presumes we cannot learn and adapt. Where 30 years ago China shunned foreign investment, it is now the largest recipient of it. Japan and Korea now trade more with China than with the United States. Chinese travelers have taken over from the Japanese as Asia's major force in global tourism.

Far from threatening the economies of Southeast Asia, China is into this global supply chain and everyone is winning. Look at any electronic device you bought recently and chances are that the parts were probably made in Southeast Asia, and assembled in China by an American-owned company. Reflecting on the lack of progress of the Doha Development Round, all trade negotiations now lead to Beijing.

New regional and bilateral free-trade arrangements are, for the most part, not really free trade: they should be renamed "preferential trade deals" because they establish new privileges and preferences, cause trade diversions, and offer new, dangerous levers to politicians. China–ASEAN, China–EU, China–India, and China–Australia negotiations are all under way but none has a binding disputes system, and all do little on agriculture. And, as yet, Japan and the Americas are still missing.

Frankly, if I were a trade minister, I would be doing the same thing. There's a cost to being left out. China's riding a tiger. But, while the dragon is undoubtedly roaring, it's not without its vulnerabilities, which China-bashers should consider before making their own problems and China's worse. (One of the great things about an integrated global economy is that bad economic moves against a trading partner damage the movers themselves.)

Between 1998 and 2005, China slid from forty-second to fifty-seventh on the World Economic Forum's Business Competitiveness Index, its absolute performance inferior to comparable economies such as India and Brazil, and deteriorating faster. Even China's trillion-dollar reserves, the world's largest, could not pay off the debts or restructure what many now claim is $2 trillion in underperforming loans. On present calculations, the hi-tech Shanghai city-to-airport train will take 160 years to pay for itself.

According to one commentator:

> Today China needs $5.4 of extra investment to produce an extra $1 of output, a proportion vastly higher than that in developed economies like Britain or the United States. But 20 years ago China needed just $4 to deliver the same result. In other words, an already gravely inefficient economy has become even more inefficient. China's national accounts tell the same grim story. China had to increase its capital stock by 9 percent every year in the 1980s to help produce 9.8 percent growth rate, but by the late 1990s it had to increase capital stock by 12 percent to produce a lower growth rate of 8.2 percent. China is now back to the Mao years in terms of the inefficiency with which it uses capital to generate growth.[2]

Credible, private polls of many government experts and businesspeople give China top marks for implementing WTO agreements. It dropped tariffs on average from 43 percent in 1992 to 8.9 percent in

2001, and nearly all licenses and quarantine import controls have been eliminated. It passed anti-monopoly legislation in 2007. Banks and insurance markets are opening as planned. The stone in the shoe of this implementation is protection of intellectual property, which is not good enough and is now the subject of legal redress in the WTO disputes system. Enforcement rates of internal legal claims are poor; only 40 percent of provincial high court decisions are enforced.[3] The old Chinese saying "The sky is high, the Emperor far away" still pertains, it seems.

In May 2006, *Asia News* reported that China had paid out more than a billion dollars in compensation to its foreign counterparts in disputes over intellectual-property rights since China joined the WTO in 2001. In October 2007, *Tech Newsworld* reported on a joint FBI–China operation in July that year that broke up a software counterfeiting ring worth $500 million. Cooperation on this scale was unthinkable a few years ago. China has now more patents pending than Germany. As the incentives begin to reverse, China will have a greater need to protect its intellectual property.

The largest single obstacle preventing improved governance is the state's overwhelming stock ownership. The fact that the government controls a majority of all shares and retains dominant positions in the vast majority of large corporations means that managers are shielded from market discipline and are pressured to act in the interests of the Chinese Communist Party—creating corporate governance with "Chinese characteristics." This leaves many firms split between the often incompatible objectives of striving to become efficient economic competitors and supporting the government's political goals.

But things are changing, as the *Wall Street Journal's* Richard Daniel Ewing has acknowledged:

> As more Chinese firms list publicly and foreign investors acquire larger stakes in them, active corporate governance, robust equity markets and shareholder protection will contribute to China's economic performance. These reforms will make China's corporations more transparent and attentive to the needs of the market. The speed of these changes will depend on three factors: the state ceding ownership to public investors, corporate boards' responsiveness to minority shareholders, and improvements in China's legal and financial systems. With clear governance structures, China's firms will have greater access to capital, new IPOs will be better received and corporate growth will accelerate.

The Chinese judicial system is still too reliant on the Party, its rules still too opaque. History has shown, everywhere and at every time, that when party, bureaucratic and commercial power mix without independent courts, rule of law, and defined property rights, the result is corruption at worst, incompetence at best, and poor allocation of resources. Here there is a need for change, and it is happening—it must or China will go bust. This raises the wider question of whether pluralism and competition can work economically without being implemented at a civic and political level. This may be possible for a short time, but then becomes unworkable. Given the fact that no nation has yet reached an annual per-capita income of $5,000 without then becoming an entrenched democracy, then China in 2025 will be a very interesting place.

China should be rich and powerful, and for most of history it has been. China in 1800 had a larger share of the world's manufacturing output than it does now.[4] As one senior Chinese official remarked to me, China had always been the most powerful nation on earth, except for the past 200 years, when it had de-globalized.

The simple act of lifting some of the horrendous government interventions that had crushed the Chinese people and their economy until the late 1970s has, we know, led to huge improvements. With the massive dead weight released from its back, the Chinese dragon can run nearer to its natural speed. Put another way, China's recent rise proves only this: if you stop strangling someone, it's amazing how well they can breathe.

Let us not forget that during Europe's Middle Ages China had great trading ships that sailed and traded with India, Africa and the Islamic world. Its fleets were twice the size of Columbus's puny collection of ships; one had a crew of more than 20,000 men. China enjoyed the benefits of magnetic compasses, drills, gunpowder, fine silks and clothes, medicine, law, and civilization's largest irrigation systems centuries before Britons learned that coal was a source of energy.

But this progress stopped when a leadership battle was won by those who looked inward. Economic and social chauvinism and nationalistic isolationism starved Chinese society of ideas and innovation. Through the middle decades of the twentieth century, new leaders opened their ears to new ideas, but sadly they were the wrong ones. Communism was a deadly blind alley that crushed enterprise, creativity and innovation, all those things that allowed the leading nations to flourish.

The greatest expansion in China's history has occurred because it has now embraced, however imperfectly, the notion of property rights and encouraged commerce. Mao's China repeated the mistakes of previous Chinese leaders. This was a Marxist response, given popular support at the time because of years of imperial arrogance, occupation and invasion by outside powers. Revulsion with this state of affairs helped cause revolution, a natural result when there's no democratic way to force out evil.

China has now turned its back on insularity, emulating the success of Japan and the Asian tigers. With the United States, it now dominates global trade, a position which attracts different, and often contradictory, responses. On the one hand, China is attacked because of its export success; on the other, people worry about the impact on global growth if China slows down.

In the early 1980s, the great cliché was that we were entering a Pacific Age, with the center of economic gravity shifting from the Atlantic. Within a few years that idea was buried: Japan had stalled, its miracle spent. Now with China's economy pumping and India's not far behind, the headlines are reappearing again, now suggesting an Asian–Pacific Age. Disturbingly, some Europeans and Americans are dusting off the protectionist speeches they made about Japan in the late 1970s. To be consistent, they would have to argue that it would have been better for the world if Germany and Japan had been left in ruins after the Second World War. The big difference between China now and Japan two decades ago is that Chinese companies are frequently state-owned and the country itself is a colossus. Japan was smaller and had been an ally of the West for decades; China is huge and a former Cold War adversary, and is competing for resources, customers and influence everywhere. The challenge the world faces with India and China is real. Together they represent 40 percent of the world's population. China is growing at 8–10 percent, India at 6–7 percent. It's a healthy, inevitable, proper challenge.

There are two big questions that need to be answered: how will China respond to the gathering pressures for reform, and how will the rest of the world respond to China's rise? China's biggest problem is not energy, inequality or the environment, but the capacity of its system to handle these problems without a responsive, accountable bureaucracy, and without a competitive political system. It's worth reminding ourselves that China had a merit-based civil service centuries before the West (top British public servants are still called "Mandarins," by the way). Today, too, there needs to be a similarly independent, professional public service in place to sustain growth and minimize corruption.

There are hopeful signs: Chinese people can now take money out of China; banks can accept more foreign investment; global newspapers like the *Herald Tribune* will be printed in China; the first sexual harassment cases have been lodged; and citizens are now able to sue the government in hundreds of areas—all unthinkable a few years ago. The Chinese media is reporting on local corruption, on citizens suing local governments, and on an increasing number of civil disturbances each year. Chinese activists are interviewed on Western TV complaining about corruption which could, according to one academic, be costing the Chinese GDP 10 percent in dead weight. There are reports of Chinese obesity and environmental health problems (the World Bank has reported that up to 750,000 Chinese die prematurely each year because of pollution). Some Chinese leaders, fearful of the facts, have tried to suppress such reports as being "too sensitive" and likely "to cause social unrest." As we know, trying to suppress reports in open societies only guarantees they will be on the front page.

Now that China is integrated into the world economy it faces the kind of threats to its reputation that all major, mature nations face. World opinion didn't matter to the Chinese during the Cultural Revolution; now it does. Take the case of Sudan, where pressure on China has mounted because of its investments and arms sales to the government of Omar al-Bashir—a leader indicted by the International Criminal Court for genocide, crimes against humanity and war crimes in Darfur. Senior politicians in the US and UK have publicly acknowledged that China is now working behind the scenes to effect change, appointing a special envoy to Darfur and pushing for a tripartite resolution involving the Sudanese government, the African Union and the United Nations.

China is going through the same process that Japan, Singapore and Taiwan experienced. As living standards rise, a middle class emerges that seeks out better social outcomes. This is the virtue of free markets and globalization. For the first time, the Chinese Government is answerable to its own laws, and citizens can now sue the Government! There are the beginnings of freedom of religion: thousands of Chinese Muslims have been allowed to go on the *Haj* and Christians have sued the Shanghai government for wrongful arrest. All this is healthy and most leaders have hit the right balance in making these points.

Critics of human rights policy inside China, particularly in relation to Tibet, went so far as to seek an Olympic boycott of China. Like the Dalai Lama, I did not support such initiatives—they would have been futile and counter-productive. It's exactly because China has re entered the global economy that she is vulnerable to and now must take into account the opinions of the world's consumers, her customers who don't live in China. Millions perished during the Cultural Revolution and the Great Leap Forward and the world didn't know, didn't care and couldn't do anything about it anyway.

The global dragon

Thanks to the wonders of the internet, we in the West were able to follow the proceedings of the 17th Communist Party Congress held in Beijing in October 2007. The media has had more access to such events and now feels comfortable "door-stopping" delegates for comment. One revealing comment to emerge from the congress came from Wang Guixiu, from the Party School of the CPC Central Committee, who noted: "Only in competitive elections can voters have choice. The increased margins between nominees and chosen candidates show that Chinese democracy has moved a big step forward."

It was at this congress that it was agreed that the Party constitution would be amended to mention religion for the first time. Much was said, too, about the environment and plans to quadruple living standards by 2025 through "scientific development." The fact that this increase is to be on a per-capita basis, rather than simply a fourfold increase in GDP, is an acknowledgement that people at the bottom were not moving ahead quickly enough.

Corruption and its costs were also on the agenda, as was a McKinsey report on social spending, which was used by the left to introduce higher public spending, new healthcare programs, unionization, a tough new labor law and the end to an unpopular rural tax on farmers. During the course of the congress, several members of the next generation of Party leaders quietly emerged, including several who have been arguing for a more open society based more on domestic spending, a more flexible approach to currency issues, and the need to address environmental and social problems. One such problem, the Three Gorges Development, was later discussed openly on television. This level of accountability and response to criticism is very new in China. The revolutionary party continues its evolutionary long march toward a new China.

China gets the message and is acting. An incompetent minister was sacked over a cover-up of the SARS outbreak; a corrupt health official was sentenced to death. Within days of a story being published in the international media exposing the practice of rural children being worked as slaves and leading to the rescue of 1,000 in Hongdong county alone, 30,000 people joined internet discussions. An appeal launched on Tianya, the largest website in China, recorded several million hits in a week. President Hu Jintao acted quickly, sending in the police and the army to clean up the mess. (On the darker side, however, the *Australian Financial Review* reported that a memo from the Internet Bureau of the Communist Party Office of External Communications to the censors read: "All websites should reinforce positive propaganda, put more emphasis on the forceful measures the central and local governments have already taken. Harmful information that uses this event to attack the government should be deleted as soon as possible.")

Corruption costs China 3 percent of its GDP, more than its total investment in education in 2006.[5] But steps are being taken to counteract its pernicious effects. In 2007, for example, BBC Online reported that an online game which allowed players to expose corrupt officials proved so popular its website crashed. In its first week, "Incorruptible Fighter," which led players through a series of moral challenges before entering a corruption-free paradise, was downloaded 100,000 times. The amazing thing was that the site was established by a regional government!

Resentment is building against a class of insiders, the relatives of senior officials and leaders, often called the "princelings." Crooked princelings and the spouses of cadres are number two—just behind baton-wielding police—on the list of citizen grievances, according to an internal Party survey. While the Party papers said that 70 percent of those named as frauds were innocent, the fact that it was actually seeking people's opinions was new and interesting.

While China is slowly reforming the Communist Party, the central fear of leaders is that a more pluralistic China will cause chaos. The loss of power and privilege, as with all centralized systems, is a huge disincentive to change. The most recent of China's leadership changes was uniquely open at the Party Congress, when nearly half the positions were filled by new faces. All but President Hu Jintao were new to the standing committee. Regeneration is under way in a manner never experienced in China before.

In the 1970s a dissident's slogan ran, "Without democracy there can be no modernization." President Hu used these same words in a speech in the United States in 2006. While the words may convey a different meaning from that understood in the West, that it's even said is new.

The powerful, in any country, often think that they are beyond their own laws. But in China this is being challenged in surprising ways. In 2002, for example, a 41-year-old Shanghai businessman waved a sheaf of property titles at three judges, pressing his claim against eviction, saying, "Any government decision to force us out is illegal, because the law of the country protects our ownership rights."[6] That a government can do anything illegal is a new concept in China.

Western trade unionists are excited over the prospect of China insisting that Wal-Mart allow unions. Wal-Mart's imports from China are so large that if the company was a country it would rank about tenth as an importer. It employs a million workers in North America but won't deal with unions (although one, lonely, endangered branch in Canada is now unionized). China's trade unions are hardly independent, and nor are the courts, but watch this space.

Napoleon once said, "China is a sleeping giant, let her sleep." That option is no longer open. The fear that China's success would hollow out the other Asian success stories has proved to be unfounded. Southeast Asia is now a vital platform in the global supply line. China's growth has helped lift Japan out of its economic stupor and has contributed more to global growth than the United States, the European Union or Japan over the past few years. Its rising power has encouraged Russia to reform and meet this old challenge.

A major issue for the United States is that it has outsourced savings. China is a major funder of the US deficit. As the biggest recipient of direct foreign investment, China's trillion-dollar financial reserves are being deployed to invest offshore. Whereas previous oil booms saw Middle East petrodollars rush into the United States and Europe, staggering new investments from the Middle East are going to China, India and Pakistan, the new Silk Road. The West, which pushed strongly for a more open investment regime as a condition for China's entry into the WTO, will face an aggressive, bold, China on a buying spree. This is the next big story.

Now that China has the world's biggest financial reserves, the big story is where and how they are invested. Inflationary pressures in the domestic economy mean much will have to go offshore. So it's worth remarking that Chinese investment managers are especially interested in companies that have reserves of intellectual property and patents.

China offered $1.28 billion for iconic appliance manufacturer Maytag, and has purchased IBM's personal computer division for $1.75 billion. But what really caused concern in the United States was the bid for the US global energy company Unocal. The bid was logical. China's oil consumption has doubled in a decade; it's gone from self-sufficiency to being the world's second-largest importer of energy. Its energy imports rose almost 40 percent in one 12-month period. China is doubling its strategic oil reserves to equal the reserves of the United States or Japan.

There is an interesting strategic element to this. Offshore oil reserves amount to about 28 billion tons. Experts contest this figure, but even if it's 50 percent wrong it would still equate to over 100 years of supply at the present rate of energy imports. And where are these offshore reserves? In disputed areas of the South China Sea. China says it is committed to diplomatic resolution of these competing claims, but the oil shortfall driven by economic expansion is having a major impact on its political, military and investment strategies, and is putting pressure on neighbors who have similar needs and ambitions. Yet very recently we have seen deals struck between China and Japan.

China is literally investing everywhere there is energy: the Middle East, Bangladesh, Canada, Indonesia, Kazakhstan, Malaysia, Mexico, Mongolia, Gabon, Pakistan, Papua New Guinea, Russia, Iran, Sudan, Thailand, Australia, and the United States. Pipelines from central Asia are being built; Siberian oil is planned to pour south. At an APEC meeting in Chile, President Hu announced a Brazilian energy deal worth almost $11.5 billion. China already invests heavily in Latin America—in Venezuela, Colombia, Ecuador and Peru—and another multi-billion dollar deal is in the pipeline with Argentina.

China now has a stake in Middle East stability. The invasion of Iraq meant that China lost important supplies. Globalization and economic integration now mean that the needs of all countries are similar. We all need predictability and stability, and being each other's customers and suppliers should force more cooperative global economic and political policies. China initially refused to consider the moral consequences of the events in Darfur by dealing with Sudanese oil magnates, but global public opinion is forcing a rethink. It was also, at the time of writing, beginning to put pressure on Mugabe in Zimbabwe. The same pressure is being exerted on China today over the problems in Myanmar.

All this unsettles some people, but we need to reconsider our perceptions and responses to trade figures and investment in our new, more borderless world. What is a trade surplus or deficit? What happens when Dell sells a computer made in China, with inputs elsewhere? On paper it looks like a United States deficit with China. But when the profits go to Dell and to Microsoft, whose operating system and the chip powering it comes from Intel, what difference does this make to the statistics?

Politicians often respond to complex issues with predictable, tired slogans rather than substance. US senators threatened China with a tough, new 27.5 percent tariff unless China revalued its currency. That would slash the profits of Standard & Poor's 500 companies by 8 percent or cost $50 billion, and save few United States jobs.

China has begun to revalue its currency upward under pressure from foreign competitors and in its own interests. But a full realignment is likely to raise input costs for every business in the global economy. US costs for financing government debt will go up and the fire sale of Chinese business will end. If China slows down its investment in US Treasury debts, the United States will have to raise interest rates. Inflationary pressures, which have in large part been tamed because of productivity increases, based on low-cost high-tech inputs and consumer costs, will rise. Eventually China, in its own interests as well as those of its trading partners, will have to move to a more mature economy based more on domestic consumption, as did Japan and Korea. A country can be too reliant on exports, making it vulnerable to its customers' purchasing power (a good thing, actually). The sequence again is the issue: how can this be done without mature, trusted domestic banking rules, and prudent, transparent institutions?

Economists calculate that the undervaluation of the Chinese currency by 30 percent adds 0.45 of a percentage point to China's growth rate because of additional export growth. Therefore, in any given year, while the People's Bank of China risks losing 3.5 percent of GDP from a potential revaluation, it is adding to the growth rate by 0.45 percent—a good rate of return until the whole fabric unravels. China is keeping its savings bottled up internally as a crucial part of its growth strategy. If it yielded to US pressure to float the *renminbi* freely it would want to stop its currency from rising. The best way to do that would be to allow Chinese savers to take their money abroad, supplying the *renminbi* that the world's markets want. It is estimated that about a quarter of Chinese savings would go abroad, which, by World Bank calculations, would reduce growth from investment. In other words, capital controls and reserve accumulation are worth about 2 percent to China's growth rate every year.

Nor is that the only consequence. If the *renminbi* rises, then Chinese agricultural prices, now keyed to world market prices, will fall.

As the *renminbi* gains in buying power, so the world market price trans-lates into lower domestic prices and lower domestic rural incomes. This would immediately accelerate the movement of the pool of 300 million agricultural laborers to the cities in search of work.[7]

Some historians suggest that China's rise and tensions arising from its success can be compared to Germany's rise in Europe in the early years of last century, with China on a collision course with Asia's other big power, Japan, as Germany was with France. The question is whether the United States and the global community will respond more wisely now than they did then, a failure which gave us 1914. The potential for a repeat if the lessons of history are not learned is obvious and painful.

History, common sense, common interests, our common future, suggest that China's progress, so important to all of us, will be main-tained. What can go wrong? Again, history is our best guide. We have learned that social cohesion and a sense of fairness are necessary to maintain progress, but 106 Chinese US-dollar billionaires sit uncom-fortably alongside the many who have yet to catch up. The 900 million Chinese who live in the countryside earn only a third as much as their city counterparts. Reaction at home and abroad, as competition for markets—domestic and overseas—results in protectionism, is a crude response. A domestic growth-led economy will not evolve until there is trust in civil institutions and commerce.

China's 15-year path to being accepted as a member of the WTO was long and complicated, and made more so by the sensitive issue of the parallel membership of Taiwan (or "Chinese Taipei" as the Chinese insist. China will surrender its claim to Taiwan when the United States gives California and Texas back to Mexico, Alaska back to Russia, and renegotiates the Louisiana Purchase with France, or when Russia returns St. Petersburg to the Swedes). With delicate handling, this was accomplished, but always with the potential threat of the severe eco-nomic and military consequences that might ensue if we botched this.

Many feared that entry into the WTO would lead China to throw its weight around like an angry elephant. In fact, the opposite is true. China is more like a python that's swallowed a buffalo, slowly digest-ing its many obligations imposed by the tough conditions of WTO membership. Many now argue that China has been too modest, that it should show more leadership and use its influence to conclude the Doha Round. But nationalism is now China's unifying ideology.

In the past, many hundreds of successful overseas Chinese in Indonesia were murdered when an angry public was spurred on by populist, nationalist politicians. Chinese were persecuted in Malaysia and elsewhere for their success and lack of "patriotism." The question arises as to whether China would accept such things in the future. It is building a blue-water navy; it will have the reach, and the means, to defend its interests. In *The Moral Consequences of Growth*, Benjamin Friedman has pointed out that it is almost inevitable where there is sustained growth, that there will be reaction, typically in times of economic stagnation.

It is my nature to be optimistic, and history and experience agree with me. How will all this end? It won't; it's work in progress. Zhou Enlai, when asked about the implications of the French Revolution, replied, "It's too early to tell." We must be engaged, be hopeful, helpful, consistent, prudent and use the rules of the WTO where we have differences—we have nothing else except self-defeating reaction.

China does have problems, and I have outlined many of them. But there's little I've said that has not been said in public at universities by students, in boardrooms by businesspeople, and by officials.

There is more to fear from a weak, unstable China than from one that is globally integrated and depending on us for business. China is a more open society. Its democracy will grow but not perhaps in a straight line, or in a form the West will completely understand or recognize. For the first time in Chinese history, those in power are being held more to account, their decisions more transparent. The government is becoming answerable to its own law. This is a work in progress. To those who, correctly, want to hold China more accountable for human rights I say this: it is precisely because the Chinese are reintegrating into the global economy that their reputation matters to them, and so global consumers have some influence over them. This is unfamiliar territory for China. When it was a closed society, millions perished and the world could do nothing. Now, this China is becoming more and more like any other country.

Curiously, the global economic downturn could accelerate this process. Alternatively, if the uber-nationalists reap the political benefit of harsh social conditions it could spin out of control and anything could happen (the nightmare scenario is the issue of Taiwan's reintegration coming into play as a distraction and as a nation-building populist strategy). While history shows that many nations have done illogical costly things before, I remain optimistic in this respect.

If China is to become like any other country, its consumers must be empowered and encouraged to spend their savings, which would be good for both China's stability and for its trading partners. People who fear for their future save and put money and gold under the mattress. This brings into play social, democratic principles of a welfare state. They must be given the confidence to spend and this can only come through the government providing public, universal safety nets for old age, health and education. Nobel Prize-winner in Economics Joe Stiglitz presents the argument that China and the US are equally dependent on each other. China has two ways of achieving growth: by financing American consumers; or by financing its own citizens who, when empowered, can stimulate economic growth.

With its growth (in February 2009) being cut by a third, and with more than 20 million new unemployed people, China knows something must be done to hold the country together and keep conservative nationalists at bay. This is important for the rest of the world, too. It's a healthy thing that all our self-interests converge. China's stimulus plan to fight the global crisis lifted Wall Street prices. The February 2009 Party Congress sounded much like a party conference in many other countries: delegates argued that the proposed stimulus package ($600 billion) could be higher; health and education should be expanded, and so on. The infrastructure spend sounded very Japanese, American or Australian, as did the record deficit predicted. The big concern is that the infrastructure spend, like that of Japan in the 1990s, will be wasted if, as feared, money is misallocated to prop-up zombie companies. But, overall, Premier Wen Jiabao's speech could have been made by Barack Obama or Gordon Brown.

The rest of the world has also to come to terms with the fact that China is going on a buying spree. A few years ago, she had just $4 billion in shares offshore; now it's more than $150 billion, and exploding. Where not so long ago governments vetoed Chinese takeovers, now, in desperation, they are more welcoming. China needs to respond with more transparency over its company accounts and the dealings of its state-owned enterprises. Reaction will set in when its state-owned enterprises, with a pipeline to the government's massive surpluses, launch takeover bids for local companies in places like Australia, Canada, or South Africa. Greater transparency and accountability would be both healthy and necessary as China becomes like any other country. Its ability and willingness to implement the necessary changes may well determine when and how the world economy comes through its present economic crisis. If China's growth stays too long under 8 percent, all bets are off.

CHAPTER 3

Enter India

The likely emergence of China and India as new major global players—similar to the rise of Germany in the nineteenth century and America in the twentieth century—will transform the geopolitical landscape, with impacts potentially as dramatic as those of the previous two centuries.[1]

India is not just a country. It is a nation born out of 29 strongly independent provinces, six major religions, a billion people—just holding the country together is a fulltime job for leaders. I first visited India as a teenager, meeting up with local Socialist Party leaders who hosted me to dinner and held an open seminar for me. (They should have made me Prime Minister at 18: I knew everything.) The most gracious of hosts, they would not let me pay for food despite their poverty. They, too, wanted to talk about how to bring about a democratic revolution and fix the world's ills, and we talked nonstop for several days. The poverty was breathtaking, life-changing, yet their acceptance of their conditions, their humility and humanity were special. At the time, in their place, I would have wanted to throw bombs.

49

India regards itself, and is well respected, as a moral superpower. Its moral, mystic, even holy, authority comes from its democratic, post-colonial inspiration, born of historic tolerance, and from the fact that so many of the great faiths of the region were born there. Its ability to navigate cultural differences, in the main, is amazing. For generations India has been the democratic leader of Third World countries that admire its independent stance. That position has been strengthened because many developing countries quietly fear the other developing giant, China.

I returned again as New Zealand's Trade Minister in the 1980s, knowing that we had much to offer in agricultural technology, food-processing expertise, pulp and paper, and that, even then, they had a middle class bigger than and as wealthy as that of Italy or Australia. The Indians seemed to be natural traders. Their love of education, knowing that it is the ticket out for their children, is legendary. Ask any taxi driver from the sub-continent, anywhere in the world, about their children and they will say the daughter is studying to be a doctor, the son a lawyer.

India's trade with the outside world, like China's, stretches back well before Alexander the Great. Archaeologists have discovered evidence of Indian products in Greece dating from the first and second centuries BC. Rome traded with India. Evidence of pre-Christian exchanges between the Arab world, Africa and China abounds, some of it suggesting interchange as long ago as 2000 BC. No-one discovered India: its products and inventions discovered us. India was described as "The Jewel in Queen Victoria's Crown," and indeed her crown did have Indian jewels in it. Such was its wealth and bounty that key military strategies during the European wars that reached their hideous zenith during the Second World War were to protect the sea links with India.

Globalization is not new to India. It was how it de-globalized that was new, a cross its leaders nailed themselves to as they followed doomed theories of self-sufficiency and restricted trade, learning from the British who also restricted competition with their local British producers in products such as textiles. For nations which had fought hard for independence from their colonial masters, it was perhaps natural that economic nationalism would seem quite attractive. The alternatives promoted by fading imperialist Britain and capitalist America, seeking to prolong their power, profits and influence, were seen to be exploitative, especially when domestic capitalists, so often protected and privileged, sought common cause and Imperial honors from their

British bosses. Then India came into the Soviet sphere of political and economic influence, with its enforced, enclosed, nationalistic policies. In the process, it simply replaced the British Raj with an often more incompetent "licensing Raj," creating a bureaucratic elite. (Georgian president Edward Shevardnadze, a former Soviet Foreign Minister, once described how the system functioned: "We had a deal with India in the old days;" he said. "We sold them tanks that didn't work and they sold us medicines that didn't work.")

Despite the well-meaning protests in rich countries (often egged on by privileged interests in India), the truth is that globalization has not impoverished India; it's the lack of globalization that held it back for years "in terms of foregone growth, the avoidable delay in the eradication of poverty, and our falling behind our competition such as China."[2]

India began to open, cautiously, inviting investment to certain areas in the 1980s. Prime Minister Rajiv Ghandi, who took over after the murder of his mother, was a progressive, and didn't accept the fatalism of the "dignity of the poor." But he too was assassinated and it was the self-effacing Minister of Finance, Manmohan Singh, who emerged as the author of India's economic reforms. Though his Congress Party later lost an election, the good Fabian influence on the secular party reinforced its dedication to the poor, building on the inherent decency of Indian culture and its history of absorbing change, tolerance, and new influences.[3] Now, Manmohan Singh has re-emerged to lead the country. It should be noted that while out of power the reforming, pro-trade Singh became a member of a WTO advisory group—a courageous move in the political climate of the time. For while China used the WTO and its ambitions for membership as a guide, a stepping stone, a ladder and rationale for domestic reform, many politicians in India did the opposite, blaming the WTO for its domestic problems.

India's annual growth is well over 7 percent and its companies and brands are world-famous and successful. Tata, which had no exports 50 years ago, is now a great multinational. It has the biggest worldwide steel empire, is the world's largest manufacturer of motorcycles and the third-largest pharmaceutical industry. As a powerhouse of innovative research, with R&D facilities for most of the major global pharmaceutical industries, India accepts WTO intellectual-property rules, after years of opposition. Only 20 years ago, the joke went that with an Indian car everything makes a noise except the horn. Just recently, Tata bought the iconic British Jaguar and Land Rover brands, and has launched the Nano, which retails for around $2,500. India is a platform for world-class technology, medicine and information, taking advantage of and leading the information age. High-tech and information services don't need an industrial-age infrastructure, which is probably just as well, given the state of India's ports and rail system.

A tradition and thirst for knowledge, backed up by a British-style parliamentary and legal system, gives India strong, skeptical processes of accountability and justification. It has been ranked among the best corporate governance and best business leaders in Asia. In recent times, Indian CEOs have headed great multinationals such as McKinsey, Citibank, Linklater, BellLabs, Standard Chartered, HSBC, United Airlines, United States Airlines, Hughes Network Systems and Hartland Financial Services, to name but a few. Some commentators are suggesting this will be the Indian century.[4]

Such is the quality and strength of India's trade diplomacy that it, more than anyone, was able to bring the Seattle trade ministers meeting to a standstill. The Indians are tough negotiators, always with an eye to their local electors. When we finally launched the new Trade Development Round in Doha, they were the last aboard. As a leader of the G20, it has fought successfully the conclusion of the round and all eyes in Geneva are on the Indian elections in May 2009. Great national interests don't change with governments. Only two elections are ever mentioned in regard to the WTO negotiations: those in the United States and India, which is evidence of India's influence and the skill of her negotiators and ministers.

Before India began its liberalizations in 1991, there was effectively only one TV channel, a state broadcaster; by 2006, there were more than 150 channels. Before the reforms, because of low growth, it would have taken 57 years for a family to double its income; now incomes will double in just 15 years.[5]

Cricket, a colonial game introduced by the British, is a national obsession. Just recently massive Indian investment has commercialized this noble game and Indian cricket clubs have gone global, offering a menu of salaries for a spread of players from all over the world in a structure reminiscent of European soccer clubs.

I find the Indians' core principles of secularism, democracy and their commitment to their poor to be enormously attractive. Their commitment at the highest levels to the United Nations and its agencies has been impressive over many years. This is not to underestimate the challenges (and opportunities) it faces. For instance, according to Gunedar Kapuur, CEO of Reliance, "organized retailing has its lowest market share in food and groceries—1 percent. India has the highest retail density in the world with 'mom and pop' shops everywhere." These inefficiencies, while superficially job-rich at very low pay, represent huge costs in energy wastage and high prices—but it's a lifestyle that will change. That is why there were huge protests when Wal-Mart opened a wholesaling operation there (note, wholesale distribution, not retail). Reliance Group is spending $6 billion to get ahead of its competition by investing in retail. Organized retail is expected to grow by 30 percent a year. Dark warnings about a Second Partition, this time between rich and poor, worry leaders. Now the poor can more easily see the rich, with their expensive cars and designer clothes, living a life of excess, causing envy which can quickly turn to political anger.

India vs. China?

India and China are rivals and competitors. This is healthy. It would be dangerous for all if China became the only Asian superpower, surrounded by weak, anemic neighbors. Trade between India and China, non-existent a few years ago, is now in the billions of dollars. At the moment, India has the software, China the hardware. The synergy is obvious and stunning in its potential. China's encouragement for India's bid for a seat on the United Nations Security Council, while at the same time opposing Japan's, was a sign of a new relationship based on respect.

A quick analysis would suggest that, since India is a democracy and its people enjoy greater freedom, India should do better in the long run. The reality, though, is a lot more complicated. India had a better start than China after the Second World War. On Independence in 1947, it had strong sterling reserves and world-class universities and institutions, but then suffered a bitter and costly partition. China's war started in 1937 with the Japanese invasion and did not finish until 1949 when the civil war was finally over. Famines and Mao Zedong's ill-considered Great Leap Forward to industrialization starved and impoverished millions. The 1966–76 Cultural Revolution killed tens of millions. Then, in the late 1970s, China began its dramatic economic return.

Before China began to open, the average Indian was twice as rich as the average Chinese. Now, however, it's the other way around, though India is catching up quickly. In 1985, 90 percent of Indians lived on less than a dollar a day. That proportion has fallen to 54 percent. Within two decades, India will surpass Germany as the world's fifth-largest consumer market. That's another 291 million people moving out of extreme poverty. When the cost of living is taken into account, this is a massive new middle class. In China in 1985, 99 percent of urban households lived on less than $3 per day per person; by 2005 that was down to 57 percent. Over the next 20 years, according to the McKinsey Global Institute, incomes will increase eightfold, cutting China's poverty rate to 16 percent. India and China will have 1.8 billion fewer poor people than before their economic reforms. All this makes me wonder why there is any debate about open economies at all.

Boasting world brands such as Tata, Infosys and Wipro, India's private sector is superior to China's, and it has better corporate governance, aligned with the best world practices. It also has functioning, albeit imperfect, capital markets, an area in which China struggles. In the bureaucratic stakes, however, China beats India in many areas. For example, securing the permits necessary to establish a business in China is said to take as little as four days, while insolvency procedures can be completed in two to six years. In India, comparable procedures would take 88 days and 11 years, respectively. China also has a much more flexible labor market than India.

China's expressways exceed those of India by some 30,000 kilometers and China has six times as many mobile and fixed-line telephones per person as India. China is ruthless in cutting through bureaucracy without worrying about popular or local opinion, which means that it has been able to build new airports, roads and ports without lengthy delays. In India, it can take up to eight days, including 32 hours waiting at toll booths, for a truck to get from Mumbai to Kolkata.

India's commitment to the rule of law and democracy should give it a long-term advantage over China, but China will not stand still. As I argue throughout this book, giving everyone the vote is not the only big idea that counts. Governance in India also has terrible challenges; corruption is still widespread. Transparency International, which monitors corruption in countries around the world, suggested in a 2005 study that Indians pay out more than $5 billion a year in bribes. Those who have exposed corrupt practices become targets of the corrupt beneficiaries and many have paid the price with their lives. But India enjoys a strong free press and a robust tradition of self-criticism. Its new "right to information" law has opened up new opportunities to further expose bad behavior and corruption.

In the West progressives often equate public service with public good, and this is often true, especially in societies with rich, honest and open histories of good governance. It is not so true in many developing countries and economies in transition. Ninety percent of India's 21 million public-sector employees are in categories which entitle them to be paid three times the salary of private-sector equivalents, and from which, under Article 311 of the Indian Constitution, it is almost impossible to sack them.

In New Delhi there are an estimated 500,000 bicycle rickshaws on the streets, but only 99,000 permits for legal drivers. Because the government will not abolish licenses or raise the quota, it is estimated that more than 400,000 drivers operate illegally and have to bribe the police just to remain in business. It's a similar story for the city's 600,000 street hawkers, who are at the mercy of both the police and customs officials and obliged to pay up to a third of meager earnings in bribes. However, that these problems are so well documented, even by government agencies, says a lot for India.

All this domestic attention and international attention puts pressure on political leaders to respond. Transparency, information, is the cleansing disinfectant of bureaucracy. The whistleblowers in India and China are great patriots, and their numbers are growing.

India has always been open to outside forces, sometimes forced by invasions. Its culture endures and adapts to these changes: that's its genius. It's dangerous to write anything definitive about India and China because things are changing so fast. Theirs is a magnificent story that is still being written.

Bollywood is now a global cultural force—and almost as much a victim of piracy as Hollywood. It would be telling to study how many patents for new discoveries are registered in India as opposed to China in five years' time.

Meanwhile, China, at the moment, is winning in the literacy stakes: 98 percent of Chinese children have spent five years in school compared with 53 percent of Indian children. It's inevitable that China's articulate, interconnected and increasingly mobile middle class will demand better outcomes for the environment, seek greater transparency and tolerate less corruption. This has been the experience in South Korea, Taiwan, Indonesia, and Malaysia. Why should China and India be any different?

The China versus India question actually doesn't matter. Both—and thus all of us—will win. The real race is an internal one, not between each other or against the rest of us. Both have greater internal disparities of wealth than the United Kingdom or the United States. China certainly faces more complex political problems in the future. India has the shock absorber of democracy in place already. It can change regimes and direction peacefully—can China?

Remember, when one cell phone comes to a village, everyone is excited; when one in 10 people have a cell phone, envy builds. Wealth and opportunity not shared and distributed inevitably brings a reaction. History has shown that the redistribution of wealth can, when done crudely and bluntly, lead to the destruction of that wealth, both current and future.

Both of these ancient civilizations will again become great powers and partners of the twenty-first century. Every country in the globe will benefit as both China and India become greater customers, consumers, manufacturers, tourists, and inventors. Every government in every country should have a minister dedicated to working with China and India. In fact, they probably do already; it's the Trade and Foreign Affairs Minister.

The Islamic World: The Need for Mutual Respect

With justifiable pride, Muslims tell the story of the Medina Charter. In 622 (600 years before the Magna Carta), the Prophet Mohammed wrote and promulgated the charter for his city-state, which had a multi-religious population of about 10,000. This charter, which laid down rules for a pluralistic society where citizens had equal rights and a say in government, was to last for a thousand years. It guaranteed religious freedom, and spoke of equality between men and women. Though it was a centralized feudal system, it delegated power to the various districts of which it was composed, granting them autonomy in certain activities. Arabic scholars and Western specialists alike have long argued that the Medina Charter was the first written constitution in history.[1]

This document gives moral strength and a religious justification for democrats in the Muslim world. In a world-values survey conducted by the Pew Institute the rejection of authoritarian rule and the belief in democracy as the best form of government is higher in Arab countries than in any other region in the world, including the United States and Western Europe.

Saudi Arabia is a unique nation. As custodian of the holy sites of Islam, it faces special tensions and deserves sensitive treatment. As the US experience in Iraq indicates, it would be foolhardy to think that any transfer to democracy as it has evolved in Western democracies could be achieved smoothly and without frictions. Success rests on more than giving everyone a vote in which the biggest or best-organized tribe can win. It is based on a host of economic, technological and social innovations. More fundamentally, it rests on big ideas, such as freedom, respect, equality, openness, reciprocity, and the rule of law. For most of the world, freedom of religion and, more important, freedom from religion are central. The separation of church and state was an important driver for freedom, innovation and the dissemination of information. Man's position in life and the future was no longer seen as being preordained. These need not be a contradiction of Islamic values, as history has taught us, and Turkey, Indonesia and Malaysia continue to show us today.

These values go to the core of our humanity, but, sadly, they are neither shared nor enjoyed universally. In the Middle East, those in power talk of a more open society and are effecting change. In March 2009, for example, Qatar opened a church, with thousands attending the consecration. In defending this move, a former dean of the Qatar Islamic Law School wrote for the local paper: "Places of worship for various religions is a fundamental human right." With literally millions of migrant workers in the region, many from non-Muslim countries such as the Philippines, this issue will continue to create tensions. Of all the countries in the region only Saudi Arabia still bans Christian gatherings. But even there, the 85-year-old King Abdullah is pushing reform, appointing the nation's first woman minister and taking strong measures against militant extremists such as Al Qaeda. Change is in the air but if it is to come about, it will have to be effected at its own speed.

Defining differences: Malaysia, Turkey, Iran and the Gulf States

The West often seems to veer toward a dangerous and self-fulfilling paranoia about the Muslim world. That emotive position is frequently matched by defensive bluster within the Muslim world. When we have such a costly invasion as the US-led takeover in Iraq, set against concerted efforts by Al Qaeda and other radical groups to strike against so-called infidels, the real commonality that exists between the majority of populations gets obscured. Yet recent polls in the region show the extremists are losing support and the recent change of administration may well see US prestige return. Such is the genius of America and its capacity to reinvent itself and correct its course.

In September 2007, I spent a few days in Kuala Lumpur, Malaysia, as a guest at an international forum of the Organization of Islamic Countries. There, leaders and scholars met to discuss, evaluate and audit the progress in implementing the Makkah Declaration, a holistic plan to lift living standards and provide an agenda for progress for the world's billion Muslims. At the meeting, Malaysia's then prime minister, Abdullah Ahmad Badawi, argued that the divide between the Muslim world and the West is *the* strategic issue of global concern. Firm about the problems of Palestine, Iraq and Afghanistan, he was equally so about the need of the Muslim world to do better, and not just in the area of lifting living standards:

> It must also mean a literate and informed society, a representative political system that gives effective voice to the people, the absence of severe irregularities, efficient and honest administration, and a commitment to the rule of law. A country cannot be considered "developed" until rights are respected, women are empowered, minorities protected, and corruption eradicated.

The Conference responded to these strong words: women's rights, corruption, and development dominated the proceedings.

The Muslim world represents some of the poorest, most desperate places, and stretches from West Africa to the Philippines. The Arab world of 280 million has a GDP, including oil revenues, that's less than that of Spain.[2] Malaysia is a progressive model of how a mainly Muslim nation can navigate great ethnic differences and succeed. But its model can no more be parachuted into other countries than the US Constitution can be FedExed into others. Malaysia has been through a lot over the 50 years since it gained independence in 1957, overcoming a powerful Communist uprising; "confrontation" with Indonesia; the split with Singapore; the race riots of a generation ago; and the dangers inherent in the financial crisis that beset Asia in the 1990s.

Where 40 years ago Malaysia was as poor as Haiti, now there is very little extreme poverty. Faced with new competition from China and a vibrant Vietnam, it has resisted the temptation to turn inwards toward protectionism and subsidies, instead positioning itself as part of the global supply chain. Malaysia's economic strategies have moved beyond "think big" projects to the point where southern Malaysia will, in the future, be little different from Singapore. Similar to Hong Kong and China, Malaysia is a major destination for Middle East investment and middle-class Muslim tourism.

Open trade and investment work. Economic growth is the best—probably the only—answer to extreme poverty. When in the 1980s Pakistan consistently recorded annual growth of 6 percent, extreme poverty dropped from 40 percent to 18 percent. When growth slowed to 3.5 percent in the 1990s, extreme poverty increased again, from 18 percent to 33 percent. Over the past few years, Pakistan has enjoyed 5 percent growth and poverty has declined to 24 percent. The lessons of history make clear that the key to sustained growth is the rule of law, property rights, education, and widening the economic social and political franchise to include women and minorities. No country has ever lifted itself out of poverty without economic growth. There's no shortage of money in the world but investment will go where it feels safe, where there are predictable laws, independent courts, and risk is minimized. Seminars and NGOs spend days debating new policies for the World Bank and IMF when their total percentage of international investment is in single figures. The same people often oppose opening their economies to investment, arguing "sovereignty."

It is the humiliation of marginalization that breeds extremism. Removing poverty of itself doesn't remove fanaticism, but where there is social justice, democracy, progress and hope, there is much less fertile ground for the seeds of fanaticism—with its contempt for human life—to take root.

There is a way through some of our more seemingly intractable problems, and countries such as Malaysia, Indonesia, Turkey and some of the small Middle East states are laboratories of hope, models of a more tolerant, semi-secular, sensitive response to these problems. There is no one single Islamic world any more than there is any one Buddhist or Christian world.

But are we listening to what the moderate states are telling us? How the European Union engages with Turkey is crucial. With European engagement and openness, Turkey can be brought into the EU environment and act as a critical bridgehead between the West and the Muslim world. (Indonesia can play a similar role in the Asian context. Positive engagement, particularly by Australia and New Zealand through ASEAN, will be critical to broader relations between Muslim and non-Muslim.)

During the past four decades of shadow negotiations, the European Union has demanded radical changes to Turkish law and customs.

This has slowly resulted in improvements in human and property rights. The process of implementing the political and economic reforms necessary to raise Turkey's standards and harmonize its laws is a painful one, and most observers don't expect the formal negotiations to conclude in a decade. Turkey has a population of nearly 70 million, of whom 18 percent live below the poverty line and 33 percent work in agriculture, with an average income not even a quarter of the European average. The genius and generosity of the European model is how the rich nations have extended a financial hand to the poorer nations who, upon joining, receive massive adjustment subsidies. All have prospered with the subsidies, advantages, privileges and opportunities in a wider, free European market. Turkey's accession will be costly, leading to many billions of dollars flowing east. Countries that have been net winners, getting more money from Brussels than they pay in, are nervous. One country at any time can veto membership or, more likely, keep pushing up demands and stall negotiations.

Turkey's membership opens a primitive fear in some European circles, dating back centuries to the siege of Vienna, when the dreaded Turks were at the gates of Christendom. Some religious and political leaders, dismayed that the proposed new European Union constitution made no mention of their Christian heritage, have been blunt about a Christian Europe being swamped by 70 million Muslim Turks. This has given rise to conspiracy literature that suggests the European Union is a Catholic plot to reinvent the Holy Roman Empire. France has six million Muslims, and two million Turks already live in Germany. The great European project, its wider membership and deeper institutions, must be agreed upon by all parliaments or, in some places, by referendum. Turkey's membership could help both sides of the argument. No-one of political substance now really argues about the economic benefits of a wider, open, free-trading Europe. The argument is between those who see a European super state, a United States of Europe, and those who see Europe as just a free-trade arrangement with weak, overarching political institutions that have no real power—a sort of United Nations of Europe.

Turkey's membership would give it a bigger voice in the election of a proposed European President than the United Kingdom or France. That specter is feared but, curiously, welcomed by some Euro-skeptics. This, they say, will stop the political integration of Europe but help build a wider economic union. Turkey's membership is supported by those who see it as a bridge to Islam, with Turkey as a model for a democratic secular Islamic state. The United States has publicly promoted Turkey's membership, causing quiet anger in European circles and comparisons to the US relationships with its Mexican migrants. Turkey is a formidable military power: its army is six times the size of Britain's, competent and well-equipped, and is an active member of NATO. Over 70 percent of Europeans would like a future Europe to be a military power to balance the United States. Demographics point to the European Union becoming an old people's home, while Turkey is a very young country.

Simply preparing to apply for EU membership has already resulted in better governance and social and environmental outcomes in Turkey. The Turks have changed hundreds of laws and are committed to adopting thousands of new rules and regulations. Turkey's risk premiums on debt have fallen with recent progress. However, some Turks are asking why Turkey's conditions of membership should be different from those that apply to any other country seeking membership. Turkey is not just another country. It shouldered much of the burden of the Cold War and now stands at the complex crossroads between East and West, Christendom and the Muslim world. Geography makes Turkey an essential nation.

A far more acute threat to relations between the Muslim and non-Muslim worlds exists around the potential of Iran to become a nuclear-armed power. Here at least is an issue over which the global community is showing some sophistication and solidarity.

It is stunning how little people understand of Iran and its history. Iran's economy is about the size of Finland's. The United States has a GDP 68 times larger and has defense expenditure that's 110 times greater. It's conveniently forgotten (except in Iran) that the West and its secret services organized a violent overthrow of a properly elected social democratic government because it had the audacity to nationalize its oil resources (something the British Government itself had just done).

One of the joys of the WTO is that it has avoided the United Nations trap of passing inflammatory resolutions about delicate issues such as the Middle East. Although none of these resolutions is implemented, they serve as good media back home but frequently lock people into positions that become very difficult to change, thereby blocking negotiations that could help resolve great divides. The Israel-Palestine issue has not been raised at the WTO. Instead, countries that normally are reluctant to share objectives come together.

Ministers and negotiators speak for national self-interest, so the ritual condemnation of each other for past grievances is normally not appropriate, although recent reports indicate that this is slowly changing as the membership widens and bad habits from the United Nations encroach. Nevertheless, where the UN has debates, the WTO has negotiations, bringing together, for the first time in years, Croats with Serbs, Armenians with Azerbaijanis, with politics off the agenda.

Iran is not a WTO member but has shown an interest in joining for a number of years. After leaving the organization, I attended a public seminar in Iran to discuss the country's WTO ambitions with officials, academics, and businesspeople. I trotted out my familiar line about the tendency towards corruption that is endemic in closed economies and was taken aback at the public strength and brutal honesty of speakers condemning the government and its economic policies—all in the presence of government ministers. If such language had been used in my country, ministers would have walked out. But then none of this appeared in the local media.

The present Iranian leadership has taken an extreme nationalistic line in economic and foreign policy. Its outrageous statements on Israel, its secret funding of terrorist groups, and its nuclear ambitions all raise the possibility of a new arms race in the region. However, many of the young people are very cosmopolitan in their outlook and are uncomfortable with all this.

Here is an ancient culture that stretches back many thousands of years before Islam. If we have a proper understanding of and respect for Persian history, then perhaps we can inch forward. The problem we have is not knowing who is in charge, who to negotiate with. Power doesn't reside in familiar places. Perhaps, from the tragedy of Iraq the great powers have learned to be patient, because they know once the nuclear genie is out of the bottle, it's hard to put back. We should look to China, Russia, India, Turkey and Pakistan as true partners if this problem is to be defused. A useful model is the coalition of core neighboring nations that is being used in an attempt to bring North Korea to a sense of reality. Libya has trimmed its nuclear ambitions and now seems to be cooperating on many levels against the fundamentalists. Working out a similar formula for integrating Iran is a global imperative.

The nations of the Gulf Co-Operation Council (GCC)—Bahrain, Oman, Qatar, Saudi Arabia, Kuwait, and the United Arab Emirates (UAE)—are creating a common economic space and there's talk of introducing a common currency that will have profound implications for the status and security of the US dollar. In substance, this would come in behind the US dollar, the euro and the Japanese yen, and a little ahead of the Chinese *reminbi*, so it's not a small idea.

The UAE is a federal state of small emirates, the most well-known being Dubai, which now hosts more tourists than Egypt. Its airport gets 30 million visitors, and its airline, Emirates, is the one of the fastest-growing in the world. Only 40 percent of Dubai's income is now resource-based; oil and energy produces only a fraction of its income. The UAE's growth is staggering. New cities—an internet city, a cinema industry ($500 million earmarked), an education city, the first-ever green, carbon-neutral city—are in the planning. The world's largest building will soon be finished. Twice as many women are at local universities than men, and women ministers serve in most Emirates. Women account for 45 percent of vehicle purchases, and outspend men in consumer electronics.

Taken as a whole, the GCC would be the seventh-largest economy in the developing world; twice the size of Turkey, South Africa, or Argentina. Its global savings are higher than China's, and its current account surplus on a par. The Abu Dhabi Investment Authority is second only to the Bank of Japan in terms of assets. UAE investments around the world range from Deutsche Bank, Citibank and Sainsbury, to Daimler, Ferrari and Aston Martin, and are growing. The IMF suggests infrastructure investment will reach $800 billion by 2010

On the respected index of economic freedom, the GCC is well ahead of Russia, China, and India. Half the GCC states score ahead of Italy. The small states are laboratories of progress and hope, where success is causing a global splash from which we can all benefit. There is a commitment to commercial law, which is why most of the world's banks and multinationals are there. All are members of the WTO and subject to its agreed rules and obligations.

People in the region speak openly of how they can evolve into constitutional monarchies. Cautiously, elections are being held, and in some places women voters have outnumbered the men. Most of these countries have migrant workers, who can outnumber the locals by as much as five to one. Labor rights remain very weak, but there is movement in the right direction. Remittances from these workers to the Philippines, Pakistan, and India are worth more to these countries than all the development aid they receive from the West.

In effect, as numerous commentators have observed, a new Silk Road is being created. Within four hours' flight lie four billion consumers.

Middle Eastern merchants were trading with India and China before Christ was born. Having 40 percent of the world's known oil reserves, 23 percent of the world's natural gas reserves, and 22 percent of the present oil supply has helped, of course. But with the current volatility in oil prices the petrodollars are being invested more wisely than in the 1970s. These nations are investing beyond energy, everywhere and at home. Qatar is always in the news for its global events calendar, and successfully hosted the world's second-largest sporting event, the Asian Games. Qatar's global TV reach through Al Jazeera is now in English.

The way forward

In the end, only Muslims can reform the Muslim world but the West and the rest of the world can assist progressive forces. Fanatics cannot be negotiated with or wished away. In facing an enemy who is ideological and theocratic, we need to wage an ideological war to give hope and opportunity to the people. When an Al Jazeera talkback show posed the question, "Have existing Arab regimes become worse than colonialism?" 66 percent of respondents said "Yes." Clearly, there is fertile ground for progress or reaction. We need to show confidence and moral clarity in the ruthless application of policies to combat the exportation of extreme Wahabism and other elements that seek to destabilize and radicalize Muslims everywhere. Our allies in this are the women of Islam and their hopes for their children. We ignore the concept of *Jihad* at our peril.

To some extent we limit ourselves in talking of the Muslim world as if it didn't include the West. The most popular name for baby boys in Belgium, and the eighth-most popular boys' name in Britain, is Mohammed. British Muslims have been found fighting with the Taliban, plotting terror attacks in Yemen, attempting to blow up passenger airplanes, and kidnapping and killing journalists in Pakistan. Two British citizens were uncovered after volunteering for suicide missions in Israel. Muslim converts—German citizens from German stock—have been arrested in Germany.[3]

After the Bali bombings in 2002, in which 202 people, many of them Australians, were murdered, Al Qaeda said the bombings were because Australian troops had helped to liberate Timor Leste. This 450-year-old Catholic enclave in Muslim Indonesia had been annexed violently by Indonesia in 1975 while the world looked the other way.

bin Laden has called for the liberation of Spain—indeed, all the old caliphate—blaming the likes of Mustafa Kamal Ataturk, Gamal Abdel Nasser and Saddam Hussein for embracing the notion of the secular nation-state. People like these want a return to the past, as do extremist Zionists who talk of the biblical borders of Israel. Both President Anwar Al Sadat of Egypt and Prime Minister Yitzhak Rabin of Israel, who opposed such views, were assassinated by extremists within their own ranks.

But then think of the many rabid right-wing radio hosts in the US who have called for the nuking of Iran; or those from Iran calling for the destruction of Israel. These extremists rail at each other from positions of anti-reason and anti-enlightenment. They have much in common and we do well to listen to them only to strengthen our adherence to the universal values of freedom, tolerance and respect for others. These are the hard-won prizes from generations of human advancement. In Part 2, we will be exploring the origins of these principles, in order to gain a better appreciation of the changes and challenges that face us today.

PART 2

BIG IDEAS THROUGH HISTORY

The concepts that I believe make a successful society—good governance, openness, choice, civil society and democracy—are big ideas, but none of them is new. None of these attributes and attitudes came about naturally, and these big ideas took centuries to unfold and to be championed. It was not obvious that a king or the person with the most powerful weaponry should be answerable to the law; nor was it necessarily a natural conclusion that all people were created equal. Engaging with strange people runs against the grain of an instinctive hostility to outsiders. That a community should accept people with different beliefs as equals was not obvious, even if it always made sense to trade. In recent centuries, the major developments have occurred in that violent, dynamic and expansionist continent, Europe, an ambitious finger sticking out from the fist of Asia. The greatest powers to emerge from its fold in the past 200 years—Britain and the United States—have led the way.

The origins of the big ideas, however, went far deeper and were more widely dispersed. What follows is my idiosyncratic (and no doubt partial) impression of the highlights of these important historical developments.

CHAPTER 5

Early Consensus Government

We begin with the basic device for preserving knowledge used by all oral cultures: story-telling. We want the young not to make the mistakes we made. Perhaps this also is a defining characteristic of our species: the ability and the need to pass on experiences and information.

Oratory, the ability to convince others, has been a hallmark of leadership since people learned the use of language. Great orators of the past knew their power. They also knew the threat represented by outside scrutiny and questioning, and thus did their best to ensure their voice was the sole source of information and authority. That power began to crumble with the invention of the printing press and the onset of the Age of Reason. Could early orators have survived in our talkback, telecratic, technological era?

In many societies around the world where oratory is still a basis for leadership, the most important occasions for the display of oratorical skills are "gatherings"—assemblies at which every member of the community is entitled to be present and participate in the discussions. These gatherings are either spontaneous (mostly those called to reach a quick judicial settlement) or formally convened (for more serious deliberations on clan activities). The decisions express the consensus of the gathering, counting on the expectation of "equivalence"— that a person "should be amenable to persuasion [and] any matter which concerns the tribe or its segments should be decided freely on the basis of arrived consensus."[1]

The clan orator is expected to retain a measure of control over these gatherings; a control that is manifested more subtly and is perhaps more difficult to maintain because only the collective assembly can enforce its consensus. These two seemingly conflicting values converge to produce an exercise that is remarkably free of coercion—a genuinely democratic function. The clan orator emerges as a figure comparable to, but less powerful than, eloquent modern prime ministers, who are limited by their parliament, their party, and the laws and values of their constituency.

In my region, the South Pacific, there is a similar pattern of giving pre-eminence to the interests of the community. Although hierarchical, the societies are democratic because they practice public discussion of all proposals and activities. Before the islanders had ever heard of the British parliamentary system, they had a deliberative body (the *fono*) that was convened to discuss issues at length, until, almost by exhaustion, consensus was reached.

I'm not suggesting that these cultures were actually democratic, or held human life or human rights in the same regard to which we now universally aspire. But they believed in consulting, and even the most bloody tribal chief felt obliged to talk to his elders and people, even if just to ensure instructions were carried out. Independent of each other, separated by thousands of miles and thousands of years, these themes emerge, time and time again. I believe they are instinctive in our species.

Just as instinctive perhaps is the need of those holding or seeking power to try and monopolize that power. Hereditary systems and tribal systems where the "holy ones" had divine insights to enable them to cure the ill and find answers to the meaning of nature, life and the universe always opposed any suggestion of merit-based power unless that merit was won by a warrior class. The rule of law, insofar as it existed, served to preserve the interests of those with power. That was always the way of things until the Enlightenment. Primitive tribal communities, whom the Enlightenment has bypassed, still operate as Europe did during the Dark Ages, with all information translated to the people through the agents of the powerful.

Karl Marx was normally scathing about peasant societies but he, like Jean-Jacques Rousseau in his day, was fascinated by the classless society of some Native Americans. His associate Friedrich Engels was entranced by *Ancient Society*, written by Lewis H. Morgan in the 1870s. Engels wrote of the league of Iroquois, for example:

> And a wonderful constitution it is … in all its childlike simplicity! No soldiers, no gendarmes or police, no nobles, kings, regents, prefects, or judges, no prisons, no lawsuits … There cannot be any poor or needy—the communal household and the *gens* know their responsibilities toward the old, the sick, and those disabled in war. All are equal and free—the women included.[2]

The Iroquois were governed by decisions made after deliberations in the tribal council at which each speaker was listened to with respect. In this respect, they have been compared to the Athenian senate.

In an essay entitled "Remarks Concerning the Savages of North America," Benjamin Franklin wrote how the Indians "have abundance of leisure for improvement by conversation. All their government is by the counsel or advice of the sages; there is no force, there are no prisons, no officers to compel disobedience or inflict punishment." At council meetings the old men sat in the foremost ranks; when they spoke, everyone else observed a respectful silence. "How different this is from the conduct of a polite British House of Commons," Franklin remarked.

More recently, Nobel Prize-winner Amartya Sen has argued that to ignore the centrality of public reasoning and leadership in the idea of democracy not only distorts and diminishes the history of democratic ideas but also distracts attention from the interactive processes through which a democracy functions and on which its success depends: "Even with the expansion of adult franchise and fair elections, free and uncensored deliberation is important for people to be able to determine what they must demand, what they should criticize, and how they ought to vote."

Oral and moral leadership

The proverb "sticks and stones may break my bones but words will never hurt me" is a religious instruction to turn the other cheek. But words can hurt as well as inspire: most wars are initiated by words; debate normally improves the quality of decision-making. That was why Barack Obama's US primary campaign was special. Obama's already much-lauded speech on race issues was both a serious, thoughtful celebration of progress and a call to do better, mindful of the great wrongs of the past. He treated his audience with respect, which made it a hard speech to report in this era of spin and sound-bite.

Winston Churchill's wartime speeches reflected his respect for Parliament and the people. He trusted them with the facts. When congratulated on the success of the Dunkirk withdrawal, he said, "Wars are not won by evacuations."

Senator Robert Kennedy's off-the-cuff speech on the night of Martin Luther King's assassination combined sympathy, empathy and respect for the intelligence of his stunned audience. Quoting Aeschylus—"Even in our sleep, pain which cannot forget, falls, drop by drop, upon the human heart, until, in our own despair, against our will, comes wisdom through the awful grace of God"—he pointed a way forward out of injustice, concluding: "Let us dedicate ourselves to what the Greeks wrote so many years ago, to tame the savageness of man and make gentle the life of this world."

Despite the tendency these days to reduce everything to 10-second sound "grabs" for TV and radio ("In one minute or less, explain your economic policy," I was once asked), such contributions to freedom and history will continue to resonate because they have in them the power of reason and liberty, a cry for freedom, cemented together by exquisite eloquence—the skill of great leaders and thinkers throughout the ages. Real leaders have to explain, convince, and inspire—that's their democratic obligation. But these same oratorical skills have been used by demagogues, populists and villains throughout history too; but how many speeches of, say, Pol Pot or Adolf Hitler inspire today? That's the difference between demagogic and democratic leadership. Democratic leaders seek the approval, consent and support of the people. Churchill went to parliament to report, as did Franklin Roosevelt. They seized the moment and the big ideas of civilization and hurled them into history: it's that intellectual courage and defiance that continues to move and motivate people today. Leadership is not just about representing the will of the people. Willing a view on others who have the power to say no is a real test of democratic leadership.

The great speeches passed down to us through history repeat key themes that still lift our spirits and horizons, bringing out the best in us all. The great Athenian statesman Pericles delivered his powerful funeral oration in 431 BC in tribute to those who had fallen during the Peloponnesian War. While honoring the virtues of the fallen sons of Greece, he extolled the value of democratic government:

> How different soever in a private capacity, we all enjoy the same general equality our laws are fitted to preserve; and superior honors just as we excel. The public administration is not confined to a particular family, but is attainable only by merit. Poverty is not a hindrance, since whoever is able to serve his country meets with no obstacle to preferment from his first obscurity. The offices of the state we go through without obstructions from one another; and live together in the mutual endearments of private life without suspicions... [I]n private life we converse without diffidence of damage, while we dare not on any account offend against the public, through the reverence we bear to the magistrates and the laws, chiefly to those enacted for redress of the injured, and to those unwritten, a breach of which is thought a disgrace.

> In our manner of living, we show an elegance tempered with frugality, and we cultivate philosophy without enervating the mind. We display our wealth in the season of beneficence, and not in the vanity of discourse. A confession of poverty is a disgrace to no man, no effort to avoid it is disgrace indeed.

Pericles captured the dignity of democracy and reminded his audience that their unique society was worth fighting for and defending. These themes reappear throughout history in almost every great act of moral leadership both in real life and in literature—from the moral courage of Socrates in the face of death, to Joan of Arc's defense at her trial, to the inspirational words of Shakespeare's Henry V before the battle of Agincourt. In this last, we find themes that are as familiar today as they were then:

> This story shall the good man teach his son;
> And Crispin Crispian shall ne'er go by,
> From this day to the ending of the world,
> But we in it shall be remembered —
> We few, we happy few, we band of brothers;
> And gentlemen in England now a-bed
> Shall think themselves accurs'd they were not here,
> And hold their manhoods cheap whiles any speaks
> That fought with us upon Saint Crispin's day.

"We happy few, we band of brothers..."—a call to sacrifice echoed in the defiance of Winston Churchill's epic speeches during the Second World War. "These are not dark days," he said, "these are the greatest days our country has ever lived; and we must all thank God that we have been allowed, each of us according to our stations, to play a part in making these days memorable in the history of our race."

His speeches to Parliament were remarkable in their candor and respect for people's ability to handle the truth. As President John F. Kennedy said of him: "He marshaled the English language and drove it into battle."

Leaders throughout history have had the unique ability to call nations to account, to shame the powerful and hold them accountable to the ideals of their own civilizations. Ghandi's unwavering defiance—"Non-violence is the first article of my faith. It is the last article of my faith"; Martin Luther King's resounding plea "to let freedom ring"; Nelson Mandela's defense of a democratic and free society as "an ideal which I hope to live for and to achieve. But if needs be, it is an ideal for which I am prepared to die"—all made appeal to what Abraham Lincoln called "the better angels of our nature." All understood that you do not change a society merely by replacing one wet-fingered politician with another. You change society by changing the wind.[3] But these arguments for peaceful resistance and non-cooperation work only when the forces being fought against have in them to some degree the principles of the Enlightenment, rule of law and democracy. Peaceful resistance to Hitler or Stalin would not have met with much success. The overreaction of British troops in India, and of the local police in Alabama, the massacre of children in Soweto: all brought ordinary people, even those without a personal interest, to their feet in righteous rage. The international reputations of entire nations suffered. Eventually the powerful had to surrender to reason; by doing so they saved themselves as well as the persecuted.

Democracy—A Universal Impulse?

It is a Western conceit that freedom, tolerance, appreciation of good governance, and government representing the will of the people originated and grew in peninsular Europe.

Europe certainly did nourish the idea of democracy, and it was Europe that gave birth to the Reformation, the Age of Enlightenment and the Age of Reason, which resulted in the separation of church and state and the establishment of the rule of law as we now know it. That's why Europe and its former colonies dominated the history of the past few centuries, and remain central to world affairs today.

But Europeans had no monopoly on the basic concepts of democracy or any of the other big ideas. More than 80 percent of the world's population did not, and do not, live in Europe. Freedom is a universal urge and wise leadership has been celebrated and remembered through the ages, passed down through oral tradition and written histories, both legendary and factual. Many societies in other parts of our planet have also found ways of responding to the will of the people, replacing tyrants and providing security for their people.

As Amartya Sen argues, "The long traditions of encouraging and protecting public debates on political, social, and cultural matters in, say, India, China, Japan, Korea, Iran, Turkey, the Arab world, and many parts of Africa, demand much fuller recognition in the history of democratic ideas."[1] The matter is important because tyrants around the world repeatedly assert that democracy is just a Western idea, and is therefore just a form of Westernization, to be resisted on nationalistic or indigenous grounds.

In a seminal work on indigenous politics, Raul Manglapus (a vociferous opponent of the corrupt Marcos regime in the Philippines in the 1980s and subsequently a minister in the Aquino government which replaced it) argues that democracy is not a Western invention, but a value that has been treasured and practiced in many cultures from as early as 2500 BC. "Yearnings for democratic freedoms," he says, "were not just an idiosyncrasy of race, but a sentiment universal in all cultures, Western and non-Western alike. The urge for justice, accountability, and integrity in the law are basic human instincts. Slavery and oppression are not the normal, nor the accepted state of man."[2]

Rebellion has arisen against the most brutal and vicious dictatorships over the centuries. Some uprisings were driven by desperation or famine, but the urge to overthrow oppression runs deeper than that—the desire for freedom is one of the key distinguishing characteristics of our species.

Isolated by geography, separated by time, long before Christ was born, and when Greece was a collection of villages, we find examples of yearning for societies based on the rule of law, with wide involvement in decision-making and accountability of leaders. These themes of freedom and self-rule persisted throughout the ages.

Sen acknowledges that it is important to note the remarkable role of Athenian direct democracy, starting from Cleisthenes' pioneering move toward public balloting around 506 BC, in the evolution of democratic ideas and practices. But he points out that while public debate and reasoning were important their use was by no means confined to the Greeks. He also reminds us that the Greeks influenced not just the Europeans:

> No great difficulty is perceived in seeing the descendants of, say, Goths and Visigoths and other Europeans as the inheritors of the Greek tradition... while there is great reluctance to take note of the Greek intellectual links with ancient Egyptians, Iranians, and Indians, despite the greater interest that the ancient Greeks themselves showed—as recorded in contemporary accounts—in talking to them (rather than in chatting with the ancient Goths).[3]

Raul Manglapus was savage with those who, in attempting to rationalize their support for totalitarian and authoritarian regimes, communist or anti-communist, claimed that democracy is un-Asian. Marcos was still the toast of Washington, DC when Manglapus attacked the conservative monthly *American Spectator* for defending Asian authoritarian regimes in its distinction "between political rights (which are a luxury of orderly disciplined people) and human rights" and its use of the word "democracy" as "a rough substitute for civic virtue, implying that all these concepts are beyond comprehension by the Oriental mind."[4]

He cited William Randolph Hearst Jr.'s denial (in the *San Francisco Examiner* in 1976) that there is any "such thing as a right—in the American sense—in any Oriental language, and since all that anyone can be in the view of the average person in the Orient is the role assigned to him by religion and society, there can only be duties—not 'rights!'"

This would be startling news to Indonesians, Malaysians, Punjabis, and Persians, who use the Arabic word *haqq;* the Bengalis who have their *adhikar* and the Sanskrit *svetve;* the Thais their *sitthi;* the Koreans their *kooanri;* and the Filipinos their *karapatan.* All mean "rights." The ideographic characters for the Chinese words *ren quan* and the Japanese *jin ken* are identical, and they both denote human rights.

India

There were many democratic republics in India; Licchavi, for instance, flourished around 600 BC. By the second century, the Licchavis had extended their rule to Nepal with kings who "were masters but also servants of the people" and could be deposed by the people if they "could not prove themselves worthy of the trust placed in them."[5]

As Minoo Masani explains:

> We are often taught that Buddha's father was a king; not so. He was really the elected president of a republic. The misunderstanding is due to the fact that he was called a *raja,* which today means king. In those days, *raja* meant only ruler and was a term used to describe presidents of republics as well as kings.[6]

Masani argues that "the assertive republican democracy of the time of Buddha" was preceded in Indian history by institutions that flourished around 3000 BC. The *Rig Veda,* the earliest publication of the Aryans, who settled and ruled large parts of India in these times, dates from at least 1500 BC. It speaks of powerful but enlightened despots who gave prominence to popular assemblies: the *Samiti*, which included ordinary people; and the upper house of nobles, the *Sabha* (the Indian Parliament is still called the *Lok Sabha*). The large number of passages in the *Rig Veda* that refer to the assemblies leaves no doubt that they wielded great administrative power and authority, and were a significant check on the exercise of arbitrary power by the king. "Political affairs were freely discussed in these bodies and debates ran high, everyone wishing to convert others to his faith."[7]

Ironically, it was the Greeks who may have first prodded Indian royalty to cross the tenuous line between claims to divine favor to assuming divine roles for themselves. Alexander the Great initiated this process when, after his first great victory on Indian soil in 326 BC, he spared the life of his gallant adversary, the king of Paurava, and cleverly gave him back his kingdom. Thenceforth, the Greeks would seek to use, rather than destroy, indigenous royalty and leaders in their conquering march.

Over the next few thousand years, divide and rule, co-opting indigenous power structures, became the model by which new empires could be controlled politically as well as militarily.

The Buddha's five great rules for life: Let no-one kill any living things; Let no-one take what is not given to him; Let no-one speak falsely; Let no-one drink intoxicating drinks; Let no-one be unchaste— advocated both peace and prohibition. In the brutal Hindu society the Buddha's message of love attracted disciples who wrote down his teachings. But Buddhism remained a small sect until it was adopted by the Emperor Ashoka, who reigned over an empire that covered India, Pakistan and Afghanistan from 273 to 232 BC. (Ashoka was said to have murdered his brother to claim the throne. He adopted Buddhism after seeing the destruction wrought by war and sent out missionaries to spread the word.)

A common thread emerges: Buddha, Jesus and Lao-Tzu (who founded Taoism in the sixth century BC) all preached kindness, love, rejection of materialism, and good, honest, pious governance.

The Buddha came from within the Shakya tribe, whose political system reads like the standing orders and rules governing parliamentary behavior in Westminster systems. The business of the clan was carried on in open assemblies. There were regular meetings, with proper seating arrangements and a whip to ensure members attended to make up a quorum.

Business began with the formal presentation of a motion, to which all discussion was restricted. In the event of disagreement the matter could be referred to a committee. If the committee could not reach a unanimous decision, a vote was taken using slips of wood of various colors. Voting was perfectly free and unfettered, and the majority view prevailed. A question once decided was not to be reopened. The procedure was thus democratic, anticipating in many respects the working of modern popular assemblies.

In India, the right of the local community to levy communal taxes was respected by all central governments before British rule. This principle of subsidiarity, which assigns power as locally as possible with individuals, families, cities, nations and regions, is still a subject of debate in the councils of Europe.

The Indian village assembly persisted until the late eighteenth century when British rule attempted to modify the system of local government. As in China and Russia, "village assemblies were left to enjoy their autonomy as long as they collected the revenue or tax (which they themselves apportioned among the inhabitants) and sent it to the royal treasury. The supreme government dealt with the village assemblies, not with the inhabitants."[8]

The Chola Kingdom at Uttaramerur, a town of 30 constituencies, chose its representatives by lot. The council was divided into committees responsible for issues such as irrigation, gardens and the settlement of disputes. The rules provided for safeguards against corruption and the monopoly of power. Service on the council was restricted to one year, after which a citizen had to stand down and could not be returned to the council for three years.

It's ironic, given Marx's view of peasant societies ("potatoes in a sack form a sack full of potatoes"), that India is the one nation that has ever freely elected Marxist governments, albeit only at provincial level; India's traditions of self-rule are ancient.

China

Until 200 years ago, China was the world's greatest economic power. China invented the screw, paper and printing, the compass, the kite, gunpowder and watertight bulkheads on ships. It organized massive engineering works for irrigation, and its poets, philosophers and astronomers mapped their inner consciousness and the outer heavens. Much of this development pre-dated ancient Greece; some was pre-Egyptian. China had the first public service based on examinations and promotion, frequently on merit, well before the West. The Chinese still revere good leaders and honest public servants in their legends, opera and myths. Even today, newspapers are likely to draw an analogy from 2000 years ago to make an oblique contemporary point.

The Chinese poet Qu Yuan (c.340–278 BC), a patriotic and passionate opponent of mismanagement at court, drowned himself after the corruption of his leaders led to the overthrow of the state by invaders. Though the story is commemorated by Chinese communities worldwide through dragon boat races, few are aware of the genesis of this celebration of a great man's sacrifice.

Lao-Tzu, the founder of Taoism, was sickened by corruption, civil war and abuse of power. His words, like those of the Buddha and Jesus, provided guidance on standards of behavior. Sayings such as: "Recompense injury with kindness. To those who are good, I am good and to those who are not good, I am also good. To those who are sincere, I am sincere, to those who are not sincere, I am also sincere, and thus all get to be sincere"[9] have resonated over thousands of years.

Confucius, born 551 BC, has also had a profound influence on Chinese, East Asian and overseas Chinese communities around the world. For 2000 years, from the Han dynasty in 200 BC to the collapse of the Manchu dynasty in AD 1912, his doctrine was the official line. But as with other doctrines, Christianity included, its implementation was neither all-embracing nor even-handed.

"My children, oppressive government is worse than a tiger," Confucius wrote. This was also the conclusion of his disciple Mencius, who said, "If the people have no faith in their rulers, there is no standing for the state."[10]

Confucius expounded on his thesis about popular government: "The essentials are sufficient food, sufficient troops, and the confidence of the people." When pressed to say which one of the three he would give up if forced, he replied, "The troops." Pressed again to decide which of the two remaining he would let go, he said, "Food. For from old, death has been the lot of all men, but a people without faith cannot survive."[11]

These tenets of political sovereignty were held 2000 years before the American Declaration of Independence proclaimed the right of revolution against a "foreign" king.

In the succeeding centuries, China began to experiment with the concrete expression of the Master's teaching on popular sovereignty. Civil service examinations were opened to "all males of any age." Democracy works best when it creates a meritocracy and has a professional public service. In China the structure of the mandarinate perfectly reconciled the needs of aristocracy and democracy; all men were to have an equal opportunity to make themselves fit for office, but office was open only to those who made themselves fit.[12] As Confucius wrote:

> When the Great Principle [of the Great Similarity] prevails, the whole world becomes a republic; they elect men of talents, virtue, and ability; they talk about sincere agreement, and cultivate universal peace. Thus men do not regard as their parents only their own parents, nor treat as their children only their own children. A competent provision is secured for the aged till their death, employment for the middle-aged, and the means of growing up for the young. The widowers, widows, orphans, childless men, and those who are disabled by disease, are all sufficiently maintained.

> Each man has his rights and each woman her individuality safeguarded. They produce wealth disliking that it should be thrown upon the ground, but not wishing to keep it for their own gratification. Disliking idleness they labor, but not alone with a view to their own advantage. In this way, selfish schemings are repressed and find no way to rise. Robbers, filchers, and rebellious traitors do not exist. Hence the outer doors remain open, and are not shut. This is the state of what I call the Great Similarity.[13]

Hundreds of years were to pass before John Locke, Immanuel Kant and Thomas Jefferson would expound similar principles.

It is one thing to express a desire for good rulers and principles of human rights and honest government; it is quite another to develop institutions that deliver good rulers, freedom and individual liberty. In neither China nor India, despite their long history of ideas and ideals, was there an equivalent of the Glorious Revolution, the Reformation or the Age of Enlightenment. In the modern era, when the world was changing so rapidly, powerful rulers were not brought to heel by the people, criticism of government was not unfettered, and so progress was retarded. Violent revolution and local uprisings destabilized the powerful but were not strong enough to do more than wound and paralyze progress.

Abraham's legacy

Abraham was the father of the great faiths: from his roots grew the great branches of Jewish, Christian and Muslim religious cultures. The *Koran* portrays Abraham as the first man to make full surrender to Allah. Each of the five repetitions of daily prayer ends with a reference to him. The holy book recounts Abraham's building of the *Ka'aba*, the black cube that is Mecca's central shrine. Apart from God, Abraham is the only biblical figure who enjoys the unanimous acclaim of all three major faiths and is thus accorded special esteem by each.

After Abraham came Moses (fourteenth–thirteenth centuries BC), who, we are told, delivered God's law from on high in the form of the Ten Commandments. These rules for living are brilliant in their focus and brevity: do not worship any other gods; do not use the name of God in vain; work six days and rest on the seventh; look after your parents; do not murder, steal or commit adultery; do not give false testimony against your neighbor; and do not covet your neighbor's wife or property.

As rules to manage life and society, the commandments have stood the test of time and have informed much of what we consider to be reasonable practice today.

Jesus Christ came to us 2,000 or so years ago and had the most profound impact on everything and everyone. In most of the world, calendar years are still counted from his life. He preached forgiveness, and love for enemies and neighbors alike. Christ argued for the separation of powers: "Render unto Caesar the things that are Caesar's, and to God the things that are God's." He expressed sympathy, lived in empathy, and stood in solidarity with the poor against the mighty.

Christ told listeners that his kingdom was not on this earth, but he encouraged the meek against the mighty, saying that they would inherit the earth. His name has been used by Christian socialists and Christian democrats, as well as invoked by fascists, from Franco in Spain to liberation movements in those parts of the world colonized by European powers. Great crimes and great acts of love have been done in his name. The cruel abuses of the Inquisition stand in stark contrast to the selfless serving of the poor undertaken by nuns and priests throughout the ages.

Christianity arose out of Jewish apocalyptic–esoteric revelations of the coming kingdom; it derives its impetus from the personality and vision of Christ; it gained its strength in the belief in his resurrection, and the promise of eternal life; it received doctrinal form in the theology of Paul; it grew by the absorption of pagan faith and ritual; it became a triumphant church by inheriting the organizing patterns and genius of Rome.[14]

A striking similarity of message runs through the three faiths descended from Abraham: forgiveness, redemption, kindness, love and reciprocity. These gifts and ideals have inspired present-day solutions, from the reconciliation commissions in South Africa—confess, repent and you are forgiven for your crimes under apartheid—to Cambodia and its uneasy coalition.

All societies have their own moral strictures, but most religions and cultures contain the concept of reciprocal treatment: you treat others as you would like to be treated yourself. This "Golden Rule of Humanity" is found in all the great religious and ethical traditions: from Confucianism, Buddhism, Hinduism and Jainism, to Judaism, Islam and Christianity.

Unfortunately, violent connotations can also be read into the various scriptures, which have been used to justify going to war in God's name. The Emperor Constantine and countless others since have used victories as signals of God's blessing. We still sang war hymns when I was at school:

> Onward Christian soldiers;
> Marching as to war,
> With the cross of Jesus going on before...
> At the time of triumph,
> Satan's host doth flee.

Such songs gave moral justification to imperialism by bringing the light to the pagans (a principle echoed today in calls to introduce the light of democracy to dictatorship by force). How God or Christ could be on both sides was never questioned. Perhaps they were—opposing both. Abraham Lincoln was a little more modest when he said, "We don't know which side God is on, but I hope we are on his side."

The consequences of such attitudes have been written in blood down the centuries. The various Crusades which took place between the twelfth and fourteenth centuries to regain or defend the Holy Lands may have disguised motives other than religious responsibility on the part of both Christian and Muslim leaders but resulted in sheer butchery nevertheless.

During the first crusade, launched in 1095, the Christian armies massacred every Jew they could find and stole their possessions. When they took Jerusalem, they tortured and killed Jews and Muslims. History records how "Piles of heads, hands and feet littered the streets of the city. In the temple of Solomon men rode in blood up to their knees and bridle reins."[15]

Over the ensuing centuries, the Holy Places changed hands several times. The Muslim general Saladin returned Jerusalem to Muslim control, but refrained from acts of bloody revenge (unlike the Christian king Richard the Lionheart who, after promising a peaceful occupation of Acre, butchered Jews and Muslims, as well as Christians not to his liking). Under Saladin, Christians and Jews seeking sanctuary from the claims of rival popes were given protection and allowed to prosper.

In a subsequent crusade, and for reasons that were as acquisitive as they were religious, Constantinople changed hands but, by the 1450s, it was firmly under Turkish control. The Turks behaved with mercy; they invited Greek and Genoese merchants to return and even re-established the Greek Orthodox Patriarch, along with an Armenian Patriarch and a Jewish Rabbi. Meanwhile in the Holy Lands, Christians were allowed to go about their business and worship, and their holy sites were respected.

While Christ has inspired freedom fighters everywhere with the principles of non-violent resistance, the effects on the behavior of Christian nations were not immediate. Evil leaders throughout history have co-opted his teaching to preserve their power, taking the opposite meaning from those teachings. Yet the big idea of reciprocity was implanted by the major faiths, even though it will take a lot more for those ideas to endure at a political level in many places. Democratic institutions and laws were critical first steps in achieving this—and to understand this branch of democracy we need to go back to Greece.

The Gift of Greece

African, Egyptian, Chinese and Mesopotamian history are older still than the Greek history that has influenced us so much. Clay tablets from Mesopotamia, 4,000 years before the American Revolution and the Bill of Rights, reveal that the King of Elba was elected for a seven-year term and shared power with a council of elders. When the king was defeated in a bid for re-election, he retired on a government pension.[1]

All societies have had laws, rules and customs, but few societies, historically speaking, have been free in the fullest sense of the word. One of the first societies to enjoy a substantial measure of liberty as we understand the term now was classical Greece—specifically Athens in the fifth and fourth centuries BC. The democracy that underlay this freedom was brief, discontinuous, imperfect and exclusive, but it was unique. It gave rise to remarkable achievements, and the memory of it has exerted an incalculable influence on our ideas about freedom and what it means. It was, truly, the gift of Greece.

It was this vision that motivated poets and leaders from the West, from George Gordon Byron to Winston Churchill, to always take the side of Greece in regional matters of conflict, especially against the Muslim Turks and their Ottoman Empire. These prejudices still exist.

Few of the ancient cultures have affected the way the modern world thinks, what we believe, and our core values system more than that of ancient Greece. It gave us ideas, ideals, and even the words that we now employ in search of those ideals. "Democracy," "proxy," "anarchy," "ethics," "quorum"—all came from Greece.

Democracy—the early days

The key to Greek democracy was the polis, the self-governing city-state, which emerged in Greece during the eighth century BC at a time when technology was advancing, trade was increasing, and developments were taking place in literature and art (such as the introduction of the new Greek alphabet). The polis was small—usually fewer than 10,000 citizens—and in its early stages it was not republican (let alone democratic), being ruled either by a king or by a tyrant, a self-appointed dictator, usually of noble origin, who had deposed the king. Even so, the polis, especially if it lay on the coast and had a port, was a lively and often prosperous place, open to foreign ideas, trade, migrants and influences and supporting a vigorous culture of its own. In the seventh and sixth centuries BC these city-states developed legal structures, coinage, stone sculpture and, newer, more expressive kinds of poetry. In particular, in certain of these city-states, the idea developed that the natural world could be explained by rational enquiry. The attempts of Anaximander and his colleagues to explain the natural world make us smile now, but they marked the emergence of a much-enhanced scientific or semi-scientific attitude.[2] This new level of objectivity, when transferred to the contemplation of politics and philosophy, yielded significant progress in the next two centuries as the Greeks debated the ideal state, the ideal ruler and the meaning of freedom.

The tyrants who ruled the polis were not necessarily bad or incompetent—many were wise and energetic leaders who promoted trade and patronized artists (Pisistratus, tyrant of Athens in the sixth century BC, transformed Athens from a number of villages into a city-state). But the ancient Greeks never lost sight of the fact that, ultimately, tyrants ruled for their own good and not that of the polis. Tyrannicides (tyrant-killers) were much admired: Harmodius and Aristogeiton from Athens, for example, were endlessly hymned and applauded, though it is not clear whether these two men were in fact the clean-cut young freedom fighters they were later made out to be. Such anti-tyrant feeling led in the sixth century BC to the establishment of republican forms of government—either oligarchic or (much more rarely) democratic—in many of the Greek city-states. In an oligarchy, such as Corinth or Sparta, citizenship was confined to a few hundred of the richer inhabitants, and actual government was carried out by a small inner council of 10 to 15 individuals.[3]

Such oligarchic government had advantages in terms of consistency and focus, but it could not, in the final analysis, tolerate *eleutheria* (liberty) or *parrhesia* (freedom of thought and speech), those two ideals so dear to the Greek (especially Athenian) soul. For these to flourish, *demokratia* (rule by the people) had to be developed.

It was at this point that Solon, the great Athenian lawgiver and the first known proponent of political liberty, rose to prominence. It was Solon who liberated the Attic smallholders, freeing them from serf-like bondage to rich landowners. In so doing he gave early Athens a citizen body with enough time and energy to devote itself to questions of politics.[4] (In a darker vein, Solon also encouraged slavery, to provide the labor that the citizens of Athens were now too busy for). It was Solon, too, who established the Boule, a powerful advisory council with 400 members, whose function was to prepare business for the Ecclesia, the ancient popular assembly, at which all free adult Athenian males (numbering in practice some 6,000 individuals) could speak and vote and which, theoretically, was the sovereign constitutional body. The Boule, which was composed of citizens elected by lot, was an extraordinary innovation; it has been called the first conscious, definitely datable political innovation in European history.[5] Together with the Ecclesia, it gave the citizen body a unique sense of involvement in the city's politics.[6]

Solon instituted other innovations too. He widened the eligibility for holding office, shifting the qualification from birth to wealth; established the *heliaia*, a popular court to which citizens could appeal if they thought a magistrate had made an unjust decision; and, crucially, made magistrates accountable to the citizen body.[7] Altogether, Solon's reforms had the effect of moving the emphasis from family to community life, encouraging the growth of democracy.[8] They gave the individual the right to bequeath his property to someone outside his clan and introduced an element of welfare: the sons of those who died in battle were to be brought up and educated by the state. Solon welcomed migrants who provided skills, and gave them citizenship. People who did not work willingly or who led a life of debauchery lost their right to address the Ecclesia, effectively losing their citizenship.

Solon introduced some fundamental ideas that strengthened and codified individual rights and responsibilities. Having done the job for which he was elected, he then returned to private life. His successor in constitutional reform, Kleisthenes, continued this work, expanding the Boule to 500 and devising legislation limiting its members to two periods of service of one year only (in this he clearly hoped to prevent the formation of a self-perpetuating oligarchic elite).[9]

The Periclean experiment

The Athens of Solon and Kleisthenes, however, was not a democracy as we understand the term. An ancient patrician assembly, the Areopagus, still regulated the Ecclesia; it held guardianship over the city's morals and could veto the Ecclesia's proceedings (it functioned, in effect, as a kind of superior Upper House or House of Lords).[10] It was only with the reforms of Pericles, the great champion of liberty, that real power was given to the citizen body. It was Pericles who, in the middle of the fifth century BC, persuaded the Ecclesia to pass a series of laws that established fully democratic institutions in Athens. Direct, ultimate power was given to the citizen body in the Ecclesia and the *dikasteria* (popular law courts); eligibility for citizenship was widened; the influence of the Areopagus was reduced; and the power of the Boule was enhanced.[11] Pericles even introduced payment for juries and public officials, to ensure that poorer citizens would be able to take part in government.[12]

This notion that barriers of class and wealth should not be allowed to stand in the way of democratic rights lay at the heart of Pericles' vision of democracy. In his great funeral oration of 430 BC, Pericles praises Athenian democracy precisely for this reason, contrasting it with the narrow, oligarchic systems of other Greek states (especially Sparta) in which the mass of citizens had no voice and no chance of winning renown for themselves through their participation in government.

Pericles won elections for 15 years straight, he gave jobs to demobilized soldiers and marines by hiring them to build the Parthenon, and he knew when to compromise. He even traded land for peace.

Athenian democracy was a fragile experiment, subject to hostile pressures from outside and to the instability produced by perennial factional fighting within. In particular, Athenian democracy was widely criticized by contemporary political thinkers on the grounds that it gave power to those without real merit or expertise (the election of public officials randomly by lot was a special point of contention).

This criticism was repeated in the fourth century BC by Plato who, in the *Protagoras*, has Socrates condemn democracy as foolishness.[13] Later, in *The Republic*, Plato again voiced his low opinion of democracy, describing it as a kind of easygoing anarchy that distributes a sort of equality to equal and unequal alike.

Plato was responsible for the philosophical underpinning of endless tyrannies from the crusaders to Pol Pot. He distrusted elected politicians. In *The Republic*, he divided society into three classes. At the top would be the Golden ones, the guardians who would own no property and would be the intellectuals, free to study. Under their command were the Silver ones, soldiers who would defend the state, and the Bronze ones, the workers, merchants and farmers. Status could not be hereditary. Writing of the masses, he suggested:

> But in war and in the midst of peace—to his leader he shall direct his eye and follow him faithfully... he should get up, or move or wash, or take his meals, only if he has been told to do so. In a word, he should teach his soul never to dream of acting independently and to become utterly incapable of it.[14]

As Philippe Gigantès has noted,

> These words of Plato describe the ethics of Stalin, Hitler, and every other dictator, brain washer, megalomaniac, self-adulatory human who thinks he is so much better than others or touched by God so people must obey him blindly. You can see these personality traits even in modern democracies. Fortunately, the rule of law and habits of democracy restrains them. Fortunately, for its citizens, Athens did not follow Plato's advice.[15]

The other great thinker of ancient Greece, Aristotle, held democracy in similarly low regard, describing it in his *Ethics* as a kind of political perversion and in his *Politics* as being about arithmetical but not proportionate equality based on merit.[16]

That Plato and Aristotle condemned democracy is a paradox. It was democracy, arguably, that gave rise to the freedom of thought and speech that allowed them to speak and write so freely. This freedom was never guaranteed, however; not even in Athens. It should be remembered that Plato's teacher, Socrates, was condemned to death at the agitation of the democratic faction in Athens.[17] This may account for some of Plato's hostility toward democracy.

Rights for some, not all: Women, slaves and foreigners

Greek democracy, where it did exist, was limited. It was the preserve of freeborn adult males. Women, young people, foreigners and slaves were excluded on the basis that only those who could fight for the state should be entitled to take part in its political life. As time passed, moreover, the requirements for citizenship (which enabled someone to participate in public life) grew stricter; by the fifth century BC both a man's parents had to have been freeborn Athenians for him to qualify as a citizen.[18]

Women appear to have had no direct involvement in political life.[19] From birth to death, in fact, they were the dependants of their male relatives, who were termed their *kyrioi* (lords). Children were the property of their father (boys till the age of 18 only); their father could expose them (leave them to die outside) at birth quite legitimately.[20] Foreigners, whose numbers increased as Athens grew and acquired overseas trade and an empire, were rarely, if ever, granted citizenship, without which they could not hold public office, be a juror or a member of the Ecclesia or Boule, own land in Attica or marry an Athenian woman.[21] In addition, foreigners had to pay a special aliens' tax if they wished to trade in the main marketplace.[22] Resident aliens, foreigners who had lived in Athens for a substantial time, were granted certain limited privileges, but in turn they had to serve in the army or navy and were required to pay a special tax. If they failed to do this they could be enslaved.[23]

The position of slaves in ancient Greece is perhaps the most startling for us today. Slaves were, quite simply, things; they could be bought or sold, hired out or bequeathed, or given away. They could not own anything; even the clothes they stood up in were their master's. They could be beaten and mistreated with impunity, since they could not initiate a legal action (though one could be initiated on their behalf by a citizen).[24] If they were lucky they could be freed by their master, in which case they assumed the status of a resident alien.[25] Very occasionally, as a signal privilege, a slave who had fought for the city could be granted citizenship. The notion of citizenship based on military service continued through to modern days. Frederick Douglass, a slave in the United States who secretly taught himself to read and write, helped convince President Lincoln to allow black people to fight with Union forces to help free themselves. In return they were to get equal rights, 40 acres of land and a mule—a deal that was not honored after Lincoln's assassination.

In ancient Greece, the idea of equality of all people was not yet obvious to the Greeks or anyone else. Greek (specifically Athenian) democracy was, therefore, exclusive, imperfect and relatively short-lived (it lasted less than two centuries, ending when Macedonia defeated a Greek alliance at the battle of Chaeronea in 338 BC). Although the level of participation by citizens in the political life of the city-state was high (much higher than it is today in our mass or parliamentary democracies), the number of citizens taking part in this life was very small (perhaps no more than 30,000 in sixth century BC Athens).[26] The bulk of the population simply didn't count at all. Its peculiar institutions—the Ecclesia, the Boule, the people's courts and so on—did not survive, even in a mutated form.

Yet this democracy was, as Pericles said, unique. The space it gave to freedom was new and unparalleled. The memory of it, kept alive in the pages of historians such as Thucydides, left its imprint on the world and served as an ideal for the ages that followed, down to modern times.

CHAPTER 8

"*Civis Romanus Sum*": Roman Citizenship and Roman Law

Athenian democracy was an inspiring experiment in human freedom, but it was a narrow, exclusive one that affected only a tiny number of citizens. The next great innovation in human freedom, through Roman civilization, vastly expanded the number of people who could enjoy certain human rights. With the help of the sophisticated legal system it developed, Rome granted its citizens a dignity and security hitherto unknown, even in the midst of horrific brutality to those outside its protective embrace.

Early rights and duties: Citizenship in republican times

Citizenship, the key to political rights such as freedom of speech and thought, appears to have been connected with the ability to fight for the Athenian state. In early republican Rome, too, citizenship seems to have been based on participation in the defense of the state. The *comitia*, the ancient popular assembly of Roman citizens that was in theory the sovereign body, had been a military gathering originally, called together when danger threatened.[1]

As in Athens, possession of citizenship made a big difference to status and rights. Roman citizens were distinguished legally from non-citizens; under the *ius civile* (the traditional Roman common law) non-Romans in fact had no rights.[2] Roman citizens, by contrast, had very definite rights, including the right to vote in magisterial elections, and the right to a vote in the *comitia*.[3] In time, these constitutional rights were expanded as the poorer citizens (the plebs) sought and, in some measure, gained political equality with the patricians. After 287 BC, for example, the resolutions (*plebiscitia*) of the *concilium plebis*, the plebs' council, were binding on the Senate.[4] Most democracies today reflect this idea, with a lower House of Representatives and an upper House of Senate.

By the late republican period, Roman citizens enjoyed a wide range of rights, including freedom from arbitrary arrest.[5] The Roman state, however, was never a democracy in the Athenian sense. At no stage did Roman citizens enjoy the right of free speech,[6] and when they voted in the *comitia*, it was not as individuals but in groups, and even then it was only to accept or reject the Senate's proposals.[7] The *res publica* (Roman state) of the republican period was in fact a kind of complex constitutional oligarchy, steered by a small number of wealthy patrician families.[8] Even so, the possession of Roman citizenship was a proud boast ("*civis Romanus sum*"), as proud as any made by an Athenian citizen in the age of Pericles. Its possession guaranteed a range of rights, as the story of St. Paul vividly demonstrates (see below).

The Romans were far more ready than the Greeks to extend their citizenship to non-Romans. This practice began early in the republican period: Roman colonies such as Ostia, at the mouth of the Tiber, were given complete citizenship, as were certain communities such as Tusculum, when their territories were incorporated into the Roman state.[9] Conquered communities in Italy were often given "social rights," a kind of inferior citizenship which permitted their citizens to trade and intermarry with Romans, but not to vote in Rome.[10] With other communities Rome merely made alliances, the most privileged receiving what were called "Latin rights." This meant they were not taxed, though they did have to contribute soldiers to the Roman army.[11]

A constitutional watershed occurred at the start of the first century BC. Between 90 and 89 BC, Roman citizenship was extended to the whole of Italy.[12] For the first time, the free population of a whole country was given legal rights, though the very disturbed state of the peninsula at this period meant that sometimes the law was used unjustly. One famous victim of the times, who fell foul of an unjust law, was the barrister-cum-philosopher Cicero, who, having pitted himself against Julius Caesar and then Mark Antony[13] and launched a ferocious verbal attack on Antony in 43 BC, was outlawed. He was killed attempting to flee Italy and his head and hands were taken back to Rome and displayed in the Forum, where he had so brilliantly argued his cases.[14]

New and brilliant ideas were emerging about freedom and citizenship, but this was still an age when the ruler with the sharpest sword and the most men had his way.

Citizenship under the empire: The example of St. Paul

The "restoration" of the republic under Augustus Caesar at the end of the first century BC was more shadow than substance (Augustus ruled in conjunction with the Senate, but there is no doubt about who held real power). It did, however, create a golden age of peace and prosperity, in which the rule of law flourished.[15] By this time, Roman citizenship had been extended to communities all over the Mediterranean. One such was the city of Tarsus, in what is now Turkey, whose most famous son was Paul the Apostle. In the Acts of the Apostles we read how Paul's possession of Roman citizenship saved him from a flogging in Jerusalem (Acts 22:25–29): the local tribune was alarmed when he found he had put a Roman citizen in chains. A little later, after he had been charged with offences against Jewish law, Paul claimed his right as a Roman citizen to have his case heard by the emperor in person and was sent to Rome. There, he was set free for want of evidence.

The fact that Paul, a Jew from a far-off city in Asia Minor, was able to appeal to the emperor and travel to the imperial capital to make his case is a vivid demonstration of the rights enjoyed by citizens of the Roman Empire.

As the empire grew in the centuries after Christ, citizenship continued to be extended. In 212 it was granted to all free inhabitants of the empire.[16] Purists might argue that such a promiscuous grant devalued citizenship, but this move was historic: it meant that all free men in the empire were citizens, enjoying citizens' rights and entitled to live lives protected by Roman law. Though their rights were, constitutionally speaking, more restricted than those of Pericles' Athenians, the actual number of citizens was far greater than that of their Greek predecessors.

Rome's great legacy: The law

Roman citizenship would have meant little in practice had it not been underpinned by a legal system capable of articulating and enforcing citizens' rights. The Greek city-states had had their laws, but these were

local and from polis to polis. Nor was Greek law especially sophisticated: it never fully developed the idea of the person as a legal entity,
for example.[17] Roman law, by contrast, was an elaborate, universal system that could be applied to every aspect of Roman life. Described as
the most original product of the Roman mind,[18] Roman law made possible the smooth running of a huge, diverse empire. In later ages, moreover, it had a major effect on European legal thinking, giving Europe a
common stock of legal ideas, a common groundwork of legal thought
and, to some extent, a common mass of legal rules.[19] Roman law is one
of Rome's most enduring legacies, and a consideration of Roman law
is of primary importance in any discussion of freedom. The Old World
produced two other great systems of law; the Hindu and the Islamic.
These were and are religious systems and so stand apart from Roman
law, which was fundamentally secular.

The Romans distinguished two types of law: public law, which
related to the functioning of the state; and private law, which regulated relations between individuals.[20] Roman lawyers were mainly
concerned with private law, which they developed into a highly
sophisticated legal system dealing with persons (rights of citizens,
masters over slaves and so on), things (possession, ownership, acquisition), obligations (contracts, thefts and so on) and succession (wills,
heirs).[21] Roman law had its origins in the ancient customary law of
republican and pre-republican Rome. By the third century, this
simple traditional law had been expanded and supplemented by
statutes deriving from the Senate (*senatus consulta*) and the emperor
(*constitutiones principis*), by the edicts of magistrates, and by the inter-
pretations of jurists.[22]

Roman law regulated and gave legal expression to a society that
was in some respects radically unlike our own, one whose concep-
tion of human rights in particular differed greatly from the modern.
According to the law of persons, for example, non-citizens (*peregrini*)
had no rights.[23] When it came to the family, the Roman father
(*paterfamilias*) had unfettered power; everything his children acquired
belonged to him, legally speaking, and he could even put them to
death.[24] Initially, in fact, there was little legal difference between a
son and a slave—both were the property of the paterfamilias and both
could be sold.[25] This power over children gradually waned, but there
were few restrictions on it till the beginning of the second century AD.
The exposing of newborn babies (that is, leaving them out to die), for
example, was only criminalized in 374.[26]

The position of the Roman wife was somewhat better than that of her children. A Roman husband had no rights over his wife's property or person.[27] Early on, his wife's dowry was owned by him, but this ownership became attenuated.[28] Divorce was easy and common, especially later in the imperial period. If the position of the Roman matron had some advantages, the position of Roman slaves had none. As in ancient Greece, slaves were things.[29] They had no rights, and up until the first and second centuries AD could be beaten and abused with impunity because they could not invoke the protection of the law.[30] Very gradually slaves acquired certain limited rights of protection (under Justinian, a master was allowed to inflict no more than reasonable chastisement).

Slavery and the low valuation of human life that it implies are alien to us today; our culture of universal human rights can find no place for it. For the Romans, however, human rights were not universal; as with the ancient Greeks, rights were for citizens. For those who enjoyed citizenship, at least, Roman law brought certainty and predictability in many important areas of life, to an extent not enjoyed by humans before.

Life after death: Roman law after 500 AD

Roman law did not disappear with the waning of the empire. In the east, Justinian's great Digest kept it alive, though since it was written in Latin (the language of the law) it soon had to be translated into Greek, which was the language of the eastern part of the empire.[31] In the west, in places such as France and Italy, Roman law declined into the "vulgar law," a simplified version of its former self; in northern Europe, which had never been more than semi-Romanized, it was entirely forgotten. In the eleventh century, however, it was rediscovered by the medieval universities (principally Bologna). Soon attempts were made to apply it to the legal problems of the time; such was the prestige of Roman law, in fact, that it was accepted as authoritative across most of Europe.[32] England, which by this period had developed its own common law, was a notable exception.

In the Renaissance, Roman law was studied in its historical context; in the seventeenth and eighteenth centuries, it was related to the notion of natural law. In the eighteenth century, Roman law was purged of its irrational elements by European jurists and made logical and consistent.[33] Its most famous expression in modern form came in 1804, when Napoleon promulgated his Code Civil. The Code gave France its first single system of laws and it was soon adopted across Europe, in the Americas and in Egypt.[34] A more detailed, rigorous modern version of the Roman law (*Pandektenrecht*) was developed in Germany in the nineteenth century; this was also adopted in Brazil and Japan.[35] Though the French and German codes contain much that is non-Roman (and even the remaining Roman elements have been considerably changed), they still retain a strong family resemblance in structure, ways of thought and essential terminology.

Though altered and modernized, Roman law lives on. The notion of the Roman citizen endures, too, in mutated form, in the idea of European—rather than merely national (French, Italian, British)—citizenship. This big idea is still at work in the European Union.

The adoption of the Christian faith by Emperor Constantine changed everything. Rome became Christian. Here was imperial power and the beginnings of state-sponsored faith. This was to have a profound impact. It was the Apostle Paul who declared war on the Greek rational tradition through his attacks on "the wisdom of the wise" and "the empty logic of philosophy," words that would be quoted for centuries to come.

The great Greek tradition of argument, rationality and evidence did not simply lose vigor and disappear (its survival and continued progress in the Arab world is testimony to that). Rather, in the fourth and fifth centuries AD, it was destroyed by the political and religious forces that made up the highly authoritarian government of the Roman Empire.[36]

Many factors contributed to the closing of the Western mind: Paul's attack on Greek philosophy; the adoption of Platonism by Christian theologians; and the enforcement of orthodoxy by emperors desperate to keep power. The rational tradition had been purged in the fourth and fifth centuries. It was left to Byzantine civil servants, Arab philosophers, and not a few Christians to protect and preserve the noble words of the great Greek philosophers for posterity.

It was about five hundred years before Anselm of Canterbury (1033–1109) would again seriously raise the potential of reason as a part of mainstream Christian thinking, drawing on the classical works preserved in the writings of Islam. A century and a half later, Thomas Aquinas (1225–1274), a Dominican, brought the thinking, ethos and writings of Aristotle into the mainstream of Church doctrine. Aristotle thought it was a natural human impulse to do good; Aquinas built on this to argue that the impulse toward good and the exquisite gift and power of rational thinking allow us to work out what is morally right (God now gave us the freedom, the will, to think for ourselves). His case for a "just war" is still used throughout the world in modern debates about the rights of nations and people, and indeed our obligations to each other. Our parliaments and international agencies still echo this elegant argument—a big idea that led to other big ideas, the Reformation and the Enlightenment.

CHAPTER

The Glorious Revolution: Freedom in the Seventeenth Century

Greek democracy has been a brilliant experiment and a shining example. Rome left its legacy of Roman law and the Roman Church, but it was the European Middle Ages that laid the foundation of our modern Western legal and political institutions. It was, largely, a feudal age, and feudalism left its imprint on most of the ideas and practices of the period, including ideas about freedom, law and human rights.

A kind of anarchy: The feudal system in the early Middle Ages

The feudal system had arisen in the Dark Ages, when leaders such as Charles Martel had been forced through lack of money to give benefices (grants of land) to their warriors in lieu of payment.[1] Originally the benefice (or fief) lasted for the life of the warrior receiving it, but over time they became hereditary.[2] Gradually, as assaults by Vikings, Magyars, Saracens and other enemies in the ninth and tenth centuries weakened royal power in several kingdoms, the relation between vassal and lord replaced that of subject and monarch. In addition, vassals came to have their own vassals, who counted as *their* men, not the monarch's.[3] Most, but not all, of Western Europe became progressively feudalized.[4]

Feudal lords and vassals were bound by a complicated set of rights and obligations. A vassal had to serve his lord in time of war, for example; in return, the lord undertook to defend his vassal, speaking for him in court cases, for instance. Beyond this relationship, lords and vassals had no general rights or duties; a knight could kill a man's serf, or rape his daughter, with impunity, so long as that man was not his lord or his vassal.[5] Feudalism of this pure, unconstrained kind (such as prevailed in France in the eleventh century) has been described as being little removed from anarchy.[6] It assumed, more or less, a permanent state of war. Might was right. Feudal courts did exist for the purpose of settling disputes peacefully, but knights were not compelled to use them—they could elect to resolve disputes through trial by combat (a Norman practice) instead.[7] Rough and ready as the feudal system of justice was, it did contain an important provision. This was that vassals could only be tried in their lord's court by their peers, other vassals (an echo of this provision remains in the fact that in England a Peer of the Realm can only be tried for a felony in the House of Lords by his fellow Peers).[8] This basic principle, prohibiting arbitrary action by the lord, was later extended to all freemen by the Magna Carta. It can thus be said to underlie our modern concept of the rule of law.[9]

During this period of high feudalism, monarchs were not totally displaced. All land, for example, was held from the king (to this day, in England, all property belongs in theory to the Crown, not to the freeholder as it does in continental Europe). All rights of justice, moreover, were delegations of royal authority.[10] But kings ruled, essentially, as feudal monarchs, exercising, and themselves bound by, obligations to their vassals (barons and other powerful nobles), who were similarly bound to them and to their own subsidiary vassals in turn.[11]

If the authority of early medieval kings was constrained on the one hand by powerful feudal nobles, it was limited on the other by the church. The notion that kings ruled by divine right had been challenged in the West since at least the fifth century; in the tenth there began a movement to free the church from secular control.[12] Great monasteries such as Cluny in France, which stressed discipline and independence from local magnates, challenged the power of the king and his barons.[13] Under Pope Gregory VII (1073–85), the struggle came to a head: Gregory asserted the superiority of the church over secular powers and claimed the power to depose monarchs, a notion that must have been deeply shocking, and revolutionary, to a feudal society based on hierarchy and respect for the liege lord.[14]

Gregory clashed with the Holy Roman Emperor, Henry IV. The pope, who enjoyed the power of interdiction and excommunication, won the battle, humiliating Henry at Canossa in 1076.[15] The Concordat of Worms in 1122 temporarily settled the struggle between pope and emperor, but the conflict boiled on throughout the Middle Ages. But it was not just a matter of popes and emperors, kings and bishops— at all levels of medieval society the church was frequently in conflict with the secular power, as each pressed its claims for jurisdiction at the expense of the other.[16] Some historians have seen this struggle as the key to the plurality and liberalism that came to characterize Western European society, contrasting it with the static orthodoxy of theocratic states such as Byzantium or the Islamic caliphates, where church and state were one.[17] The germ of the idea of a secular state was present this long ago.

Kings and barons: Rights and the law in the high Middle Ages

A number of different types of law coexisted in this feudal world. In England, the popular local assemblies of the Anglo-Saxons had developed into communal courts, presided over by the king's sheriff.[18] In the tenth century, great landowners increasingly took over the administration of justice in their districts; their own courts stood side by side with the communal courts.[19] By the end of the tenth century, the king's officers were selecting 12 men in each district to decide whether there was a prima facie case to justify prosecution (the origin of the grand jury). Guilt was not established through careful analysis of evidence, as in our courts, but through ordeal by fire or water, which people at the time thought would deliver an accurate verdict. In addition, an accused man's friends could swear an oath testifying to his innocence—this was termed compurgation.[20]

The Anglo-Saxon communal courts continued to function for several centuries after 1066, but their importance waned while the influence of the courts of the great landowners (now called "feudal" or "seigneurial" courts) waxed.[21] To trial by ordeal the Normans added trial by combat, in which the two parties in a court case fought it out (God, it was believed, would give victory to the innocent party). Trial by combat sounds brutal to us, but in their time the Normans were regarded as comparatively merciful. Under pressure from the church, which disapproved of the taking of human life, the old capital

punishments of the Anglo-Saxon period were abolished in England
(except for certain very serious crimes) and the relatively milder
penalties of blinding and castration were introduced.[22] Courts were
male affairs—women could not testify[23]—and slaves and serfs had few
legal rights.

Running in parallel to the old communal courts and the local
seigneurial courts, and assuming increasing importance as kings
gradually extended their power, were the king's (or royal) courts. In
England, Henry II had instituted the practice of sending itinerant jus-
tices into every county in England to hold assizes.[24] This had brought
the king's justice within reach of many of his subjects; in addition, the
king's law (unlike Anglo-Saxon communal law and local feudal law)
was common to all England; hence the term "common law." The king's
court functioned as a kind of court of appeal—someone who felt
they had not obtained justice from their local seigneurial court could
mount an appeal to the king's court.[25] Roman law, which had been
rediscovered in the eleventh century, was taught as an academic subject
in places such as Oxford, but it was never "received" in England. To
this day the legal systems of English-speaking countries, which descend
from the common law, stand in marked distinction to the legal systems
of continental Europe (and much of the rest of the world), which are
adaptations of Roman law.

A more serious rival to the king's law in England came from the
ecclesiastical or canon law of the church. Unlike the king's law, this was
an international system, in use across Europe. It controlled, or sought
to control, large areas of the behavior, such as marriage, inheritance
and family life, of lay and religious people alike.[26] In particular, it
claimed the exclusive right to deal with any crimes committed by religious people, generally imposing lighter punishments on wrongdoers
than the seigneurial or king's courts.[27] This "benefit of clergy" was
much resented by secular rulers, who frequently challenged it. It was
in defending this claim against the demands of Henry II that Thomas
Becket, for example, lost his life and became a martyr.[28] Canon law,
though not an active element of the country's legal system today,
lingers on in modern England.

CHAPTER 10

Magna Carta and Beyond

The growing authority of common law in the twelfth century reflects the fact that at this time the king's own authority was increasing. This change occurred unevenly, and at different times across Europe. In England, for example, the authority of the king was established early on, whereas it was slow to spread in France, and even slower in Italy and Germany, where power passed increasingly to feudal princes, city magistrates and petty tyrants (the *signori* of Italy).[1] By the end of the thirteenth century, royal supremacy was well established in France and England, with kings exercising powers of taxation and legislation and controlling the administration of justice.[2] The kings' increasing power was supplemented by special advisory bodies such as parliaments or "estates of the realm": these can be said to mark the first stirrings of representative government.[3] As the feudal system decayed, the relationship of the monarch to his vassals altered; increasingly, the king began to rely on the paid services of specialists, such as professional soldiers and agents.[4]

Feudalism did not die without a fight, however. In England in June 1215, a group of disgruntled northern barons, alarmed at what they saw as King John's encroachment on their ancient feudal rights, forced him to sign a document containing 63 demands, all but one of which he accepted.[5] The document (known as the Magna Carta or the Great Charter) has gained iconic status; it is taken to enshrine such basic Anglo-American rights as the right to bear arms and the right of the

English to be secure in their own houses ("an Englishman's home is his castle"). It is regarded as the foundation stone of political liberty in England and America.[6] Many historians, however, see it as a conservative, reactionary agreement between an unscrupulous king and opportunistic barons. The barons, it appears, considered it a means to gain time to prepare for war; almost immediately, for his part, John tried to have the agreement declared invalid by the pope.[7] Most of the demands made on John in the Magna Carta related to the barons' feudal obligations (especially regarding the provision of money to the Crown), which the barons wanted to see fixed at old feudal rates; they also wanted to halt the encroachment of the king's law on their own feudal courts.[8] It has been argued, indeed, that the Magna Carta merely hastened the end of the feudal system it was designed to protect: by freezing the revenues of the Crown, it forced monarchs to find new, non-feudal ways of raising funds.[9]

Yet the Magna Carta acknowledged some important demands. Some related to taxation (excessive charges were not to be levied by overlords); others to property (the king's men were forbidden to seize property without the consent of the court). Three demands in particular were to have far-reaching consequences and have been taken by some historians to be the foundation of our modern liberty.[10] The first was that no man should be condemned without due process of law—thus establishing our modern right to a fair trial.[11] The second was a restatement of the old feudal practice that no man should be convicted except by judgment of his peers, which has been seen as enunciating the principle of trial by jury.[12] The third related to taxation: the king was not to levy taxes without the consent of his Great Council, which has been described as enacting the doctrine of no taxation without representation.[13] These were ideas that had the power to alter the course of civilization.

Crucially, these and the other provisions of the Magna Carta were not reserved just for the barons and other nobility; all freemen in effect acquired the same legal status as knights.[14] As more men in England became free, more came to enjoy the rights assured by the Magna Carta. Serfs, however, gained nothing.

Perhaps the most remarkable thing in the Magna Carta, however, was the clause that, in effect, authorized revolution. Under this clause, the barons agreed to elect a committee of 25 men to check that King John was observing the charter. If he was not, he would be given 40 days' notice that the committee would call upon the people of England to "harry" the king with war until he complied.[15] This was basically a legalization of revolutionary resistance, and inaugurated the Anglo-American tradition of citizens' revolt.[16]

In signing the Magna Carta, John accepted a limitation on monarchical power that was to assume immense importance. Subsequent English kings were forced to reissue the charter some 30 times (Edward I, for example, confirmed and extended its provisions in 1297). The Magna Carta stood as a symbol of the king's subservience to the law, even if its actual clauses were obsolete or forgotten.[17] Under the despotic Tudors, the Magna Carta was ignored, but in the seventeenth century it was resurrected, being seen as a document which set the precedent for a contract between king and people, which the people could enforce, if necessary by revolution.[18] In rather different form, the same notion, so radical in an era of absolute monarchs, reappeared in the eighteenth century in the writings of the French philosopher Jean-Jacques Rousseau and of the American revolutionary Thomas Paine.

"Town air makes a man free": A new world emerges

Attempts to limit monarchical power and reassert feudal rights were not confined to England, of course (in France, the States-General, which acted as a brake on kingly power, met for the first time in 1302).[19] In truth, however, despite the efforts of John's barons and others like them, feudalism was in decay. In the calamitous fourteenth century, the collapse of the population following the Black Death hastened its demise by making it impossible for manorial lords to keep serfs tied to their manors (serfs were also able to work as freemen for wages).[20] At the same time, the growth of towns in the late-medieval period encouraged liberty, for burghers were free of the yoke of feudalism and able to acquire freedoms unavailable to peasants living in the countryside. As a German saying went, "Town air makes a man free."[21] Technology also played its part in the destruction of feudalism: the advent of powerful cannons, for example, meant that kings could knock down the castle walls of recalcitrant nobles. The eclipse of feudalism made it possible for centralized nation-states to emerge in Europe, ushering in a new chapter in the history of freedom.

After about 1500, history, as one historian has put it, "speeds up."[22] For hundreds of years, energy had gone into defending the existing social order and preparing for the afterlife.[23] After 1500, ideas about freedom began to change. The seventeenth century in particular witnessed intense debate on liberty, especially in Holland and England. By 1700 many of our modern freedoms had been established in north-western Europe. More modern liberties (such as religious freedom—freedom to be Catholic or Protestant, or even an atheist) and tolerance would take longer to arrive, but the process had started. Later freedoms, such as votes for ordinary men and women, were simply an extension of rights established in this early modern period.

Liberty enlarged: Society in early modern Europe

This enlargement of freedom in the seventeenth century had many fathers. The old feudal system, with its complicated web of rights and obligations, had broken down. Peasants now paid their lords rent in money, or developed sharecropping tenancies, thus freeing themselves from the necessity of unpaid labor on the estates of their masters.[24] The power of the nobility had been progressively weakened, despite attempts to protect old feudal rights; the influence of the church, too, had been limited, in a series of concordats agreed between the church and the monarchs of states such as France and Spain in the early sixteenth century.[25] Monarchs such as Elizabeth I of England, thanks to expanded armies, navies and bureaucracies, exerted a political and military control unimagined by their medieval predecessors.[26]

This control made it possible to impose order on a whole kingdom. Although this order was by no means democratic, it was welcomed by the increasingly powerful townsfolk and mercantile classes, who relied on conditions of peace and stability to guarantee the development of the trade on which their prosperity depended. How these newly wealthy burghers and merchants could have a say in the government of these new nation-states had yet to be resolved, though it was clear that the small-scale citizen democracy of ancient Athens, or the narrow republicanism of ancient Rome were not appropriate models for states that possessed many millions of citizens.

The establishment of powerful monarchies, while good for peace and stability, led in some instances to a loss or contraction of liberty. Religious dissent, which had blossomed in England with the Reformation in the middle of the sixteenth century, was viewed by nervous monarchs as a danger to the state (King James I of England sought to create "one worship to God" in England).[27] As soon as they were able, many monarchs banished religious freedom from their

territories. Protestants were expelled from Austria in 1597; in Bohemia
and Moravia, Catholicism was the only permitted religion after 1621.[28]
Louis XIV, for his part, forced French Huguenots to choose between
conversion to Catholicism or expulsion in 1685.[29] Only in some countries, such as Holland and England, did limited religious freedom
come to be tolerated, though grudgingly at first.

Fortunately for the development of liberty, a number of factors
militated against the establishment of uniform, absolute monarchical
rule right across Western Europe at this time. There were barriers of
culture and language, which slowed the acceptance of the king's (or
queen's) sovereignty; there were the privileges of the church, which
remained immensely powerful. Newly annexed towns and provinces
frequently had charters of liberties which could not be easily ignored;
when they were, revolts were liable to break out, as happened in
Holland several times in the sixteenth century.[30] More intangible, but
perhaps of even greater consequence, Protestant Christianity encouraged a habit of self-examination and adherence to the dictates of conscience that permitted citizens to resist what they saw as the immoral
demands of government.[31] The seventeenth century was full of sects,
usually of Lutheran or Calvinist origin, whose members were prepared
to defy the ruling power of the day.

The new monarchies were in fact quite fragile. In France, Louis
XIV was chased out of Paris during the Fronde, an uprising of the
judges and people of Paris that lasted from 1648 to 1653.[32] Only in
1655 was royal control restored; when it was, Louis set about making his rule absolute with the greatest determination, inaugurating
France's *siècle d'or* (golden age). The centralization and extension of
power enabled by absolute rule led to advances in French civilization
such as the codification of laws and improved provincial administration. It even led to street lighting in Paris, which vastly increased the
physical safety of its citizens.[33] It did not lead to representative democracy, however, nor to freedom of religion (even of a limited kind). For
these one has to look to Holland and, especially, England.

Death and debate: The English Civil War

In England, the despotic but efficient rule of the Tudor monarchs
had been followed by the less adept sovereignty of the Stuarts. James
I developed the theory of the "divine right" of monarchs to rule, and
his son Charles I adhered to this doctrine unswervingly, until the

moment in early 1649 when he mounted the executioner's block.[34] Charles's relations with parliament were always tense and it was parliament (purged of its royalist sympathizers) that condemned Charles to death. In 1629, Charles had sought to rule without parliament; when through lack of funds he was forced to recall it in 1640, he was obliged to accept a number of reforms that greatly reduced his power. Henceforth, control over the calling and dissolution of parliament was to be in the hands of MPs, together with choice of government ministers and control over the army; in addition, unconstitutional legislation was rescinded and the power of Anglican bishops was to be curtailed.[35] It was the first time that parliament had asserted its rights over the king.

Charles, who did not really believe that he should have to rule with parliament at all, invaded the House of Commons in 1642, but failed to arrest his most significant opponents.[36] It was a dangerous move. Feeling in London ran high against the king and he was forced to flee the capital. Parliament declared that Charles was conspiring to wage "civil war" on his own subjects and shortly afterwards the fighting began,[37] causing immense loss of life and huge destruction to property.

The English Civil War also intensified the debate about freedom. Not for the last time, Scottish ideas of liberty had been influential. The self-governing, democratic Kirk, inspired by John Knox, had coexisted uneasily with monarchs such as the Stuarts. When Charles tried to bend the Presbyterian church to his will by forcing it to accept the Anglican Book of Common Prayer in 1637 the Scots signed a national covenant. As Arthur Herman wrote in *The Scottish Enlightenment*:

> The National Covenant was more than just a petition or a declaration of faith. It was the Presbyterian version of democracy in action. In the name of true religion, it challenged the king's prerogative to make law without consent, and affirmed that the Scottish people would oppose any change not approved by a free General Assembly and Parliament ... The English Civil War would destroy for ever the façade of absolute monarchy in Britain. A new political idea, that of government with the consent of the governed, had arrived. But it took its original impulse from the Scottish Covenanters.[38]

The English Civil War gave rise to a vast number of pamphlets, theses and books on the rights of the king and parliament, prominent amongst which was Thomas Hobbes' *Leviathan* (1651). Hobbes viewed society as a pitiless war of the strong against the weak. The only asylum from anarchy, he argued, was the surrender of liberty to an omnipotent sovereign (the "Leviathan") in whom all individuals would be subsumed.[39] It was a revolutionary notion, for it denied that government derived its authority from tradition or pedigree; the only thing that bestowed authority was the ability to offer security and justice. Given the turbulent times, it was perhaps a realistic notion, but scarcely one that enlarged human freedom.

The Levelers, who were especially active during the 11 years of the republic that followed the Civil War, were one group determined to enlarge human freedom.[40] The Levelers did not want to "level" society (their name was given to them by their enemies); in fact, they thought of themselves as moderates, and even called their news sheet *The Moderate*.[41] Though scarcely communists or anarchists, they did hark back to the Magna Carta and the Anglo-Saxon rights they believed Englishmen had enjoyed before the imposition of the Norman feudal yoke.[42] They wished to transform England into something like a representative democracy, a change they proposed to effect by giving the vote to all male householders over the age of 21. Certain categories of people would be excluded, but the Levelers' program of electoral reform was liberal; it proposed that everyone above the level of pauperdom should be able to take part in the political life of the nation.[43] Parliaments would be annual and members would be debarred from sitting for consecutive terms. The tithes supporting the clergy were to be abolished; and the law was to be simplified and made accessible to everyone.[44] Most revolutionary of all, women were to be regarded as the equal of men, "alike in power, dignity, authority and majesty."

One MP, Thomas Rainsborough, declared:

> For really I think that the poorest he that is in England hath a life to live, as the greatest he; and therefore truly, sir, I think it's clear, that every man that is to live under a government ought first by his own consent to put himself under that government; and I do think that the poorest man in England is not at all bound in a strict sense to that government that he hath not had a voice to put himself under.

Needless to say, the men who ran England at this time were appalled. Oliver Cromwell and his senior officers were frightened by such doctrines, which appealed to certain radical elements in the republic's New Model Army. General Henry Ireton argued strongly against the sovereignty of the people, asserting the sovereignty of property. "No person hath a right to an interest or share in the disposing of the affairs of the kingdom," he wrote, "that hath not a permanent fixed interest… those persons together are properly the represented of this kingdom."[45] The Levelers were persecuted, and their followers in Cromwell's army were hounded and, in three instances, summarily executed.[46] The need for strong, authoritarian government was rarely questioned at this time; the argument was where power should be located.[47] England was not yet ready for the kind of liberal, representative democracy that was to evolve in the succeeding centuries.

When the monarchy was restored under Charles II in 1660, parliament quickly reverted to its traditional role of advisory body, though it was careful to retain the power to approve or reject the king's appeals for money from taxation.[48] The later attempt by Charles' successor, James II, to roll back the Reformation and re-establish Catholicism, however, caused alarm that led opponents to demand that James accept the "fundamental law" of parliamentary government and agree that parliament was an equal partner in government.[49] When it became clear that James would not accept this, in 1688 the parliament invited William of Orange over from Holland to replace him, in what became known as the Glorious Revolution.

Before William and his consort Mary were crowned in 1689, the Declaration of Rights was read, solemnizing the Crown's commitment to the parliamentary reforms of the previous 50 years. There were to be no more standing armies; no more extra-parliamentary taxation; no more special courts and tribunals, ecclesiastical or civil. Freedom of petition was guaranteed, as were free elections; parliaments were to be annual, as the Levelers had demanded a generation earlier.[50] William and Mary were Europe's first constitutional monarchs. They presided over a political system that was unique and that served, ultimately, to prevent the formation of absolute monarchies.[51] The notion of the divine right of kings, which had so haunted and retarded the debate on political freedom in the seventeenth century, was banished with James to France.[52]

A triumph for tolerance: John Locke on religion

Freedom was in the air, and the debate found one of its most powerful spokesmen in the philosopher John Locke, who had been forced into exile after an attempt on the life of Charles II and his brother James.[53]

Locke had fled to Holland, where he came under the influence of the Remonstrants, a Calvinist sect who believed that it was up to each individual to read the scriptures and come to his or her own conclusions about religion.[54] Locke was fascinated by this notion, and subsequently produced his *Letter Concerning Toleration.* In the letter, written in Latin so that any educated person in Europe could read it, Locke argued that it was blasphemy for the state to enforce a particular version of Christianity. The church was not a monolithic body, he suggested, but a disparate institution of mutually tolerant religious societies.[55] Even so, Locke had his limits: atheists and Catholics would not be accepted in his tolerant Protestant state. Most fundamentally, Locke's ideas form the basis of our modern idea of the separation of church and state. Civil power, he argued, was limited to "civil concernments," which by their nature excluded religious matters.[56]

Locke's ideas about religious tolerance were put into effect when an *Act of Toleration* was passed in England in 1689, allowing Baptists and other Protestant nonconformists (though not those who denied the Trinity) to worship God in their own way. Freedom of conscience, one the most fundamental modern freedoms, can be dated to the passing of this law. Though the Puritans have long been satirized as kill-joys, in the seventeenth century they were the shock troops of liberty.

In examining the gains in human freedom made during the seventeenth century, it would be well to keep in mind what "liberty" meant to Englishmen of the period. It meant, first of all, freedom from papal dominion; toleration of the Catholic religion would not become a reality for nearly a century and a half. It meant parliamentary consent to taxation; regular elections, and *habeas corpus.*[57] Liberty, popularly conceived, meant the Magna Carta and the 1689 Bill of Rights; its heroes were Hampden and Milton, and its villains the Stuarts.

Liberty to take away another's: The establishment of the trans-Atlantic slave trade

English liberty still had its appalling blind spots. While liberty was being discovered among the green fields of England, the trans-Atlantic slave trade was established. Between 1650 and 1807, when slavery was abolished in the British Empire, British ships carried up to four million slaves to the New World plantations; the total carried by European ships probably numbered between nine million and 12 million.[58] It has been called the greatest abduction in history, and is a lasting stain on

European civilization[59] (though it should be noted that other cultures participated, even in Islamic societies where such activities were contrary to the Prophet's instruction from God).

While Englishmen talked so obsessively about liberty and the rights of men, these were reserved mainly for white, male Europeans who possessed property. The history of freedom in the succeeding two centuries would be about the expansion of those rights to groups (women, the poor, other races) hitherto excluded from the culture of liberty.

11

Revolution and Reform: 1775–1914

The Glorious Revolution of 1688 had been a signal event in the move toward political freedom, but the true "Age of Revolutions" lay ahead. Between 1775 and 1914 a series of revolutions took place in different spheres of life (agricultural, industrial, political, ethical and social). They all had the effect of changing perceived notions about liberty. This is the period when many big ideas took root, ultimately altering human experience for the better. The ideas flowed through to reform: the steady, patient but determined attempt to improve the lives of ordinary people, increasingly by direct state intervention. Whether human beings were "freer" in an absolute sense by 1914 is a matter for debate; what is certain is that in the West they were more numerous, healthier, better educated and politically more enfranchised than at any time in history.

The first two revolutions, the agricultural and industrial, are epics in themselves. Their impact on freedom is difficult to assess, in the sense that many gains in liberty they produced were, arguably, offset by losses. Thus, in Western Europe, the agricultural revolution of the eighteenth century can be seen as a positive, in that it increased food production and food exports.[1] This enabled Europe's population to grow to about 200 million by 1800; in particular, it freed Europeans from the specter of famine. This was an extraordinary achievement— in less-developed regions, such as Russia, India and China, millions continued to starve. But it came at a cost: the enclosing of land in

England, for example, forced tens of thousands of people out of the countryside into the new industrial cities. Ireland's population fell to a little over half its previous size before the potato famine.

Similarly, the Industrial Revolution created vast wealth and was, generally, astonishingly successful in raising living standards.[2] Britain was first out of the blocks and as a result propelled itself from a modest power in 1700 to world leader in the nineteenth century. But this, too, came at a price: conditions in the new industrial cities were often appalling, especially in the revolution's early phases.[3] Much of the health and welfare reform of the nineteenth and early twentieth centuries was instigated in an attempt to ameliorate these dreadful conditions, which were graphically highlighted by writers such as Dickens.

Political revolutions: America and France

Isaiah Berlin described the Enlightenment as "the best and most hopeful episode in the history of man." It was a period, he said, which questioned everything: the role of government, the rights of man, women's rights, trade and economics, the nation-state and the proper place of the church within society. "Reason and logic would free the individual in the intellectual and moral world. The individual, free from economic restraints, on his private initiative could rise to a career open to the talented."

As Isaac Kramnick wrote in *The Portable Enlightenment Reader*, "virtually all Enlightenment theorists followed the lead of Locke in demanding religious tolerance. Religion, removed from public life and public authority, would be reserved for the private sphere of individual preferment and practice." Voltaire approvingly described the Royal Exchange in London as the place where, "The Jew, the Mahometan and the Christian transact together, as though they all professed the same religion and gave the name of infidel to none other than the bankrupts."

"Have courage to use your own reason, that is the motto of Enlightenment," wrote Kant in 1784. Free-thinking was fueled by a reading revolution that took place in the eighteenth century: an unprecedented 5,000 newly published books were available at the Leipzig book fair in 1764. Coffee shops became places where books, pamphlets and ideas flourished. Trade prospered; cocoa, tea, sugar and coffee became fashionable addictions.

Paradoxically, perhaps, Enlightenment thinkers turned back to the heroic age of Greece and Rome, or to isolated communities further afield, for inspiration. The eighteenth-century French philosopher Denis Diderot was much taken with the recently discovered Tahitians, seeing them as being "closer to the origin of the world." Like many Enlightenment writers, Diderot argued that the "noble savages" were like spyglasses into heroic phases of European culture, replicating those of Greece and Rome in their earliest phases. He, along with Rousseau and other Enlightenment thinkers, argued that crowded cities and court society led to moral corruption and the emotional manipulation of one man by another. They went in search of simpler times.

Every society has its problems, but people have long projected their hopes and fears on to other groups. Nearly 200 years later similar things happened when the people of Samoa teased and mischievously misled anthropologist Margaret Mead, who went on to make a good and interesting living out of her Pacific studies, reporting how sex without guilt was the natural order of things. We can still see strong strands of this thinking in the hippies of the 1960s and some Greens today.

At bottom, the Enlightenment was about being open to new ideas. Since the Christian faith had been central to most ideas for so long, arguments within the faith came first. The Age of Enlightenment stood on the shoulders of the Reformation. Together these great periods of thought forged a secular society and political entity. Those countries that put these ideas into practice—the Dutch, the English and, eventually, the Europeans and free Americans—had the edge. Those that didn't—most notably the Islamic countries—missed out.

Enlightenment ideas of religious freedom fed into political and ethical revolutions that also occurred at this time. The first of the political revolutions, the American, was in some senses a rerun of the Glorious Revolution of 1688. For all its Enlightenment rhetoric, the American Revolution was essentially a conservative affair, launched to safeguard existing freedoms (legal, customary and practical) which had seemed threatened by a distant, unaccountable government.[4] Few American colonists at the start of the war in 1775 conceived that their protests would result in a break with Britain and the establishment of an independent republic; their concern was to protect particular, established rights (especially those belonging to white, property-owning, adult males), not to uphold a notion of universal human rights that might apply, say, to African-Americans or Native Americans.[5]

The establishment of this independent republic created something new: a written constitution and a government composed entirely of elected officials.[6] This was the first large-scale example of open, accountable government. To this day, it stands as an inspiration for those who yearn for freedom.

The radical genius of the American Constitution was the checks and balances it contained and the limitations it placed on power. The colonists started out by expecting "the rights of Englishmen." But after the War of Independence they started from scratch and created something of their own. In contrast to revolutionary France, which ultimately sought to replace one form of unitary, sovereign power with another, at the core of the United States constitution was powerful judicial autonomy and the development of a system of political parties whose competition was accepted as legitimate. The American experiment was all about reducing and checking the power of the king and the state. These radical innovations laid the foundations of a unique political structure that showed how democracy might work in practice without executive tyranny or mob rule.

The American colonists had many sympathizers in Britain, among them Tom Paine, who believed that each individual had rights that it was the duty of society to protect.[7] The best way to achieve such a society, he believed, was through a radically republican form of government that eschewed monarchy and hereditary succession. Such views, set out in early pamphlets such as *Common Sense* in 1776, made him popular with many American colonists and their supporters in Britain. They also drew him to France in 1787, two years before the outbreak of the revolution there.

The French Revolution was a very different affair. The Enlightenment rhetoric about the "rights of man" that had graced the American Declaration of Independence was taken to its radical conclusion in France. It is intriguing that the French bill of rights included property rights, which Thomas Jefferson excluded in favor of the pursuit of happiness. Freedom, said Diderot, was a "present from Heaven," which all men, regardless of color or station, had a right to enjoy.[8] When the revolution was attacked, Paine defended it warmly in his hugely popular *Rights of Man* (1791–92), which he dedicated to George Washington and Lafayette, the French nobleman who had fought with the Americans in the War of Independence.

Initially, it is true, the revolutionaries of 1789 sought only to establish a constitutional monarchy along the lines of Britain's

(Britain's constitutional arrangements, hammered out at the end of the seventeenth-century, were hugely admired by eighteenth-century French thinkers such as Voltaire and Montesquieu). Certain reforms, long overdue, were undertaken (the powers of the church and the nobility were reduced, for example) and a uniform system of administration was created, which abolished the old provinces and their local assemblies.[9] By 1791 a new constitution had been drawn up, based on a limited monarchy and a National Assembly elected on a narrow franchise of wealth.[10] Such arrangements did not, however, satisfy the more radical members of the National Assembly. In 1793, Louis XVI was executed and the constitution was abolished; a secular, anti-clerical, revolutionary republic was established, with a government centered on the National Convention, whose members were elected by universal male suffrage.[11] Events spiraled out of control. Thousands perished in the ensuing Terror: Paine, who had pleaded for Louis' life even though he loathed kings, was imprisoned (the fact that he was an American citizen appeared to have saved him from execution). France descended into something close to civil war and only the taking of power by Napoleon in 1799 restored order.

The killing of Louis XVI and the establishment of a republic in France caused profound shock throughout Europe.[12] Whigs such as Edmund Burke, who had sympathized with the American revolutionaries, saw this as a profound threat to the social order and condemned it in the strongest terms.[13] Governments across Europe reacted by arresting and imprisoning political agitators; even in England, regarded as the most liberal of the European nations, all public meetings and public lectures were banned in 1793.[14]

But the idea of a secular, democratic, republican state, active in the protection of its citizens' rights, remained enormously influential, not the least because the Americans had shown that this was possible without chaos. While few such republics were established in Europe (and those that were, were swept away after 1814), a whole series were set up in South America in the wake of the wars of independence against Spain that occurred in the first quarter of the nineteenth century.[15] The overall gain in human freedom was questionable in South America, because entrenched elites tended to retain their hold on power. Yet certain definite advances were made: slavery, for example, was progressively abolished throughout South America from the 1820s onward.[16] The notion of universal human rights was gaining hold.

The idea of a state guided by "the will of the people" had its darker side, though. Military service was a *quid pro quo* for citizenship and this resulted in huge standing armies in countries such as France and Germany—which was to have bloody ramifications in the trenches in 1914. The will of the people was not always enlightened.

Britain, which had avoided a revolution in the French style and had retained its monarchy and House of Lords, was unusual among European nations in not having conscription (it was introduced only in 1916). More generally, the atheism and oppression associated with republican government in France and with its imitators elsewhere left a lasting legacy of bitterness and division.[17] We see this being played out now with the fundamentalist right in many democracies.

Europe experienced another revolutionary convulsion in 1848, with governments overthrown in Vienna and Berlin and unrest in France, Britain and Italy. At the very end of the period, moreover, in 1905, Russia nearly had a revolution.[18] Even so, the period from 1814 to 1914 was, generally, an age of reform rather than revolution. Rapid economic and social change, combined with the spread of radical new ideas, led to a tide change in favor of increasing political rights across the board.

This was especially true in Britain, where political stability and the great wealth generated by the Industrial Revolution permitted increasingly radical humanitarian measures to be taken as the nineteenth century progressed. Reform in the areas of the slave trade, labor conditions, suffrage (male and female) and social welfare revolutionized the life experience of the mass of the people and laid the foundations for all-important social mobility. By the early 1900s many enjoyed the right to be free, the right to work in safe conditions, the right to vote, and the right to government support in old age. Such rights, however imperfect in practice, shone like a beacon from a few rich countries and would be demanded by people across the world as the decades passed and word spread.

The Scottish Enlightenment

While less glamorous than Voltaire, Diderot, Rousseau and the other leading lights of the French Enlightenment, the Scots arguably had a greater influence, with their clear understanding of human nature, society and commerce. Any list of the books that molded the thinking of Europeans in the last quarter of the eighteenth century would have to be dominated by Scottish writers: Adam Smith, David Hume, William Robertson, Adam Ferguson, Francis Hutcheson and Lord Kames.

The Scottish Enlightenment presented man as the product of history. Our most fundamental character as human beings, they argued, even our moral character, is constantly evolving and developing, shaped by a variety of forces over which we as individuals have little or no control. We are ultimately creatures of our environment: that was the great discovery that the "Scottish school" brought to the world. At the same time, they also insisted that these changes are not arbitrary or chaotic. They rest on certain fundamental principles and discernible patterns. The study of man is ultimately a scientific study.[19]

Smith's observations on the division of labor and the link between commerce and cultural progress helped to create an environment that inspired greater effort. As we continue to specialize and become increasingly more productive, Smith wrote, the fruits of our labor are no longer things we consume ourselves. They become "commodities" which we buy and sell in exchange for other goods. We start to think about our labor in a new way. We look for ways to improve what we make and save time in making it, in order to sell it at market to get the things we really want. Capitalism was born, the system of economic production behind commercial society.

Capitalism is so successful because it brings intellectual as well as economic change. Smith argued that it alters the way we think about ourselves and about others: we become buyers and sellers, customers and suppliers, who strive to improve the quality and quantity of our output, in order to gratify our needs. Eventually, the division of labor produces people who do nothing but think about improvements: engineers, scientists and those "whose trade it is not to do anything, but to observe everything"—philosophers, teachers and professional managers of every sort. It lays the necessary foundation for technological innovation, as well as the gift of cultural refinement.[20]

Christian gentlemen and French *philosophes*

Agitation to abolish or at least mitigate the worst effects of the slave trade had begun in the second half of the eighteenth century. Evangelical Christianity drew on a long-cherished Reformation strand of thinking which stressed the dignity and value of all human beings as "children of God." If we are equal in the eyes of God, then we must treat each other equally. This notion guided the towering figure of the debate, William Wilberforce. The abolitionist cause also reflected new, humanist notions of how man should behave toward his fellow man. Voltaire and other French philosophers were active in the encouragement of tolerance and enlightenment.[21] Montesquieu, in particular, had attacked the enslavement of Negroes in North America; Diderot's *Encyclopédie* (1751–80), meanwhile, had also condemned slavery as a violation of human freedom.[22]

Practical steps toward the abolition of slavery were first taken in England when a group of Christian gentlemen, citing the Magna Carta doctrine of *habeas corpus*, had succeeded in 1772 in freeing a slave who had been brought to London by his master. The court's ruling was that there could be no slavery on English soil.[23] Encouraged, the Abolitionists began a campaign to expose the horrors of the trade, despite strong opposition from merchants and planters, who after 1792 resorted to accusing the Abolitionists of being French revolutionary agents. A bill to abolish the slave trade in the West Indies was twice defeated in the House of Commons, and twice in the House of Lords; eventually it was passed in 1807.[24] The Royal Navy was used to suppress the trade from this date, and slavery itself was abolished throughout the British Empire in 1833. Though slavery continued in other parts of the world (notably in the southern states of the United States, parts of Africa and Arabia), the institution, which had lasted almost as long as civilization itself, was at last in retreat. This argument also provided the rationale, the principle that it was right and proper to intervene in the affairs of other countries, to bring them "civilization," and it still does. Even in "backward" states like Russia the influence of reform movement was felt, with serfdom being abolished in 1861.[25]

As Victor Hugo and other nineteenth-century writers pointed out, it was all very well to shed tears for one's "black brothers" but concern had to be shown, too, for the urban poor in the new industrial cities at home. At first, reform was timid: in Britain the *Factory Act of 1802* limited to 12 the number of hours a child could work, and even this stricture applied only to certain establishments.[26] Gradually, however, legislation became more progressive: the *Factory Act of 1819* prohibited the employment of children under nine years of age, while the *Act of 1830* required certain safety measures to be set in place. Finally, the *Factory Act of 1842* prohibited the employment of women and children underground (in mines), while the *Ten Hour Act of 1847* set further limits on the working day.[27] Legislation was not always so humane. The *New Poor Law of 1834*, introduced to discourage paupers from applying for public relief, was brutal in its provisions and the way it was applied.

The great doctrine of equality: Suffrage in the nineteenth and twentieth centuries

In the twentieth century, the extension of suffrage in the West to all but children, criminals and the mentally incompetent arguably marks the endpoint in the evolution of democracy.

Progress toward this goal began in the nineteenth century. Rousseau had believed that man's original condition was one of happy, solitary equality; in Rousseau's ideal state, moreover, all men were to be equal.[28] Radicals such as Paine, meanwhile, had argued against hereditary succession and monarchy. In England after the Napoleonic Wars, workers' movements such as the Chartists began to agitate for electoral reform (their demands had included universal male suffrage, abolition of the property qualification for MPs, voting by secret ballot, payment of MPs and annual general elections).[29] Their demands were fiercely resisted by the middle and upper classes, however, and universal male suffrage did not become a reality in Britain until 1918.

Running counter to the notion of equality in the nineteenth century was the widespread fear that mass democracy was a threat to liberty. The most influential liberal political writings of this period— John Stuart Mill's essay *On Liberty* and Alexis de Tocqueville's *Democracy in America*—were devoted to exploring the threat to liberty posed by the prospect of widening political participation beyond the small circle of educated, propertied males.[30] Many feared the Greek lesson: democracy degenerated into tyranny, due "in no small part to the baleful influence of demagogues and populists—eloquent, unscrupulous orators who ignited the baser passions of the populace and led it astray. Democracy would lead to mob rule, ending in dictatorship, which would stamp out liberty."[31] The extension of the franchise in Britain, therefore, was slow and cautious. Electoral equality for women took even longer to arrive, despite a prolonged and sometimes violent campaign by Mrs. Emmeline Pankhurst and her daughters and sympathizers in the first decade of the twentieth century (in Britain, women did not gain full electoral equality until 1928).[32]

Progress was faster in Britain's colonies or former colonies, where the pioneer society was more egalitarian and caution was thrown to the wind, because the powerful had not yet become firmly entrenched as a governing establishment. The American state of Wyoming gave its women the vote in 1869, for example, while New Zealand did so in 1893, the first nation-state to do so; a universal male franchise had been granted earlier. To the surprise of many, liberty and political equality proved to be compatible in Britain, the United States and most Western countries (and joined by many others after the Second World War). Institutions held, trust remained and competing interests managed to knock along without minorities being oppressed unduly, although certain liberties had to be yielded (such as the rich keeping most of their incomes). As one commentator puts it: "Democracy does not abolish differences. Rather, it provides a framework for resolving or managing them without violence. A crucial feature of the liberal political system is the widely held and therefore often self-fulfilling belief that political differences will be resolved peacefully."[33]

Suffrage for indigenous peoples was generally slower to arrive (Australian Aboriginals, startlingly, did not gain the right to vote by Federal law until 1967), although there were exceptions. New Zealand Maori had special parliamentary seats reserved for them as of right in 1867, and still do: indigenous people can choose to vote on a Maori roll of electors or be on the general roll.

Equality in all its forms has become, like liberty, or democracy, one of the defining human-rights watchwords of our age.[34] It is now assumed that the state has a duty to correct inequality in whatever form it appears. This basically socialist notion is now widely espoused across the world, except by conservative thinkers who worry about the trade-off between equity and liberty, but they are in a minority. We have come far indeed from the hierarchical notions of the past, where inequality was accepted as a fact of life. The culture of human rights in our modern "socialist" civilization is similarly far removed from the narrow culture of citizens' rights we saw in Periclean Athens, or the semi-anarchic culture of feudal rights in early medieval Europe.

The modern world appears: Trade unions, state pensions and income tax

Progressive political movements, the heirs of the Levelers and Chartists, and grass roots organizations like trade unions were active in campaigning for improved conditions for workers (especially women and children) in the nineteenth century, and trade unions themselves benefited from the climate of reform in this period. In England, where any kind of worker "combination" had been illegal since 1799, trade unions were given legal legitimacy in 1825.[35] Factory owners, who saw the new unions as a threat to the laissez-faire economic system of nineteenth-century Britain, resisted union demands fiercely, and there were bitter strikes in the 1830s and 1840s. These strikes were unsuccessful. The position of unions improved only after 1870, when Gladstone's and Disraeli's governments successively removed nearly all restrictions on them.[36] The Trades Unions Disputes Act of 1906 exempted trade unions from liability to pay damages for any action they had initiated while on strike, in effect turning unions from victimized organizations into privileged bodies with extraordinary power.[37] Under the same reforming Liberal government, national insurance and the first old-age pensions were introduced, steps that would eventually result in a fully fledged welfare state. Increasingly, it appeared, the state would not only protect its citizens from exploitation, but would also actively care for them in sickness or old age. These measures were paid for by increased taxes for the rich—progressive income tax (up to 5 percent in 1908) and death duties (up to 15 percent on large estates). Greater freedom for the majority was bought by reducing the financial freedom of wealthier citizens. The use of redistributive taxes was only made possible by the extension of the voting franchise and economic growth brought about by the conditions of more open trade and commerce.

This quiet electoral revolution led to the delicate trade-off between liberty, efficiency and equity that has been the stuff of Western politics ever since. The scope for the majority to oppress the minority is still wide, requiring robust political and civil institutions and a strong sense of social cohesion and fair play to keep excesses in check.

Painting the globe red: Freedom and the question of empire

Ideas of equality, freedom and democracy improved the lives of ordinary citizens in Britain, the United States and Western countries enormously. And yet, the period in question saw vast growth in European power across the globe, especially after 1870.[38] By 1914, indeed, European nations, thanks to their advanced, industrialized economies, superior weapons technology and aggressive self-confidence, controlled most of the world and its inhabitants. Britain alone ruled over one-quarter of the population of the planet, and it was a proud boast of Britons that they had "painted the globe red."[39]

This imperialism clearly had many unfortunate consequences for the human rights and liberty of subject peoples, including the destruction of local cultures and institutions, and the exploitation of their resources. At one level, of course, this was a gross infringement of the right to self-determination of the subject peoples. Economic development roared ahead at the center of the empire and tended to stagnate in subject countries. Between 1757 and 1947 Britain's per-capital GDP increased in real terms by 347 percent, India's by a mere 14 percent.[40] And yet, colonization and empire brought new ideas. The coming of European civilization, with its Enlightenment culture of human rights and respect for the law, often did result in an improvement in the lives of ordinary people. In India, for example, the advent of British rule brought the abolition of *suttee* (widow-burning), the eradication of the Thug cult, a modern judicial and civil service, and a tenurial system guaranteeing property rights in land.[41] It also brought the railway, giving countless ordinary Indians the opportunity to travel around their country with speed and safety. Not everyone in India benefited equally, however; some historians judge that British rule benefited the rural propertied classes rather than the very poor and landless.[42]

Adam Smith, who is often portrayed as a right-wing fanatic, questioned the cost of empire, although in economic rather than moral terms. If Britain had got rid of its empire in the mid 1840s, it could have reaped a "decolonization dividend" of a 25 percent tax cut, enabling reinvestment in the very industrial areas in which both the United States and Germany were beginning to compete with the British.[43]

As we have learned, and are still learning, institutions and habits are hard to change. The moral justification of empire was also to civilize the heathens and bring them to God. The same language is used today about bringing democracy to the world at bayonet point. Empires throughout history have overstretched, and this has been their downfall as more and more resources are spent to maintain their presence and their ambitions. Evangelical imperialism records many martyrs.

Beneficial as it sometimes was, imperial rule was not remotely democratic, and liberty in the European or American sense was not available to subject peoples. Indians, for example, were ruled either directly by British officials, or indirectly by native princes kept in power by the

British.[44] Nor did Indians live in a self-determining nation-state of the kind that had been fought for and established all over Europe. With the support of progressives in Britain, Indians began to agitate for self-rule the first mass protests sponsored by the Indian National Congress taking place in 1905.[45] Denying "savages" the rights which European nations claimed for themselves could not be defended indefinitely.[46]

The same Royal Navy that chased down slave-owners' ships also used force to open China to opium exports from British interests. In due course, under pressure not so much from national insurgency as from rival, and far more ruthless, empires, the British Empire was relinquished in the mid-twentieth century, sometimes with good grace, sometimes not.[47]

Colonial legacies remained: the rule of common law, for example, is still upheld (at least in theory) in many of Britain's former imperial possessions, which generally practice, or claim to practice, some form of Westminster-style parliamentary democracy. More generally, Anglo-American and European notions of freedom, justice and equality were exported all around the world via the colonial empires.

CHAPTER

12

Modern International Institutions

What is good for the individual and the family is generally good for the community; what is good for the nation evolves into a good for the family of nations. Just as individuals cooperate in all sorts of ways for the wider community good, so must nations. The nation-state evolved to resolve problems that individuals, tribes and feuding princes could not. Internationalism has, in turn, grown in significance as a means to broker disputes between nations. It is the new frontier of institutionalized freedom and the rule of law.

Reciprocal treatment is the basic principle of all the main international forums and agreements: the United Nations and the World Trade Organization (WTO), the Law of the Sea, the European Union (EU), and hundreds of other agreements governments have entered into.

Today the true patriot and good citizen must also be an internationalist. We serve ourselves best when we serve others. The nation-state needs the cooperation of others to progress. International rules and institutions protect and promote individual nations' interests. They enhance independence, which in a modern world is best achieved by interdependence.

The age of empire is over: the age of enlightened internationalism is, I hope, nearly upon us. We are now reaching nationalist goals by means of international institutions. Far from threatening the independence of the nation-state, robust internationalism should be its guarantor. I see internationalism as the next step in an evolutionary process that gives voice to a wider democracy and is a force for peace and progress.

National rights and international rights are fraught with dangers and life will never conform to clean theories or management lines. Nationalism taken to extremes is inevitably perverted to racism. Hitler perfected the double standard of in-group morality and out-group ferocity by calling his movement National Socialism. Socialism stood for communitarianism within the tribe; nationalism for its vicious exterior.

The so-called internationalism of Marx set back the post-colonial Third World for two generations. The siren call of Marxism and its anti-imperialist, colonialist message was seductive, given the horror and the suffocation of human, political and economic rights experienced under colonial rule. But international communism was really a new sort of empire. Internationalism that tries to control how nations act is dangerous and impractical.

Yet no single encyclopedia could store all the treaties, constitutions, and bilateral and international agreements that have made the world safer and better over the past decades. There is a staggering collection of conventions and treaties covering air law, postal services, human rights, armed conflict, aliens, refugees, immigration, extradition, governmental cooperation in customs and just about every other government agency, diplomatic law, self-defense, genocide, labor, the environment, indigenous rights, commerce, trade, the seabed, adoption, nationality, outer space. It's never-ending, though it's not perfect and never will be. But the continuing drive toward that better world is a distinguishing feature of our species. A world without these imperfect mechanisms would be a much more dangerous world.

But none of this is an argument for so-called World Government, which would be unworkable and wrong. Any such campaign would force a reaction that would blast apart the progress we have achieved through the evolution of civil and democratic internationalism and the rule of law.

My argument is that global and regional laws and rules are necessary if we are to save our environment, protect the world's stocks of migratory fish and fowl, establish fair rules for trade and labor, and provide more-effective political and economic security. Through the international institutions outlined above, we have built up a treasure of case studies that serve to confirm this view.

The ideas of liberal democracy and the Enlightenment spread from Europe and the English-speaking peoples in the nineteenth century through colonization and empire. The transmission was only partial. The other great victory of ideas in the twentieth century was the development of international institutions, also drawing on Enlightenment values. Here was a big idea.

I've always seen democratic internationalism as the highest form of civilized behavior: the rule of law, not force; cooperation, not coercion. Our species has evolved from tribe to state and is now evolving to save and advance itself through new forms of international cooperation at every level. Internationalism's purpose ought to be to strengthen, protect, and advance the rights of peoples and the nation-state—not to replace them.

No nation will or should willingly surrender its power and responsibilities. Most things are best managed democratically at a local level. Governments are already too distant from their owners, the people. Internationalism without consent and approval will cause revulsion and revolt that will undo the virtues of cooperation.

But there has been a failure at the highest political level to explain the peaceful, democratic functions of international organizations such as the United Nations, the WTO or the European Union, and the benefits they can bring.

For some reason the United Nations and the International Labor Organization (ILO) are seen as noble, but their sister structures, the WTO, IMF and World Bank, as sinister. This is a hangover from the Cold War, when the communists saw them as instruments of capitalism and a threat to their influence. Western Europe was reborn after the war because of the Marshall Plan, but the Marxist masters in Moscow refused to let Eastern and Central Europe avail itself of its funds and ideas. Thus Hungary and Czechoslovakia, whose industries were the equal of France's and Britain's before the war, lagged well behind the West by the 1950s.

US Senator Daniel Patrick Moynihan has expressed the current role of international law succinctly and well:

> The point is that international law is not higher law or better law; it is existing law. It is not a law that eschews force; such a view is alien to the very idea of law. Often as not it is the law of the victor, but it is law withal and does evolve. There was little that could be called human rights law in Dr Johnson's time; there is much today.[1]

In 1910, on accepting his Nobel Peace Prize for mediating between Russia and Japan, President Theodore Roosevelt (one of those who later broke the mold of United States isolationism) shared a grand vision: "It would be a masterstroke if those great powers honestly bent on peace would form a League of Peace, not only to keep the peace among themselves, but to prevent, by force if necessary, its being broken by others." Thomas Jefferson had said in 1791, "No court can have jurisdiction over a sovereign nation." As we shall see later, this is still being fought out in modern America.

As individuals, tribes and nations we live by violence, or by customs and law; good law and customs become a habit of trust and expectation of decent behavior. The weak and modest need the protection of law more than the mighty, but the mighty also need peace, predictability, law, trading partners and a clean planet.

If we accept that civilization can be measured by the growth of civil society and respect and reciprocity between tribes and nations, a few minutes' thought on how international law evolved is worthwhile. Two thousand years before the birth of Christ, the city-state ruler of Umma and Lagash in Mesopotamia carved out on a stone block the defining boundaries that were under dispute.

A thousand years later, Egyptian Pharaoh Ramses II and the King of the Hittites signed a "paper" for a defense agreement acknowledging respect for one another's territories. The Old Testament prophet Isaiah stated that "sworn agreements, even when made with the enemy, must be preserved." The Old Testament urged warring parties to spare the fruit trees of their enemies, even when laying siege to their cities (advice presently ignored in Palestine).

Centuries ago, international trade and commerce created the need for international law to handle disputes and to guarantee safe passage to merchant shipping. In the past 30 years the Law of the Sea has been developed to handle ownership questions over 200-mile economic zones. One of the world's first interstate treaties was the 1885 convention for the uniform regulation of fishing in the Rhine. Treaties, customs and conventions establishing the integrity of embassies, and asylum for political refugees, are not new to the last two centuries. Such moves represent early evolution toward international civil society. Without such rules, there would be international anarchy.

The 1815 Congress of Vienna, after the Napoleonic Wars, represented the first systematic attempt to regulate major political differences at an international level. For a hundred years, it institutionalized the balance of power and became a semi-formal international order. The First World War changed everything. European empires and ideologies had ruled the world but the Great War undermined the foundations of European civilization, giving life to two new European theories: fascism and Marxism.

The League of Nations

In 1919, Paris was the capital of the world. The Peace conference was the world's most important business, the peacemakers the world's most powerful people. They met day after day. They argued, debated, quarreled and made it up again. They made deals. They wrote treaties. They created new countries and new organizations. For six months between January and June, Paris was at once the world's Government, its court of appeal, and parliament.

This is the opening paragraph of Canadian writer Margaret Macmillan's wonderful book *Peacemakers*. She continues:

The war to end all wars was finally over, 10 million had perished, millions were maimed, poisoned, traumatized, and broken. The proud, self-confident Europeans had descended into barbarism and carnage made more deadly and efficient by the technologies from the Industrial Revolution. Technology and industrial capacity had moved quicker than the world's political system and instruments were able to cope. An industrial age was fought out with pre-industrial age state and international institutions.

However, revolution was in the air. The Tsar had been overthrown in bloody revolution, empires were falling apart, the days of the Hapsburgs, Romanovs and Ottomans were over, Imperial Germany was now a republic, ancient nations submerged by empires raised their flags and hopes. Poland, Estonia, and component parts of Yugoslavia and Czechoslovakia sought to reassert their suppressed national dreams of independence.

At Paris the international order had to be recreated. After the apocalypse of war, hopes and expectations were high. Though the menace of Russian Bolshevism loomed large in the minds of the statesmen present, many ordinary people saw in it the hope of a new classless world order based on solidarity between peoples.

It's not an exaggeration to say the hope of the world resided in the Paris meeting: Irish freedom, votes for women, labor rights, petitions, personalities great and not so great found a place. A Parisian waiter, Ho Chi Minh, knocked on the door seeking independence from France for Vietnam, to be turned away. Paris hummed with schemes, for a Jewish homeland, a restored Poland, an independent Ukraine, a Kurdistan, an Armenia. Petitioners came from countries that existed and ones that were just dreams. Some, such as the Zionists, spoke for millions; others, such as the representative of the Aland Islands in the Baltic, for a few thousand. Some arrived too late.

President Woodrow Wilson's arrival in Europe was a triumph. His new "permanent peace" precluded the acquisition of territory by conquest and gave recognition to the equality of rights between all nations, great and small. It promoted the idea of an association of nations to guarantee the territorial integrity of each. Wilson also called for the removal of barriers to international trade: free trade was, along with disarmament and democracy, a pillar of a peaceful world.[2] All of these were big, big ideas.

Wilson's Draft Covenant for a proposed League of Nations set out 26 articles covering such diverse matters as the structure of the League, disarmament, the future of colonial possessions, conditions of labor for working people, international shipping and commerce, and the rights of racial and ethnic minorities within nations. The most important, and soon to be most controversial, feature came in Article X, which made international enforcement—what later generations would call "collective security"—the heart of the League of Nations. Article X guaranteed the political independence and territorial integrity of League members against external aggression, and it required members to take action, using military force if necessary, against violators of this guarantee.

Article X was Wilson's singular contribution to the Draft Covenant and was an especially daring move for an American president. If approved at home, it would overturn his country's traditional isolationism and would commit the United States to helping to maintain peace and order throughout the world.

The loaded gun of Wilson's proposal was the bold idea that every nation had the right to self-determination. Self-determination and sovereignty are powerful words. Does every tribe have a right to claim nation status? Partition is the most feared word in the language of diplomacy. Displaying considerable prescience, Wilson's advisor, Robert Lansing, thought his boss had made a huge mistake:

> It will raise hopes that can never be realized. It will, I fear, cost thousands of lives. In the end it is bound to be discredited, to be called the dream of an idealist who failed to realize the danger until it was too late to check those who attempted to put the principle into force.[3]

(Lansing's misgivings soon proved to be well-founded. Wilson's principles were betrayed in China, where hopes of self-determination were dashed as Japan was awarded Germany's Chinese concessions.)

In this way, global leaders groped their way toward extending ideas of freedom, equality and the rule of law to the rest of the world. Contradictions abounded and hopes would be dashed, but the idea was out there.

When the Treaty of Versailles was finally signed in June 1919, Wilson sighed and said, "It is finished and as no–one is satisfied, it makes me hope we have made a just peace, but it is all in the lap of the Gods." The savage reparations imposed on Germany are now almost universally regarded as short-sighted and counterproductive, but Wilson's failure to win over the Republicans in his own government proved equally damaging.

That the United States failed to ratify was a tragedy. Wilson's speech challenging the Senate to adopt his Treaty "or it would break the heart of the world," came true. The jury is still out on whether this failure was a result of Wilson's ill-health or the result of a deep flaw in his idealistic character.

The idea of collective security, global law and global institutions died for a generation. Of the many organizations suggested by the Wilsonians, only the International Labor Organization remains in its original form today. However, a generation and a holocaust later, Franklin Delano Roosevelt had taken note of Wilson's failure and applied that experience in the creation of the United Nations and the Bretton Woods institutions.

With hindsight, it's clear that the League broke new ground that was to yield a great harvest several seasons later: the idea of collective security, the rights of minorities, an international labor organization and the idea of an international court of justice to hold leaders accountable for offences against humanity. Of course, there were mistakes at Versailles for which the world is still now paying a dreadful cost in the Middle East and elsewhere. Margaret McMillan sums the whole attempt this way:

> They tried... to build a better order. They could not foresee the future and they certainly could not control it. That was up to their successors. When war came in 1939, it was a result of 20 years of decisions taken or not taken, not of arrangements made in 1919.[4]

The United Nations

President Wilson's dream of effective international institutions smoldered through the 1920s and 1930s and was rekindled at the first meeting of Roosevelt and Churchill, even before the United States had entered the Second World War. The post-war peace and its institutions were being thought through even then. These were big ideas and big men.

On January 6, 1941, Roosevelt delivered his famous declaration of hope for "a world founded upon four essential human freedoms"—of speech and expression; of religion; from want; and from fear—which were, he said, "a definite basis for a kind of world attainable in our own time and generation." The four freedoms, which became the moral cornerstone of the United Nations, marked what historian William Allen White has called "the opening of a new era for the world."

As the war drew toward its conclusion, the focus shifted toward establishing Kant's dream of "perpetual peace through international institutions." However, Roosevelt's judgment of Stalin as a partner with whom to share global problems was overly optimistic. Exhaustion and illness play a greater role in the events of man and history than we care to acknowledge.

The horror of war encouraged radical ideas. John Foster Dulles led a commission in 1942 to study the "Basis of a Just and Durable Peace." The commission called for a world government. Seven state legislatures supported a Federation of the World. Realists quickly responded that the new post-war order would remain "a world of power politics in which the interest of the United States will continue to demand the preservation of a balance of power in Europe and Asia."[5]

In April 1945, 282 delegates from 46 nations arrived in San Francisco. The United Nations they created was not perfect. Regional groupings soon reappeared in the Cold War setting. The American-led North Atlantic Treaty Organization (NATO) and the Soviet-led Warsaw Pact would order the world. Regional bullies still crushed weaker nations, and tyrants continued to rule unmolested. The United Nations played a secondary role and is marginalized still. But even the most aggressive coalitions of the willing eventually seek legitimacy in the form of the United Nations' blessing.

By the end of the 1990s, after the Somalia debacle, and the genocidal slaughter and ethnic cleansing in Rwanda and the Balkans, people everywhere were shaking their heads with frustration, asking if we had learned anything over the previous 50 years. The reality is that military action must be appropriate, have a widespread consensus, and come with an exit strategy. Perhaps after successful direct action in the Balkans and Serbia, some agencies become overconfident about their ability to bring the ballot by the bayonet. Nevertheless, the United Nations has lasted the distance and continues, slowly, to advance the ideas encapsulated by FDR's four freedoms. Imperfect as it is, most agree that if there was not a United Nations, we would have to invent one.

When the United Nations was founded in 1945, there were 51 member countries; now there are 190. So much for predictions that globalization would cause the death of the nation-state.

The Cold War is over, global economic integration is accelerating for better and, at times, for worse, and we now live in a world where a company like AOL-Time Warner can attain—and lose again in a matter of a year or so—a market value greater than the GNP of some 120 countries, including nations such as Norway, Finland, Colombia and Israel. We live in a world where upward of 30,000 national NGOs utilize an ever-more pervasive media to spotlight corporate and political shortcomings and promote their agendas; where borderless fanatics threaten peaceful coexistence and economic security; where diplomacy has gone from being the preserve of a ruling elite of kings, kaisers and cardinals to a point where a stateless pressure group can have a ban on land mines accepted through the multilateral system.

These trends make the powerful uneasy and apply useful pressure on the United Nations system. They are testing the limits of international institutions and conventions, which are now struggling to find a legal and moral compass to handle these new forces. The issue for our times is that while the global landscape has changed dramatically, the institutions serving the world have not. Leaders face the challenge of managing conflicts and challenges based on the concept of the nation-state with global institutions that are not equipped to cope and often immobilized by outmoded procedures. There are now dozens of inter-governmental agencies whose roles, agendas and locations were often part and parcel of old Cold War priorities. Functions overlap, mandates conflict, objectives become blurred, institutions have lives of their own and different systems of accountability or unaccountability to their owner governments.

My reforms at the WTO, for example, were focused in part on trying to address the real and perceived democratic deficit of this and other multilateral inter-governmental organizations. This deficit is the fault of governments which devolve global and regional responsibilities to institutions and treaties, without imposing corresponding account-ability on the institutions, or adequate supervision by these governments and their parliaments. We must re-establish accountability and good governance in our global institutions by connecting better with governments, democratically elected representatives and wider civil society. We have begun; we now have to build upon those initiatives and age-old principles and ideals.

Unfortunately, many nations don't even have the capacity to maintain embassies in New York or Geneva. I established a unique initiative to involve small countries in the WTO by putting information online, sending out daily summaries of news clippings. We paid for regular briefing trips to Geneva for ministers and officials from poor countries. We established a fund to provide legal assistance and advice for our smaller members so they could take advantage of the WTO's binding disputes-settlement mechanism. This was an international legal "first" and was, of course, resented by some countries which disliked the idea of having to pay to have a competitor take action against them. (This same argument was once used in mature democracies when, in domestic legal systems, the idea of public defenders or legal aid to enable suspects to defend their rights in courts was first considered.)

The common denominator of implementing the will of the people democratically through elections is the peaceful transfer of power through predictable, agreed, transparent voting systems. More people in the world now live under a Westminster-style government—the first-past-the-post, electorate-based system where the party which wins the most electorates forms the government—than any other democratic system. Coalition governments are not uncommon and local conditions often create unique hybrids. The United States system, copied and admired in many places, is very careful in its studied separation of powers between an elected president with strong executive powers, an elected legislative, and strong independent courts to interpret legislation and its relevance to its revered Constitution and Bill of Rights.

Many countries enjoy federal systems, the better to devolve and localize power in state and provincial governments. All democracies enjoy elected municipal governments which have local duties and whose powers vary greatly. A key principle is votes of equal value. This is nearly always true of the House of Representatives, but not true of elected Upper Houses, where regional balance is usually paramount. This argument usually outweighs the idea of equal votes, equal value. Thus a few hundred thousand votes can elect a senator from Vermont, while it takes tens of millions of votes to elect a senator from California. How to handle regional, racial and minority representation is always a complex question when democracy is based on majority rule.

Federalism, proportional representation, and reserved seats for indigenous people are mechanisms often used to handle these contradictions. Strong safeguards within constitutions are also a legal, lasting mechanism to protect the minorities from the tyranny of the majority.

In many countries, proportional representation ensures large minorities are guaranteed parliamentary representation. The problem with this is that politicians naturally campaign for their ethnic and tribal base, which can lead to extremist, potentially divisive, policies. Mauritius, which has large numbers of Hindus, Muslims and Christians, and the potential for racial conflict between people of African and Indian descent, has equal electorates with a number of seats reserved for minorities, but to get elected one must stand in a general seat, thereby needing to appeal to the wider population. Those from minorities who win the greatest number of votes, but not necessarily enough to win a seat, are appointed to parliament as "best losers."

Strong democracies need strong, well-researched, funded, transparent, and democratic political parties to provide stable and constructive alternative governments. That's why many countries provide government funding for their political parties. Though this can lead to maintaining the status quo and the corruption that privilege breeds, it is still important.

Parliamentary process and the WTO

I went to Geneva to take up my role with the WTO full of internationalist zeal but I was shocked at the pettiness of many of the great institutions, which acted like municipal and national political organizations. This was especially so after the collapse of the Seattle Ministerial. The head of one agency put out a press statement deploring the lack of transparency. The trouble was that his statement went to the media before the conference began, and riots delayed the start of the meeting. Later, I found that his organization's transparency and democratic accountability to member countries amounted to a half-day meeting each year in Geneva and New York. WTO ambassadors meet most weeks. Another agency gained great headlines with a report saying that the WTO was not democratic, yet the author of the report had not visited the WTO or even met with any of its staff. Things weren't always like that: Kofi Annan and Jim Wolfenden of the World Bank were helpful partners. Our international institutions exist to serve governments and their peoples, not the other way around; a fact too often forgotten.

I met with the international institutions that act as coordinating agents and meetings of the political parties from the left to the right: the Socialist International, the Democratic Union, and the Liberal International. (Unfortunately, at that time there was no structure to assist the various Green parties internationally.) This was the first time they had met together and they were suspicious and uneasy. What they had in common was their acceptance of the peaceful transfer of power according to the will of the people. My idea to get them as observers to the WTO didn't quite work, although I did get some along to seminars. Such groups are capable of being a very important force in nation-building and democracy-building, but have very few staff and minimal funding. These very old traditional institutions have global reach and, in proper partnership, have much to give. While none of these internationals ever tries to tell national political parties what to do they are unique clearing houses to share policy ideas and to promote the understanding of the political process. Protecting grand brand names of political parties is no small thing. Why should just anyone suddenly call themselves Social Democratic, using a 100-year-old brand and tradition, or call themselves Green, or Conservative? No-one has yet seen the value of enlisting the global umbrella organizations of political parties or assist with their funding in a substantial way to do this work. Former Secretary of State Madeleine Albright's initiative to assist democracy-building through the United States Democratic and Republican Parties, which are funded by the State Department to help and advise in emerging democracies, is a creative concept which should be extended and built on by other governments. Under this initiative, election monitors—eminent persons—are sent to talk quietly to leaders in troubled places and promote the democratic process.

The European Union

The most profound example of how internationalism can work is the European Union, which was born of the vision and patience of men like Schuman and Monnet in proposing a European coal and steel community. The proposal was that coal and steel resources in Western Europe be pooled and administered by both the nation-states and by a pan-European authority, with the objective of gradually reducing tariffs in these heavy industries. It was a bold first step toward European integration. These men were visionaries who set in train the steps that have created what idealistic men and women (and quite a few villains) had dreamed of for centuries: a European Union. The world is safer, stronger and better because of this. The great tribes of Europe are mainly now at peace.

European solidarity is emerging. A few years ago, I was talking to the children of a Belgian friend and asked them how many medals Belgium had won at the Olympics. "Europe won the most!" was the excited reply. One poll revealed that when French people were asked who France's best friend was, the overwhelming response was "Germany," not the United States, as their parents would have answered 50 years earlier. This splendid European project has largely, at least in a military sense, abolished or sidelined European nationalism. Alas European nationalism and tribalism raised its ugly head again the Balkans with the collapse of communism and Europe was shocked to see ethnic cleansing at its doorstep. It took time but the world acted. Recent ominous nationalistic rumblings from Russia remind us that history has not been abolished. Europe is now the largest donor of development aid, representing over 50 percent of all aid from OECD countries.

Yet history in Europe has recently slowed down, as it were. Further European integration was put on ice when French and Dutch voters said no to a new constitution. In October 2004, the 25 leaders had signed up in Rome to what was to be a new set of rules to manage the enlarged European Union. The existing rules and procedures for managing 10 countries were inappropriate for the new grouping of 27 nations and 495 million people in wider Europe.

The constitution, put together by the political elites, brought together sensible new procedures and then called grandly for a European bill of rights, a European President, and a new foreign policy czar for Europe. The 400-page constitution, announced in ringing triumph as the biggest, most historic decision in generations, was dead on arrival. It had tried to be everything for everybody and therefore pleased no-one.

With unemployment in France and Germany running at record levels since the Great Depression, the scene was set for major reaction. It's normal for politicians to try to have it both ways. But when, for years, they had attacked the European bureaucracy in Brussels for all their domestic problems, and then asked the voters to give Brussels more power, it didn't wash. Domestic politicians who find it a vote-winner to bash the EU or the WTO can hardly expect it to be easy with their voters when they wish to strike a deal. The Irish caused further displeasure among the elites in Brussels and Dublin when they rejected a rewritten treaty in a 2008 referendum.

The glue that held the original European Community together was a generation that had experienced two devastating world wars, and faced an Iron Curtain. The recent expansion of the European Union was driven by the collapse of the Soviet Union. A big fear of voters was the noble objective of some European leaders to get Turkey into the European family. Turkey, which would become the largest country in the European Union, is 95 percent Muslim. High unemployment, ungrounded fears of Polish workers flooding into Europe, and competition from the rising economic giants, China and India, drove the anti-migrant protectionists, from the left and the right, to attack what they called "neo-liberal Anglo-Saxon economic strategies." Right-wing French President Jacques Chirac said at the time that liberal economics was as bad as communism. Never mind that the countries that they slammed for such policies had lower unemployment, lower inflation, and less debt than their own.

This is not the end of the European project. But the idea of a European superpower has been dealt a serious blow. The nation-state has asserted itself and its sovereignty. The people don't want their political power outsourced. Interestingly, all those who voted against the idea wanted a successful Europe; perhaps the argument is between those who want a United Nations of Europe but not a United States of

Europe. The world needs a strong, growing Europe. Perhaps the worst thing the European Union and Brussels have done is to provide an excuse for politicians of economic appeasement, allowing them not to face up to their own economic weaknesses and shortcomings.

Rapid change unsettles people and mistakes are made, but even so, freedom, peace and economic development are spreading rapidly over what was one of the benighted regions of the world only 30 years ago. To join the European Union, candidate nations need to agree to common European laws on human rights, environmental standards, and commercial law. Serbia, for example, surrendered war-crimes suspect Radovan Karadzic just days after a pro-EU government was installed in July 2008. This is an outside peg to drive, benchmark, and introduce the best of the European experience.

The WTO has similarly tough criteria for membership in the form of negotiated, legally binding agreements to introduce common rules that benefit all. To get first-world results, nations also need to have first-world standards. Raising standards through membership of international organizations is one of the least-observed benefits of globalization, with profound developmental implications.

The euro, which came into being in January 1999, added further dynamism to the European economy as it challenges the United States dollar and Japanese yen as a reserve currency. Europe is a clumsy superpower, however, because of its decision-making structure, which quite rightly gives sovereignty to the nation-state, except where the nation-states agree to delegate such authority or share its obligations.

After Nato and the United States put a stop to the slaughter in the Balkans, the United Nations handed over responsibility for policing to the EU. The European Union provided the most peacekeepers, and most of the international aid, and is opening other markets to the Balkans: a contribution to peace that unfortunately took more than a decade to bring about. The integration of the Balkans into the EU is wildly popular in the region but less so in the rest of Europe, where, as always, many are fearful of cheaper competition for jobs and business.

The European Union has reaped the rewards of the generosity of its wealthy members: Germany, the United Kingdom, France, Denmark and Holland gave massive grants to assist poorer countries such as Spain, Portugal and Ireland to integrate into the wider EU. Economic integration works and is in everyone's interest but there are short-term upfront costs that test electors' patience, and frequently make cowards of political leaders.

The European project worked. Now Ireland, Spain and Portugal are booming, and we should accept that the recent global economic is a wretched setback but not a collapse as the antiglobalizers predicted. Watch carefully the emerging problems in the Baltic States and many of the countries that wish to join the EU because of the precarious nature of the banks. Economic integration means bad debts and poor decisions will be contagious. This will not be fatal but can stall progress. It remains to be seen if they, in their turn, will be as supportive of new members from East and Central Europe. Those who disdain "aid" as a signal of failure might find it instructive to study how EU aid and grants have given a leg-up to poorer new members, making every country, rich and poor, better off.

The big gap in the international architecture is that great development agencies such as the World Bank don't work in a coherent way with the WTO and its trade negotiations. Ministerial talks in July 2008 in Geneva again failed to push forward the Doha Development Trade agenda. How easy it would be if the European model of firm structural assistance were available to negotiators, and if the WTO with the World Bank and IMF would write out the checks to poor countries to assist them during transition. What if we could promise, and mean it, to assist with local infrastructure, from ports to a professional public service. This should now be the focus of global leaders if they want to prosper in a more-inclusive international system. I can only envy the ability of the EU to match restructuring funds with market openings between member nations. It's a splendid model to use when we negotiate trade rounds to ensure developing countries have the backing to build the capacity and infrastructure to take advantage of the opportunities that open markets offer each other.

Alas, this model does not exist internationally. In international institutions, as in national governments, the agenda and priorities of the relevant institutions always trump a global, holistic approach. Ownership of the programs is more important than the people the programs are meant to benefit.

International organizations—powerful and transparent?

Having experienced public-sector reform, I was keen to restructure the WTO, which is not a United Nations agency. I tried, but to my surprise and horror, ambassadors were reluctant to pursue reform, saying the WTO was the best-organized of the institutions. They may well be right, which is a worry.

In my disappointment, I wrote a paper on how we might rebuild the trust in and capacity, coherence and relevance of global institutions by revisiting the global international architecture. The Security Council reflects the world as it was in 1945, which means that it excludes both the world's biggest democracy, India, and its second-largest economy, Japan. This clearly won't do in this day and age, so I prepared some ideas but could get little support. Perhaps the time was not ripe, or perhaps some major players were relaxed about the inefficiencies of the global institutions. Perhaps some saw a danger in having more relevant, effective institutions. Eventually, a high-level panel on the future of the United Nations (but not the Bretton Woods Institutions) was created, about which I'll say more later.

The responsibility to protect

Few things irritate me more than reading headlines criticizing the United Nations for failing to act to stop violence, prevent a civil war or solve some humanitarian crisis. The United Nations, like the WTO, can only do what its members allow, fund and mandate it to do. Correctly, it has no army; it cannot force its way in. Frequently, leaders call for action and then will not fund or equip the United Nations to do the job. The politics of the Security Council and the veto stop direct action, or a weak mandate puts peacekeepers in an impossible situation where they are powerless to enforce a peace. The most appalling acts of barbarism have been committed under the noses of lightly armed United Nations soldiers who are instructed not to use force. This happened when the first-ever UN contingent was deployed in the Sinai after the Suez crisis and has happened on countless occasions since. The United Nations is often mandated to maintain the peace where there is no peace or where, at best, there's an uneasy standoff. There has to be a peace to keep.

Take present-day Afghanistan, for instance. The way in which governments call for action and then deny the United Nations and a vulnerable new government the resources necessary to rebuild and reconstruct their nation is both heartbreaking and breathtaking in its cynicism. For centuries, the principle that governments have the right to conduct their own affairs without outside interference has been at the center of international relations. However, does this mean sovereignty allows the dominant domestic political force to maim, torture and commit genocide? Article 51 of the United Nations Charter sanctions force only in self-defense, or when approved by the Security Council to stop an act of aggression. Intervention is illegal in matters which are essentially within the jurisdiction of an individual state, and this is the legal premise that Sudan has used to warn countries to keep out of its domestic affairs. However, the 1948 UN convention on genocide can give states the legal authority to take measures or can be used to enlist UN action where genocide is established.

Despite visits to Sudan by the then Secretary-General, Kofi Annan, and condemnation by United States and numerous world leaders, the United Nations resolution called only for sanctions, not intervention. Kofi Annan then urged nations to assist with funds for what has been called the greatest humanitarian crisis in the world. At the same time, Sudanese president Omar al-Bashir was in Belarus purchasing weapons to continue the genocide in Darfur. President Aleksandr Lukashenko of Belarus also cheerfully ignored UN sanctions and sold weapons to Saddam Hussein during the embargo, and is now reported to have traded arms with six of the seven nations on the US State Department's list of state sponsors of terrorism. Yet he goes unpunished. The Sudanese government claimed it could not disarm the Janjaweed militia it created and claimed immunity from an enforced solution in the name of sovereignty.

One interesting factor for those who believe in international law and order is that the Sudanese president's indictment to appear in the International Court in the Hague to answer charges of crimes against humanity makes him the first head of state to face such charges while still in office. Knowing there could be a process of international justice against murderous leaders might change behavior.

A new theory of international engagement is emerging that brings this dilemma and these contradictions into sharp focus. The age-old theory of sovereignty, the right to self-determination, the right to non-indifference, just won't do any more. This doctrine is a new "right" and "obligation"—the responsibility to protect.

The threshold for direct action must be very, very high. First, it must be doable. Diplomacy must be given every chance. Action must be followed through with resources, a plan for post-conflict stability, institution-building, and democracy. Military planners talk of an exit strategy. Equal to this must be the plan for reconstruction. As we have learned from Iraq and elsewhere, winning the war can be the easy part. Winning the peace is a long, expensive, dangerous and difficult process.

In the new world of terrorism, the high-level panel, appointed in 2002, on the future of the United Nations has driven the new doctrine of pre-emptive defense, the responsibility to protect. That means, with UN authorization, where governments are unable or unwilling to protect their citizens, pre-emptive force can be used. This is an historic moment in global diplomacy for it challenges a long-established diplomatic principle: that of the absolute sovereignty of the nation-state. Murder, the harboring of terrorists, and the destruction of life and property can no longer be brushed aside with the old excuse that this is a domestic concern and no business of the international community. In its measurement of the threshold for UN action, the panel expresses five principles of legitimacy that should be considered by the Security Council: seriousness of the threat, proper purpose, force as a last resort, proportional means, and ensuring a balance of consequences. The report also suggests a peace-building commission to prevent the collapse of failed states, and to assist nations to make a peaceful transition to peace and recovery. This could provide much-needed coherence and focus between the global institutions whose contradictory advice and policies often cause much confusion, waste and inaction. How this report is implemented will shape the future of global diplomacy for the next half-century of the United Nations.

I frequently attend the Forum 2000 in Prague, a think-group organized by one of my heroes, Václav Havel, former president of Czechoslovakia. Poet, dissident and leader of the "velvet revolution" that saw a free Czechoslovakia, Havel presided over the peaceful separation of the old Czechoslovakia into two independent republics. At a Gorbachev Foundation meeting in Italy I observed Lech Walesa, Mikhail Gorbachev and Wojciech Jaruzelski, some of the great characters who oversaw the demise of the Soviet empire, chatting about their heroic past. (Jaruzelski made one of the most important phone calls in history, seeking Gorbachev's response to an overwhelming victory at the election of Walesa. Do nothing, advised the Soviet leader, and in so doing removed the cement that held the Soviet empire together.)

Some claim that individuals don't matter; that history has exhausted the need for heroes. The disappointing reforms of the United Nations that came from the high-level panel did at least suggest abolishing the embarrassing and discredited Human Rights Commission with a new

Human Rights Council—a good step which, however, has apparently changed little in practice. The idea of a peace-building commission is more dramatic. If funded and led properly, it could implement the new doctrine of the UN's responsibility to protect.

There was some good news, however, from the 2005 UN *Human Security Report*, which reported an 80 percent decline in the number of armed conflicts involving 1,000 or more battle deaths in a year since the early 1990s. There was a dramatic decline too in the number of battle deaths, in both absolute numbers and the deadliness of each individual conflict. In the 1950s and for years thereafter, the average number of deaths per conflict per year was 30–40,000. By the early 2000s this number was down to around 600—reflecting the shift to low-intensity conflicts, and geographically from Asia to Africa. While this is only a small part of the misery of war (as many as 90 percent of war-related deaths are due to disease and malnutrition rather than direct violence), the trend is both significant and highly encouraging.[6]

There has also been a dramatic increase in the number of conflicts resolved through active peacemaking, involving diplomatic negotiations, international mediation and the like. More civil wars have been ended by negotiation in the last 15 years than in the previous two centuries.

Still, none of this should make us complacent or smug. There's much to do, and we should all be haunted by the tragedy of Rwanda, the Balkans and elsewhere. But we have learned what works and what certainly does not. Conflict prevention and conflict resolution are better than forceful peace-making. Even in post-conflict peacekeeping we have learned valuable lessons about resources, focus and the patience to win, slowly, calmly, over a long period of time. That's where the proposed Peace Building Commission could prove to be the best new idea in years.

Fundamental to this is democracy and here again we have something good to report. Less than 10 years ago only one-third of nations were democratic. By 2002, two-thirds of nations were democratic. Now, three-quarters of the world's population live in a form of democratic self-government.

GATT/WTO

The General Agreement on Tariffs and Trade (GATT), and the WTO, the structure that manages this 23,000-page treaty, are probably the most misunderstood of all the great international institutions. Yet the

WTO has far more effect on people's daily lives and living standards than the United Nations, by providing trading and economic certainty between nations.

The WTO is unique in the international architecture because of the binding nature of its disputes mechanism, which handles differences when countries disagree with the interpretation of agreements they have entered into, or regard another member as having broken the rules. "Trade war looms," is an all-too-frequent headline. Yet logically, it should read: "No trade war: peace resumes, talks begin, panel established, WTO dispute system working." I bet the UN Secretary-General wishes he had binding dispute mechanisms to use in other areas of international disagreement.

It is an article of faith among opponents of the WTO that the system is "undemocratic." The irony is that many of the things its critics do not like stem from too much democracy. They want the WTO to introduce labor standards, protect animal rights, preserve the environment, protect indigenous people, save the developing world from growth and capitalism, and a lengthening list of other goals—even when these goals are resisted by sovereign countries. They grasp that the dispute-settlement system, and its threat of trade sanctions, gives the WTO unique power to impose policies on recalcitrant governments—if only it could be made to exercise those powers.

Its very success makes it vulnerable. Critics ask why we can have a binding disputes mechanism in trade, and not in human rights, women's rights, indigenous, labor or migration rights. Many say the WTO is too powerful, and then insist it take on wider powers and responsibilities, which would make it impossible to manage.

This myriad of issues is beyond the competence of an organization with a staff of 900. Instead, governments might look at adopting similar mechanisms in other institutions which have mandates in these areas—the International Labor Organization (ILO), the World Health Organization or the Commissioner for Human Rights—and which are better funded and staffed to cope with such demands. These are matters of jurisdiction, not principle.

There is a need for a World Environment Agency armed with real teeth. The present UNED organization that handles environmental issues is staffed with good people but is an advocate rather than a management agency. Nor does it facilitate treaties and agreements that are binding. And because of the compounding complexity of tax law and internet-facilitated business transactions, there will soon be a need to multilateralize tax treaties. Perhaps we will have to create a new World Tax Standards Organization, building on research done by the OECD Secretariat. Governments one day will want to drive some common standards or they will see their tax base continue to erode. Perhaps such a body should also have oversight on currencies; after all, it was competitive devaluations in the 1920s that also prolonged and created the conditions for the Great Depression. How to do this without making things worse is a challenge. We can only hope that the current global economic crisis will provide the impetus for governments to agree to new rules, having learnt from our failures of the past few years.

The "undemocratic" claim against the WTO is based upon a fallacy. WTO membership is not imposed on countries; countries choose to belong to the organization. Each of the WTO's agreements is negotiated by member governments, agreed by consensus, and ratified by parliaments. If the WTO has more power than other international organizations this is because governments have given it that power. Countries choose to participate in an open, rules-based multilateral trading system for the simple reason that it is overwhelmingly in their interest to do so. It is difficult to conceive of a system that could be more democratic.

This explains the multilateral trading system's remarkable expansion, and why so many countries are queuing up to join. No nation has ever left the WTO, although they are free to do so. It began as the General Agreement on Tariffs and Trade (GATT) with just 23 members in 1947. Today the WTO has 144 members and this number could easily exceed 170 within a decade. This also explains why members have repeatedly agreed to widen and deepen the system's body of rules. The multilateral trading system was initially concerned mainly with trade in goods, and it was based on a provisional treaty, the GATT. By the end of the Uruguay Round in 1994, the system contained sweeping new rules for services, intellectual property, subsidies, textiles and agriculture. The new WTO was established in 1995 on a firm institutional foundation, with a strengthened mechanism for settling disputes, but without an increase in resources or much-needed internal reforms.

No other international body oversees rules that extend so widely around the world, or so deeply into the fabric of economies. Yet, at the same time, no other body is as directly run by member governments, or as firmly rooted in consensus decision-making and collective rule. The multilateral trading system works precisely because it is based on persuasion, not coercion—rules, not force.

Two fundamental concepts underpin the equal rights of WTO members: non-discrimination and consensus decision-making. The principle of non-discrimination ensures that the WTO treats all members alike. Underpinning this principle are the "most favored nation" obligation (which prevents members from treating products from one member better than those from another) and the "National Treatment" rule (which obliges governments to treat like goods from foreign and domestic sources equally). Non-discrimination has been key to the system's success. It is widely accepted that in the 1920s and 1930s competition and conflict among trade blocs was a major cause of global instability, leading to tit-for-tat protectionism and the Great Depression.

The multilateral trading system was designed precisely to avoid having a world of inward-looking, potentially hostile trade blocs and self-destructive factionalism. From a national perspective, the principle of non-discrimination has also allowed countries to liberalize their economies and integrate into the world trading system at their own pace. Non-discrimination has provided the essential underpinning for the huge expansion of global trade over the past half-century, and for the broad political consensus to move the system forward into new sectors and wider responsibilities. It has enshrined universality as a central objective of the trading system. It is certainly one major reason why the GATT/WTO system has emerged, especially after the Cold War, as a major force for integrating developing and transition countries into the world economy.

Equally central to the system is the principle of consensus decision-making. Unlike other international agencies, the WTO has no executive body with delegated authority to take decisions on behalf of member governments. With a few limited exceptions, there are no provisions for majority or "weighted" voting. The small WTO secretariat has only limited independent authority but no grants or loans to hand out, no licenses to issue and no influence over individual countries' policies (although technical advice is offered, and some analytical comments are provided in regular-trade policy reviews). In short, the WTO does not tell governments what to do. Governments tell the WTO, and that's how it should be.

Each WTO member has equal rights and an equal vote under the agreements. Because no decision is taken unless all member governments agree, effectively every country has the power of veto and a consensus is needed to even have a vote. The rules are enforced under agreed procedures by the members themselves. Sometimes enforcement includes the threat of sanctions. But those sanctions are imposed by members, not by the organization.

This is not to say that the day-to-day workings of the WTO are perfect; far from it. One problem is that the system continues to rely on major new negotiating rounds—and "package" deals of trade openings—to create or clarify rules. This means that reforms are episodic and infrequent. Seven years elapsed between the end of the Tokyo Round and the beginning of the Uruguay Round; eight years between the Uruguay Round's completion and the launch of the Doha Development Agenda in 2002. When the WTO arose out of the GATT, I thought we would have a permanent negotiating mechanism, with no further need for trade rounds. I was wrong. Peeling layers of the onion off in single-issue negotiations didn't work. Governments cannot just pick the low fruit that they like. A wide agenda is required for there to be trade-offs, so all member nations and ministers can sell a package to domestic interests. It's called a single undertaking. Ministers now often have more difficulties with their domestic interests than they have with each other.

Before 1995, under the GATT, panels that met to consider complaints published reports which were not binding. Now cases are heard by an independent panel, and dissatisfied members can appeal to a higher authority, the Appellate Body, which gives a final ruling. With billions of dollars at stake and political prestige on the line, there has never been a hint of scandal or of national self-interest influencing the panelists. This is a tribute to the WTO rules and culture that have developed over many years of professionalism and public service. Inside the present Doha Development Round there are new ideas to improve these rules.

Since the WTO came into being in 1995, nearly 400 complaints have been brought before the Disputes Settlements Body. Many are withdrawn before getting to the panel stage, while more than half are not pursued because consultations show that there is no serious problem, that the case is not strong enough, that the other side has already removed the alleged infringement or a settlement has been reached or is pending.

The WTO's dispute-settlement mechanisms have been likened to "having a fuse in the electrical system of a house—better the fuse blows, than the house burns down."[7] This was well illustrated during my time at the WTO, when a republic of the former Yugoslavia took another to the WTO to settle a dispute. This was, in the words of the republic's ambassador, "good news [because] it's the first time in hundreds of years we are settling a major difference through a legal, binding mechanism."

Developing countries are increasingly active participants; in 2001 they filed about 80 percent of all complaints, of which 20 percent were against developed countries. There were 23 requests for consultations, 19 from developing countries and six against developed countries. These figures show that, contrary to the widespread disinformation spread by its critics, the organization provides justice for all countries, assisting in developing countries' dispute-settlement needs. In 1999, for example, New Zealand hosted a meeting of APEC leaders, including President Clinton. The United States had just stopped New Zealand's lamb exports and Clinton was asked about this. "I know, it's terrible," he drawled. "If I were you, I'd take us to the WTO!" (which was a bit like saying, "I know, I robbed your house. If I were you, I'd ring the police."). New Zealand took his advice and eventually won the case.

What's curious is that none of the many popular anti-globalization books really mention the importance of this disputes-settlement process. Best-selling author John Ralston Saul, in his book *The Collapse of Globalism*, suggests there should be an arbitration court for trade, but fails to mention the binding disputes system that already exists.

If civilization is defined as the rule of law by parties entering into free contracts, rather than being a target of ill-informed abuse this process should be a model. No nation has yet failed to abide by these rules. If the WTO did nothing else but manage disputes successfully, that alone would be a major contribution to global stability. Where else in the international architecture does such a system exist?

Precious though the system undoubtedly is, it is vulnerable and can only thrive with the continued support of member governments, which must be willing to abide by the rules. The next few years will see whether the system improves or becomes sidelined. Rules must evolve, stay relevant, or they could be brought into disrepute. It would indeed be a shame if the WTO, like the League of Nations, became a good idea that was ignored and bypassed for regional and bilateral deals. We must never forget that one of the reasons the GATT/WTO was established was to prevent the rise of hostile trading blocs that had such disastrous consequences in the 1930s.

Economic globalization has outpaced the capacity of sovereign governments and post-war institutions to cope, and capital flows in dollar terms are greater than conventional trade in goods and services. Yet, the system is silent on global standards and rules.

Some of the criticism about the excesses and failures of recent economic history is fair. Yi Gang, the disputes governor of China's Central Bank, has pointed out the IMF's deficiencies in its surveillance of countries that have enjoyed reserve currency status, which has enabled them to run "easy" deficits. Double standards do exist: the IMF would have been appalled, for example, if governments had bailed out industry during the Asian crisis. The humiliation of President Suharto at the hands of the IMF in 1998 is not forgotten. Governments swore never again to have to go, cap in hand, to the IMF. Southeast Asian countries now have $4,000 billion in reserves.[8] Asians dryly note it would be good if the Europeans and Americans applied their prudent "conditions of transparency" to themselves first. A new geopolitical, economic order is emerging and all must be included in the world's global institutions.

The root causes of the global economic crisis are clear. When banks and commercial organizations operate beyond their national borders, there is dangerously little transparency, disclosure or accountability. National decisions now have global implications. Some have suggested that financial institutions need to be brought into a WTO-type setting. I disagree: there would be no consensus; it wouldn't work. We failed even to get financial services liberalized within the context of the Doha Development Round. The world doesn't have time for decades of negotiations or to start again from scratch, as they did in the dark days of the Second World War.

What could be a starter is an ISSO, an international standard-setting organization. That is, if perhaps the top seven economies—US, EU, Japan, India, Brazil, South Africa and China—agreed to a set of standards on disclosure, transparency and early-warning procedures about economic health to which others could then sign up voluntarily. Negotiation would be limited to the seven founding members. What gave Western economies the edge 200 years ago was, among other things, having common, transparent, agreed standards: railway gauge, time, electricity systems. The global economic system needs such standards and disclosure because, at present, the financial system lacks a circuit-breaking function similar to that of the WTO's binding disputes system.

It is good that the G20 meets on a regular basis and has an agenda for the way ahead. The old Chinese proverb about "crossing the turbulent river by feeling your way through the surging water by placing

your feet carefully on the stones below" comes to mind here and
it took two years of private negotiations before the Bretton Woods
Conference came to be. Everything centers on good, clean housekeeping now. If the top seven economic groupings can agree on a set of
standards, then there's credibility for others to join up and not dilute
or pollute these. While this may seem elitist—and it even flies in the
face of my life's work in widening and deepening global institutions
and multilateralism—it is necessary elitism to provide and hold to firm
transparent standards. This would evolve into a model more like the
international standards-setting organization mentioned above, which
would set credible global standards on all sorts of products.

Amid great fanfare and high expectations, the G20 met in London
in April 2009 under the chairmanship of UK Prime Minister Gordon
Brown. The world's media was transfixed, not least because it was
President Obama's first international outing. The meeting was historic,
not so much for the decisions reached or the flaws exposed as for the
fact that it is now a "process" that will be more formalized, more tightly
managed, as everyone's economic needs demand more integrated
attention.

As always, vanity and domestic politics played their usual role.
Brown, a social democrat, and French president Nicholas Sarkozy and
German leader Angela Merkel, both conservatives, eventually generally agreed on what should be done. The core differences in approach
to the crisis lay in the question of whether this is just another, more
severe, cyclical crisis such as the Asian crisis or the 1987 crash, or if it
is something bigger—a structural crisis. In the main, though, governments have responded with common policies of expenditures and tax
cuts to boost consumption. Most are within the suggested IMF targets
of 2 percent of GNP, and the World Bank and IMF have been allocated
more resources. In recognition that 17 of the 20 governments had in
varying degrees adopted protectionist policies, in breach of their commitments at an earlier G20 in Washington DC, there will be a new system to "name and shame" the offenders. This is important because it
gives governments a useful tool to combat some of the protectionist
pressures at home. The process itself is important because it provides
the framework for future work and against which countries can be held
more accountable.

Despite the fact that it represents a big step forward, the meeting
was disappointing in that it didn't go far or fast enough and it failed to
address the big question of our generation: the structural imbalance

between nations with trade surpluses and savings and those countries that have poor savings and trade deficits. Concluding the Doha Trade Round would help, but it needs more than that. China's savings and surplus flooded the US with cheap money, which encouraged slack regimes to recycle that money into the poor-quality lending that created a sub-prime market. We are all now living with the consequences. We are all in this together. Our prospects, incomes, and security are so interwoven that to act unilaterally is to ignore the fact that our own self-interests are also the interests of others. Saving ourselves means saving others. The genius of our species and democracy is our capacity to learn, albeit slowly and painfully, and to adjust. The framework put in place by the G20 is a work in progress. Evolution is in the air.

As the founding father of the European Union, Jean Monnet, said "The only things that can be left to future generations are strong institutions." Benjamin Disraeli claimed that nations and civil society must be governed by rules and institutions or anarchy and violence. Eventually these rules and institutions become habits and conventions which, thankfully, are hard to break. The United Nations, the WTO and a host of other international institutions and systems draw us nearer to the goal of an effective rule of international law.

International civil society will be built on integrity, and respect will be earned on the basis of results. It's a long, imperfect process. We should dream, plan and move on knowing our limitations, and be modest in our pragmatic principles. We need an evolution, not a revolution, to build the new international architecture. Then, perhaps, we may witness a world in which, to quote Lord Alfred Tennyson, "the kindly earth shall slumber, lapt in universal law."[9]

The grandeur of Versailles: the 1919 Peace Conference, where leaders met with high hopes to build the new world after "the war to end all wars."

The Wall Street crash marked the beginning of the Great Depression.

Even the richest countries struggled to feed the people in the midst of plenty. The Great Depression changed expectations regarding the role of governments in the West and the way they operated. But, until the recent advances of globalization, most people had never known anything but poverty. This is still true in the less-globalized parts of the world.

The Soviet ambassador to the UN harangues the UN Security Council in August 1953, while the US and UK ambassadors are less than impressed. After the idealistic beginnings of the United Nations, the reality of the Cold War paralyzed the Council (AP Photo/John Lindsay).

Mike Moore with Chinese Trade Minister Shi Guangsheng and Qatari Host Minister Youseff Kamal celebrating China's membership of the WTO at the Doha Ministerial meeting in November 2001. (Photograph courtesy of the Agence France Presse).

China's material success has lifted hundreds of millions out of extreme poverty but presents huge environmental challenges.

An active civil society, born out of a growing middle class, normally demands better social outcomes. The Kuznets curve famously shows that once incomes reach a certain point, then environmental outcomes improve. However, development without standards and community values can come at a cost to the environment. Environmental damage is being severely exacerbated by climate change, the effects of which are starkly illustrated in the Aral Sea (below).

Anti-globalization demonstrations in Washington DC, in which the author is accused of "starving the poor."

Big numbers, but who's counting? Zimbabwean currency 2008, which the author carries in his wallet to make the case that bad governments and bad policies have consequences.

PART 3

THE PILLARS OF FREEDOM AND PROGRESS

Democracy asserts a strong hold on the imagination of the peoples of the world. Even the most vicious dictators feel obliged to cloak their regimes with its veneer. (The Kim dynasty's repressive grip over the "Democratic" People's Republic of Korea is but one example.)

Though many dictators continue to schedule controlled elections in order to claim legitimacy, this fools nobody: legitimacy can be conferred only where there is genuine, freely exercised choice.

There are many types of democracies, but all share the peaceful transfer of power through the will of the people exercised at elections. Democracy is about choosing leaders within constitutions; the rule of law is about setting the parameters within which governments can rule within the checks and balances brought about by having transparent institutions, an effective, honest and well-paid bureaucracy, independent courts, trial by jury and a professional merit-based public service. These are the necessary preconditions—established over centuries— for creating a healthy democracy and an absolute prerequisite for the social mobility that promotes sustained economic development.

No-one is suggesting that any of the many liberal democracies operating around the globe is paradise. They all suffer to varying degrees from the usual symptoms of wealthy countries: family breakdown, alienation, loneliness, drug abuse, and gang violence. The cycle of disappointment, despair and social disrepair among marginalized people, frequently minorities, still presents a social sore that threatens to infect modern societies.

Liberal democracy is constantly undermined and challenged, whether from neglect or delusion or by groups seeking special advantage. That's the nature of things. A democratic inheritance needs always to be defended against the lobbying of special interests and politicians who are tempted to use the levers of state to defend themselves. The redistribution of wealth and income is part and parcel of social democracy and this keeps alive the ceaseless jostling and jockeying by those holding different points of view: this is the stuff of democracy.

CHAPTER

13

The Need for Good Governance

Douglass North won a Nobel Prize in Economics for his pioneering work on the value of institutions in economic development, and has made a useful contribution to the United Nations Commission on the Legal Empowerment of the Poor. The higher the quality of the institutions, he argued, the better the result—a point recognized by the World Bank when it observed, for example, that if Cameroon could lift the quality and efficiency of its public institutions, it would more than double its per-capita income within a few decades.

Governments do matter, despite the right-wing mantra that government is the problem, not the solution. The dreadful response to the Katrina disaster in the United States shows just how much we need effective government. Of course, too much government is almost as bad as no government. It is the quality, predictability and honesty of government and its agencies that matter, more than the quantity. If you think globalization has meant that governments no longer matter, explain the differences between Chile and Argentina, North and South Korea, or Myanmar and Thailand. Where there is a problem in economics, seek out the cleansing disinfectant of competition. Where corruption is a problem, seek out transparency and competition. Where there is a political problem, seek more competition via democracy. Without powerful institutions, it is impossible to expel the rent-seekers and the privileged who make use of their insider knowledge to extort and steal.

I have spent time in Peru, a place of fabulous resources: gold, gas, gems, phosphate, fish and great agricultural opportunities. Peruvians should be the wealthiest in the world, but there are huge disparities in wealth. In the cities the wealthy, imprisoned behind high walls, barbed wire, electric fences and guards, live in fear of the poor. Outside the walls, 50 percent unemployment and seething resentment give life to extremist politics in the region.

In 1900, Chile, Argentina and Uruguay, the Latin American flag-ships, were richer than Canada or Australia but they all fell prey to protectionist, nationalist economic policies, where the rich sought privileges and subsidies, where government was swayed by big business, big church, big unions, and big politicians. The institutions, legal or parliamentary, were not powerful enough to withstand this onslaught. Throughout Latin America the military, often supported by the West, moved in, ruthlessly suppressing everyone who disagreed, especially if opponents could be branded as "communist." Don Hélder Câmara, the Catholic Archbishop of Recife in Brazil, famously declared: "When I give food to the poor, they call me a saint. When I ask why the poor have no food, they call me a communist." The social demo-cratic impulse to widen the economic base and increase social mobility through equality was suppressed, and polarization and popular resent-ment were unleashed.

Things have improved. Thirty years ago all the governments in the region were neo-fascist or pretend socialists; through their "corporate state" policies they ran these rich countries into the ground. Now all Latin American nations, with the exception of Cuba, are democracies, albeit fragile ones in some cases. Because recent economic changes have not rewarded those who live in the shadows quickly enough, a new form of economic nationalism and populist politicians, such as Luiz Inácio Lula da Silva in Brazil and Hugo Chávez of Venezuela, have emerged. Chávez is funding like-minded politicians in many countries in the region: a strategy of interference and a destabilizing policy. From the marginalized shadows, indigenous people are taking advantage of their numbers and marshalling legitimate grievances in a new expression of what are labeled "left-wing" ambitions. Chávez excuses his actions by talk of countering American imperialism. This backlash against the interests of the open economy is a heavy price to pay for the years of "right-wing" suppression of democratic progress. President Lula is a star among present world leaders. He has given the very poor in Brazil their first regular payments but there's a catch: they must ensure their children go to school, accept health checkups for Aids and take the free medicine provided. For years the joke went that

Brazil is the country of the future ... and always will be. Now, Brazil is in the front rank of nations.

Westerners working in developing countries find themselves stunned when corruption is standard, when it is expected that people will take personal advantage of the political and economic opportunities that so often exist when politics, bureaucracy, business and nationalism collide. This corruption is endemic when the state is intrusive in business and public affairs, creating a moral hazard on which the ruthless and the opportunists graze contentedly.

These realities have been brought home to me both during my days at the WTO and subsequently in my business life and my travels as a do-gooder. I have spent time with members of the UN sponsored Commission on the Legal Empowerment of the Poor, which included the Peruvian economist Hernando de Soto, who co-led the commission with former US Secretary of State Madeleine Albright. De Soto's book *The Mystery of Capital*—one of the most important studies in the past 20 years—explains that the poor in poor countries have assets but that these are used mainly in the informal economy outside the legal system. The story of successful economies is their capacity to protect private investment and allow people to borrow against their assets— most start-up businesses in the West are based on loans against properties. Yet most jobs and businesses in poor countries struggle outside the legal system because people don't trust the rule of law. Consider this:

- Throughout Latin America 80 percent of all real estate is held outside the law.
- The extra-legal sectors in the developing world account for 50–70 percent of all working people and are responsible for anywhere from 20–67 percent of the total output of developing countries.
- The assets of the poor in Egypt alone are more than 50 times all the foreign investment ever recorded, including the funding of the Suez Canal and the Aswan Dam.
- In Haiti, the value of extra-legal real estate is 10 times the value of the government's holdings. The assets of the poor are still 150 times greater than all the foreign investment received in 200 years.

Perhaps such figures can be explained, at least partly, by the inadequacy of the institutions and the strangling bureaucracies that exist in those countries. In Haiti, for example, it can take 65 bureaucratic steps and two years to lease land for five years with the right to purchase, and in Egypt acquiring and registering a "lot" on state-owned desert land can take 77 bureaucratic procedures at 31 public and private agencies. This can take from five to 14 years. It can take two years and 45 steps to establish a barber shop!

Roughly half the world's people live in makeshift homes in squatter settlements and work in shadow economies. In many countries, more than 80 percent of all homes and business are unregistered—in the Philippines the figure is 65 percent; in Tanzania, 90 percent. More than one-third of the developing world's GDP is generated in the underground economy, a figure that has increased steadily over the last decade.

Bringing people out of the shadows formalizes what they own already, helps to safeguard them from predatory bureaucrats and the local mafia, and widens the domestic tax base; this in turn makes people look to their politicians for accountability rather than for favors.

Credit for empowerment

Powerlessness and poverty go hand in hand, yet neither is inevitable, as the experience of the Grameen Bank in Bangladesh has made abundantly clear.[1]

In 2006, the Nobel Peace Prize was awarded to Bangladeshi economist Muhammad Yunus for his pioneering work in the field of microcredit, which has assisted millions. Having witnessed the failure of his government's Soviet-style economic-planning model which meant that local fields lay idle and unproductive for several seasons during the devastating 1974 famine, Yunus realized he could multiply productivity with a small water pump. The cost involved was so small that no bank was interested. The transaction costs were too high, and the people who needed the pump had no money or assets to borrow against. From this simple realization, he established the Grameen (meaning "village" or "rural") Bank. Its first loan came from his own pocket—$27 shared among 42 people for weaving stools. By the end of February 2008, his bank had lent out $6.82 billion, of which more than 98 percent had been repaid. Most loans are under $100 and 96 percent have been to women.[2]

The borrowers own 94 percent of the Grameen Bank and the government 6 percent. Such small sums elbow out corrupt bureaucrats, and politicians are sidelined because such small stuff is not newsworthy enough for them.

This is another big idea that works. We need to study how to eradicate poverty through profits. A look at purchasing power parity shows that India, China, Brazil, Mexico, Russia, Indonesia, Turkey and South Africa combined have a GDP of over $12 trillion, larger than that of Japan, Germany, Italy, the United Kingdom and France. Enterprising companies are tapping the bottom of this market, lifting living standards and providing jobs and consumers with a better deal. The poor are price-sensitive, ambitious and canny, and they welcome technology. The number of mobile-phone users is growing by 1.5 million a month in India, which now has more than China (which, in turn, has more than the whole of Europe). Brazil already has 35–40 million. New low-cost PC kiosks are liberating villagers in many countries. Internet connectivity increases the incomes of poor farmers and fishermen by 5–10 percent. Big global brands that meet the needs of the very poor can make good profits. Avon has 800,000 women managing distribution in Latin America alone. In India, Amway has 600,000 representatives running their own small businesses.[3] The 4 billion people in the developing world who have the opportunity to become consumers represent a profound change in the global economy for the good of all.

Poor countries need to be pointed in the right direction. Visiting Timor Leste, which is among the worst places in the world to do business because of its confused bureaucracy, I found myself wondering whether it could become the first of the least-developed countries to escape the resource curse, whether it could use its newfound wealth in oil and gas to assist people and develop without serious corruption. While no-one pretends this will be easy, it's not rocket science either: the evidence and literature showing that it is achievable is overwhelming. The way forward must not be allowed to be interrupted by muddled thinking, no matter how well-intentioned. Meanwhile, however, the generous Europeans are spending huge amounts of aid money to establish a working justice and court system which will operate in Portuguese, a language few Timorese speak! People need to be able to trust the institutions which govern their lives, and trust is something that needs to be built and earned.

Building social trust

We have too easily forgotten fundamental aspects of Europe's earlier advance. The invention of property rights, and the genius of the limited liability company, which preserved savings, protected a family's investment and intellectual property, allowed borrowing and minimized risk, created an explosion of commercial adventurism. Trustworthy financial institutions and rules for holding and passing on wealth are fundamental for growth and development. Scandals erupt from time to time, but they attract attention precisely because investors and the public are horrified, and they force a political correction, and sometimes an overcorrection.

France, one of the laggards among the major European economies over the past two decades, suffers from a "trust deficit" that shackles its capacity to adapt, reform and innovate.[4] This distrust can morph into a fear of competition itself and create a demand for protection and privilege. The Swedes are the most trusting of all Europeans. They believe they will get a fair deal from those in authority, and this boosts confidence. There is an economic cost, followed by a social cost, when trust is absent. If the French were as trusting as the Swedes, the French economy could be boosted by 5 percent and its high unemployment could drop by almost a third.[5]

Trust and confidence in commercial and financial rules have been developed over centuries. A great benefit for societies that develop these attributes is that trust begins to permeate society. Societies where social cohesion functions without the need for rigid or violent enforcement by the state tend to do better. Germany and Japan are examples of this, both economically and socially. The larger a country's police force, and the more detailed and intrusive its laws, the more expensive the transaction costs of monitoring and enforcing civil agreements. Nobody has got it completely right. Even the United States still has a medical system where each doctor must pay $100,000 or more a year just for insurance against litigation.

The will to cooperate without coercion is the key to success. It is the basis of civil society. Countries, companies and individuals that litigate, sue or blacklist in frustration at the failure of another party to cooperate join in the common failure to resolve a problem.

Plato spoke of an ideal republic where the citizen was so well educated and trained as a citizen "that no enforcement against him of particular duty, nor system of sanction, would be required, nor anti-civic act, willful or inadvertent, be committed by him." Cooperation with the authorities when people are part of the democratic decision-making process is proper and acceptable. However, when the state is too powerful or politicians are too strong and take liberties with their power in the "common good," bad things always happen. Even Rousseau, in

The Social Contract, warned against worship of the state, which he said was the act not of a free citizen but of a subject or slave.

Institutions, customs, habits and culture build strong civilized societies. That is social capital, and it is based on the fundamental concept of reciprocity: the expectation that your neighbor, competitor, teacher, the courts, the police and the suppliers of goods you purchase will do the right thing; that they will act in accord with civil and honest behavior; that they will display integrity and honor, based on common values. Once embedded, reciprocity becomes a habit, normal behavior, and we are shocked when these principles are broken. Trust is central to the success of society and is good business, and the reverse is equally true. Decency is also an economic good—another big idea.

Where that social trust is broken, society retreats. When politicians lie to the people they betray trust and show by their example that civil order can be broken. The same is true of a police officer who has taken a bribe, a teacher who has given up caring, or a parent who is more interested in bingo than in his children's education. If the very wealthy appear to pay no tax while the poor battle on, it is seen as immoral and wrong. It destroys social trust, betrays our common values and erodes our ability to progress. It is people's mutual cooperation within the accepted rules that makes for a civilized society.

Compatriots who interact in many social contexts are apt to develop strong norms of acceptable behavior and to convey their expectations to one another in many reinforcing encounters. These norms are reinforced by the network of relationships that depend on the establishment of a reputation for keeping promises and accepting the norms of the local community regarding behavior.[6]

Networks of civic engagement facilitate communication and improve the flow of information about the trustworthiness of individuals. Trust and cooperation depend on reliable information about the past behavior and present interest of potential partners, while uncertainty reinforces dilemmas of collective action. Thus, other things being equal, the greater the communication (both direct and indirect) among participants, the greater the mutual trust and the easier they will find it to cooperate. Individuals in high-trust societies spend less to protect themselves from being exploited in economic transactions. Written contracts are less likely to be needed and they do not have to specify every possible contingency.[7]

People have to cooperate, even in competitive situations, by accepting rules of behavior. This "prosociality" becomes more entrenched because it works. The market may not teach people to trust but it certainly makes it easier for them to do so.[8]

Václav Havel, the last president of Czechoslovakia, said that political repression in Eastern Europe had robbed those nations of a healthy civic life and worthwhile public institutions:

> Trade unions, democratic involvement and management of our health systems, public ownership of our energy system, are important to our life, our way of doing things. Eastern Europe's problems were not only problems of shortages of private investment, but because public investment and structures, from phones to roads to schools, were in disrepair.

Alexis de Tocqueville remarked often how the democratic American experience and the civic virtues of associations, clubs and groups had bought democratic life and social mobility to many. An open, successful society is as much about unwritten laws as it is about formalized written law. Individual enterprise and innovation should be rewarded and cherished. Such enterprise needs to be protected and upheld by the law.

Good governance and good institutions themselves take us a long way. They are necessary, but not sufficient. We still need to add openness to ideas, trade, people, tolerance, an active civil society and democratically accountable politicians and policies to promote social mobility via equality.

Much has been written about how to make government more effective and responsive. Given that the last decade gave us the most sustained economic growth in history, not enough thought has been given to corporate governance (except in the industry that has developed around the social and environmental responsibilities of corporations). If we accept Thomas Friedman's argument that the only responsibility business has is to its shareholders, then it follows that much more thought has to be given to ensure companies are responsible to shareholders through providing information upon which to make decisions. It should come as no surprise that some executives are as greedy and self-serving as any politician or government institution. For almost a generation the pervasive cliché created by President Reagan—that government wasn't the answer, it was the problem—ruled. To question business seemed negative and anti-business. It isn't. If as much public space had been made available to question business accounts and what their new financial instruments actually were, perhaps the economic hoaxes that have been brought to light recently would have been exposed much earlier.

Advancing Africa

But perhaps nowhere on the globe is in more need of sound, trustworthy institutions and good governance than the African continent. When he was prime minister of the United Kingdom, Tony Blair reminded us that Africa was a scar on the world's conscience. Colonialism left a terrible inheritance. No other continent has so many artificial political boundaries. Colonizers often claimed they were bringing civilization, but bayonets, bullets, booze and the Bible did untold damage. When the European empires retreated, they left behind a trail of devastation. (At the time of Angola's independence, for example, there were only 68 black high school students in the whole country.) But it wasn't always so.

Africa was once host to many ancient, pre-Christian empires. We know of the glories of ancient Egypt and Carthage, and that Timbuktu was a university city which at its height in the fourteenth century had 20,000 students.

The earthworks around Benin City in Nigeria—a world heritage site—are very likely the largest ancient earthworks anywhere and testimony to a robust trading culture which flourished from around the fourth century AD and vanished around the fifteenth (trade goods from Egypt, India, and even from southeast Asia have been found unearthed there).[9]

Evidence exists that Africans were smelting iron as early as the seventh millennium BC—earlier than Europe and China. Their steel foundries were at work at the same time as Europe's. In Burkina Faso I purchased a beautiful bronze horse cast in a traditional manner, with an expertise developed well before Europeans learned how to do it. The old empires of Ghana and Zimbabwe that peaked in the Middle Ages were extensive and sophisticated, to the point of having councils of elders with the power to replace the rulers who failed to perform to their expectations.

Yet Africa today is often the worst place to live. One of its biggest problems is that of global perception: the entire continent is blamed for the problems in Zimbabwe or Darfur. (Curiously, no such blame is attached to Asia for the excesses of Myanmar or North Korea.) And

Africa's leaders are often to blame for its unsavory image: kleptomaniacs and civil war exact a predictable, terrible toll. It has been estimated that an average war, civil war or insurgency shrinks each affected country's economy by 15 percent a year, with the continent losing $18 billion annually as a result. Africa continues to be crippled by higher tariffs and costs, its countries even limiting trading with each other—though the African Union, which replaced the tired Organization of African States, offers some hope.

Though the United Nations has said that more economic progress has been made in the last 50 years than the previous 500, Africa has been the only continent to go seriously backward. Per-capita income in the poorest African countries has fallen by 25 percent in the past 20 years. Half of its inhabitants live on less than a dollar a day—not enough to buy a cup of tea in London. Despite what some protesters outside the WTO have claimed, it is not trade or investment by the multinationals that has caused this: it is the lack of trade and investment.

Sub-Saharan Africa represents 10 percent of the world's population, but has two-thirds of those infected with HIV/AIDS. Corruption costs the continent nearly $160 billion a year.

Some things have improved. Growth is now 5 percent, almost the level needed for sustained growth. Dictatorships are on the decline and, since 2000, two-thirds of sub-Saharan nations have had multiparty elections. The Blair Report recommended the total cancellation of debt for the poorest countries and increasing aid by 300 percent. These bold moves to open trade barriers to African exports, plus the abolition of agricultural subsidies, would return up to five times more than all the aid put together.

Calls for debt relief, channeled through transparent accounts to prevent abuse, echo those championed by Keynes in calling for the cancellation of Germany's post-First World War debt. Failure to do so, he warned, could result in "a conflagration that may destroy much else as well." Much the same could be said of Africa today as many of its best people pour out as economic refugees. It is disturbing to note that 80 percent of African university graduates do not work in Africa.

In 2005, the G8 also called for increased levels of aid. There is much merit in that position. Forty percent of Europe's budget is used to subsidize farmers and make food dearer. A cow in Europe receives more than $2 a day in subsidies, while two billion people live on less than that, and 30,000 people die each day because of poverty. Some

200 million Africans suffer from intestinal worms that could be cured at a cost of just 25 cents per person. Globally, one-third of deaths, 18 million a year, are because of poverty. Half-a-million women die in pregnancy and childbirth every year; one a minute.

Aid can work. Forty years ago, smallpox killed up to two million people in one year; by 1980 the world had been declared smallpox-free by the World Health Organization, a triumph of dedicated resources, political will, and management. Malaria still kills three million per year in Africa and costs the African economy $12 billion a year, but it can be stopped, as it has been elsewhere, at a cost of about $2 billion a year for five years. The same can be achieved for HIV/AIDS and TB, given the necessary resources and commitment.

Aid-delivery systems urgently need restructuring. Tanzania suffers a thousand aid missions from well-meaning agencies every year to check out projects and write reports. The lack of coherence in international aid efforts is mind-boggling. Tied-aid—asking for receipts, to ensure that the money got to those targeted—was seen as a form of colonialism in the 1970s. The wheel has turned and now the much-hated "conditionality" is accepted as encouraging good housekeeping.

The need to build African infrastructure and remove the red tape that provides an opportunity for corruption is now being recognized. Computerized management systems introduced into some African ports save weeks spent in sorting out paperwork and allow governments to raise more revenue while reducing opportunities for corruption. It is now recommended that aid be reoriented toward infrastructure— $20 billion a year for five years, rising to $40 billion a year for the following five years. All these issues are on the Doha Development trade agenda, including trade facilitation, fishing and agriculture subsidies.

Of the world's 20 poorest economies, 18 are in Africa. Yet there is reason to hope and invest in Africa. Of the world's top 10 fastest-growing economies in 2007, four were in Africa—Angola, Sudan, Equatorial Guinea and Ethiopia. Between 2002 and 2007, real GDP growth in sub-Saharan Africa averaged 6.6 percent a year, having registered 4.6 percent for the preceding five-year period. Resource demands account for some of that growth. Development in other sectors has also been notable, helped by improvements in infrastructure (particularly telecommunications) and in fiscal administration.

Other developing nations have played an important role in this development. Africa's exports to China have increased 40 percent per year since 2002; sub-Saharan Africa's natural-resource exports to China in 2006 were seven times greater in value than in 2001. A million Chinese live and work in Africa. In 2007 the largest-ever investment in Africa was made by the Commercial Bank of China, which spent $5.5 billion purchasing 20 percent of South Africa's Standard Bank. Brazil, India and Russia have also been important sources of foreign direct investment. An indication of the importance for India of its relationship with the region was the launch in June 2008 of an India–Africa Forum Summit. Indian conglomerates are investing widely and Indian policymakers view the provision of its technology expertise as the key to competing with China in Africa.[10]

Africa is undoubtedly recovering from the Cold War and extremist governments; the decline in commodity prices between 1975 and 2000 has been reversed. Debt relief has cleaned up the books somewhat and credit confidence is returning. Most important for this process is the fact that better governance has come, and elections are now commonplace.

Much has been written about South Africa's successes, but there is little about Nigeria where, in 2003 and 2007, power was passed on peacefully and, albeit with difficulty, democratically—a notable achievement considering the country's history of military intervention. The Nigerian economy was growing at 8 percent in 2007. In 1999 Nigeria had fewer than 500,000 telephone subscribers; today it has 36 million. Its population is 150 million, and it has productive land and a lot of oil and other resources. While success is far from assured, Nigeria is taking steps away from the curse of the resource-rich nations discussed in the Introduction.

Nevertheless, we should not forget that over the past 20 years more Africans have gone to North America and Europe than were shipped by force across the Atlantic during 200 years of slavery. A million economic refugees in Libya alone are waiting to escape to Europe. The real indicator of whether change is real and trusted is when people begin to go home. The great historic tragedies that created mass migration from places as diverse as Ireland, Cambodia and Armenia have also provided the phenomenon of these expatriates and their children returning to help in the reconstruction of their homeland, as tourists, as investors and, in many cases, as key bureaucrats and ministers. Their ability and willingness to help represents a valuable asset that a few countries still ignore to their cost. Africa's diaspora has yet to return.

It is hard to keep claiming that debt relief and more aid can work while corruption and poor governance continue unabated, which becomes an excuse for donor countries to hold back. It is easy to call for yet another Marshall Plan for Africa, but Africa has already had five times the aid that went to Europe. The contrast is striking. In Europe, civil society, businesses, universities and parliaments were ready and eager to be rebuilt in 1945. Building sound governmental structures, property rights, independent courts, and democratic, accountable politicians and parties is essential if Africa is to succeed.

CHAPTER 14

Openness

Over the past two decades, it has become clear that nations that embrace the global economy prosper; those that don't, falter, fail and fall behind. Compare Singapore with Myanmar, Belgium with Belarus. So much for the argument that under globalization governments are irrelevant. The opponents of the open economy and globalization have no success stories of closed economies to point to as models to admire. It is not just a matter of national resources, and nor is it a new phenomenon. The march of civilization has been a story of vibrant, often violent, internationalism by daring explorers and traders, of colonial conquest and the exchange of ideas and products. Inward-looking societies have perished or limped behind as history and progress strode over or around them. In the current global economic crisis, those who argue in the name of fairness had better beware. If policies turn inward, this decade will become known in history as the Great Contraction, or the Great Step Backward. The evidence of history is again the best roadmap to the future.

Our distant cousins, the apes, live in family tribes, as did our prehistoric relatives. The family tribe was the basic political social unit for thousands of years. Over the 12,000 years of mankind's most rapid march we separated into two types of existence: hunter-gatherers on the one hand, and those who domesticated animals and crops on the other.

The latter established the first permanent villages, the most basic collective social unit. Here was a society that did not live by self-sufficiency; it traded its surplus grain or pottery for other things it did not produce. Here were the beginnings of economic specialization.

Specialization led to the development of the basic political, religious and social structures—in short, civil organization. Increasing wealth and surplus time allowed expeditions in search of riches and new technologies, ideas, crops and animals, which in turn refined specialization, improved living standards and created a new world in which the ideas of others could be utilized.

Specialization and the division of labor may have kick-started civilization, but it took millennia for our species to articulate the intellectual underpinning of that ancient and fruitful discovery. Indeed, it was not until 1771 that David Ricardo formulated what is perhaps the best-established of observations: the theory of comparative advantage. He argued that specialization at the level of the group was the basis of economic success. Some assume that the logical extension of this is that the most efficient nation or company would consume the whole market, but this ignores the competitive advantage afforded by innovation, new product ranges and consumer emotion. Initial success which is not tested through competition usually leads to the organization eventually going backward.

Swapping and trading products is as old as time. It reduces the risk of shortage and is a more efficient use of resources. The old arguments about divisions of labor also apply between countries, tribes and groups. What's true between business and towns should be true between nations.

Ricardo had explained what our forefathers were doing anyway. The law of comparative advantage is one of the ecological aces that defines and separates our species.

Maybe the need of our species to expand, control, record history, store grain and accumulate wealth goes much deeper than political and economic theory. Perhaps at its base lies an evolutionary imperative; perhaps that's what defines and makes our species more successful than the others. In the main we enjoy and are enriched by change and new experiences. Isn't that what travel, the arts, books and cinema are all about?

Reciprocal advantage

Evolutionary biologists and historians write of the "selfish gene," central to which theory is the argument that people do things not solely for the good of themselves or their group, but for the benefit of future generations. Genetic nepotism, the determination to ensure the survival of the species, is seen as the source of ambition, industry and drive. None of our ancestors died celibate.[1]

If we accept absolute rationalism we become "rational fools."[2] There is a morality, whether we accept the selfish-gene theory or a more biblical interpretation of the point and purpose of our species. The Ten Commandments are rational as well as common sense, and these principles, applied more widely, become the basis of good governance. The biblical theories of reciprocal treatment as the basis of a just life (which, as we have seen, are to be found in all the great religions) are as profound for nations as they are for individuals.

All societies have their own moral structures, but all religions and cultures are based loosely on the concept of reciprocal treatment: we treat others as we would like to be treated ourselves. This was one of humankind's earliest and biggest ideas. And very early on man learned that the basis of reciprocity is cooperation. No-one can survive alone. History and evolution teach us that one and one can make three when we cooperate. It is called synergy. As Adam Smith said:

> Among men... the most dissimilar geniuses are of use to one another; the different produces of their respective talents, by the general disposition to truck, barter and exchange, being brought, as it were, into a common stock, where every man may purchase whatever part of the produce of the other men's talents he has occasion for.[3]

Both Adam Smith and Charles Darwin have been co-opted by economic and social extremists to justify racist and criminally exploitative policies as being the natural order of things. Most have not studied Smith's other work, *The Theory of Moral Sentiments*, in which he argued: "...benevolence is inadequate for the task of building cooperation in a large society, because we are irredeemably biased in our benevolence to relatives and close friends; a society built on benevolence would be riddled with nepotism. Between strangers, the invisible hand of the market, distributing selfish ambitions, is fairer."

In the opening chapter of his landmark book *An Inquiry into the Nature and Causes of the Wealth of Nations*, Smith chose to illustrate the point with the example of a pin-maker. Somebody not trained in pin-making could probably make only one pin a day, and even when practiced would probably be able to make only 20 or so. Yet, by dividing labor between pin-makers and non-pin-makers, and by further dividing the task between a number of specialist trades, we vastly increase the number of pins that can be made by each person. Ten people in a pin factory could produce 48,000 pins a day. To buy 20 pins from such a factory therefore costs only 1/240 of a worker-day, whereas it would have taken the purchaser a whole day at least to make them himself. Smith believed that specialization, by causing better allocation of resources to achieve the maximum returns, also led logically to free trade between nations.

The absurdities of protectionism were pointed up, perhaps inadvertently, when in his later life as a customs officer, he declared: "Upon examining the list of prohibited goods, and to my great astonishment, I had scarce a stock, a cravat, a pair of ruffles, or a pocket handkerchief which was not prohibited to be worn or used in Great Britain. I wished to set an example and burned them all."[4]

Despite being appropriated recently as a champion of the "right," Smith also said that the government could, without injustice, pay for education but that the market might do a better job of motivating teachers.

Specialization had its problems. Adam Smith and Karl Marx both wrote of the danger of the mind-destroying social alienation that comes if there is too much specialization and not enough time for leisure, social and intellectual pursuits: what we might call the "satanic mill" theory. But both Smith and Marx also identified specialization, and the international trade that would result, as a means of securing peace and development through economic cooperation. Societies that specialize and trade advance in medicine, public works and living standards. Specialization, trade, an outward-looking disposition and openness to new ideas are all linked, and are a good guide to success.

History underscores this fundamental insight. Man has always been curious and hungry enough to look and wonder what is beyond the horizon. This is in the nature of our species. People were on the move before national boundaries were drawn and war and conquest became inevitable. In this and other areas farmers and settlers had an advantage over the hunter-gatherers. Technology and invention accelerated urbanization and surplus rural labor, which could form the basis of fulltime standing armies. The hunter-gatherers, with their focus firmly on day-to-day survival, could not maintain troops in the field for long periods of time.

Africa was a continent with great empires that reached out and traded across the Indian Ocean and into the Middle East well before the Crusades.[5] Islamic traders sailed from Africa to Asia and India, taking with them ideas and culture, as well as commercial products. Their society prospered. The Ottoman and Islamic empires stretched from North Africa across the southern Mediterranean to the gates of Vienna until they were stopped by a Europe finally united by fear, the sword and the cavalry of Christendom.

As we saw in Chapter 2, China was a great trading nation, its ships trading with India, Africa and the Islamic world. But the nation that considered itself "the center of the world" looked inward and lost its way. Economic and social chauvinism and nationalistic isolationism starved Chinese society of ideas and innovation.

Throughout history, outward-looking peoples and leaders have prospered and won, while inward-looking peoples and leaders have lost and their people's prosperity has suffered.

The enterprising Portuguese adventurer Vasco da Gama, who in the fifteenth century became the first European to sail around the southern tip of Africa, picked up a pilot from the Kenyan coast who took him to India. Voyages from China and India predated this epic "discovery" by centuries. Tiny Portugal and Holland in time became great trading nations. Holland is still a great trading nation, a major exporter of tobacco products and a great oil exporter. Yet none of these products is gathered locally. Portugal and Spain, on the other hand, retreated because feudal leaders and then fascism pulled them back from the front line of open, competitive and curious societies.

Historian J. H. Elliott composed an epitaph to imperial Spain's decline in the seventeenth century:

> Heirs to a society which had over-invested in empire, and surrounded by the increasingly shabby remnants of a dwindling inheritance, they could not bring themselves at the moment of crisis to surrender their memories and alter the antique pattern of their lives. At a time when the face of Europe was altering more rapidly that ever before, the country that had once been its leading power proved to be lacking the essential ingredient for survival—the willingness to change.[6]

Japan, too, suffered from an unwillingness to change, surrendering its technological expertise in modern weaponry because the samurai were unwilling to let go of the traditional, highly ritualized code of warfare. When peasant soldiers discovered that guns were a great equalizer, laws were passed in Japan restricting their use. Equality and the democratization of power are always resisted by those who enjoy its monopoly at any one time.

Genghis Khan swept all before him and his army was poised to take Europe. But his untimely death put paid to this scheme because of the cultural (that is, political) requirement that he be buried in his homeland. This meant the withdrawal of the greatest and most effective military force of its time.

Peter the Great took Russia from being a superstitious, primitive society to the front line of European nations of the day. Brutal but brilliant and thirsty for knowledge, he was the first tsar to travel beyond his nation's boundaries. He worked in shipyards, steel factories and hospitals, employing hated foreigners to modernize his nation. He learned to sail so he could develop a Russian navy, and later built a new capital, St. Petersburg, a naval base that looked west, not east. He stripped the religious leaders of their power. His openness to new ideas and his willingness to modernize meant that the Swedes, Poles and Turks were no longer a threat to his people. Literacy rose, infant mortality dropped and Russia prospered.

Unfortunately, Peter's heirs reverted to the old beliefs in their divine rights as God's representatives and stopped the modernization programs. They perished, to be replaced by another elite which was equally convinced of the rightness of its cause. The Union of Soviet Socialist Republics was in the end little different from the Russia of the last tsars.

In the 1980s Deng Xiaoping famously said in defense of open investment and new ideas for China, "It doesn't matter if the cat is black or white, so long as it catches the mice." He also told the Communist Party Congress, "We can make people equal but they will be equally poor." Poverty is something governments can always deliver—except, of course, to the new elites, party officials, appointees and bureaucrats. Deng's policies provided the impetus for the economic freedom that has seen Chinese people recently enjoy unprecedented rises in living standards. Famine is no longer a daily danger, because people produce more if they own their products.

Kemal Ataturk was another great leader who transformed his country by opening it up to fresh thinking. Ataturk gave women in Turkey equal rights and removed the power and privileges of the high priests of Islam. He also looked to Europe, calling for a new Latin alphabet to replace the Arabic script.

What did such leaders have in common? Absolute power, indeed, and often used brutally; but they also had a curiosity about the outside world, a determination to utilize the best the world had to offer and the courage to break with the past in that process. They broke the religious and cultural straitjackets of their nations. They respected their history and culture and at the same time drove toward a new age. Is it possible that leaders can be divided between those who embrace modernity and those who reject it?

15

Free Trade

The free flow of goods and ideas has lifted living standards worldwide and strengthened human rights. Globalization and open societies have proven to be forces for perpetual improvement and thus better, sustainable outcomes.

In 1840, the French diplomat François-René de Chateaubriand said of railway, telegraph and steamships, "Distances will disappear; it will not only be commodities which travel, but also ideas which will have wings. When fiscal and commercial barriers have been abolished between states... how will you be able to revive the old mode of separation?" He was getting a bit ahead of himself, but ultimately he was correct.

Sir Robert Peel, Prime Minister of the United Kingdom from 1841–46, who championed free trade by repealing the Corn Laws that protected home-grown grain, adopted the motto: "Advance, not recede." Britain did just that and continued to lead the world for the best part of 70 years afterwards. He recognized that tariffs and subsidies are essentially a tax on the poor to pay the rich, a concept that some European social democrats have yet to fully understand.

The Great Depression was made deeper and prolonged by the outburst of protectionism and economic nationalism that it triggered. By March 1933, the volume of international trade had fallen 33 percent from its 1929 level.[1] This provided further justification for the European nationalism and vicious tribalism that fueled the twin tyrannies of last century—fascism and Nazism. After the Second World War, the great democracies followed a path exactly opposite to the one they had chosen in 1919. The Marshall Plan was unique in that the victors funded the reconstruction of vanquished nations and encouraged the rebuilding of their infrastructure, industry and democratic institutions.

The advantages of open borders have been clearly demonstrated. A recent World Bank study showed that 24 developing countries that increased their integration into the world economy over two decades ending in the late 1990s achieved higher growth in incomes, longer life expectancy and better schooling than those that did not. These countries, home to some three billion people, enjoyed an average 5 percent growth in per-capita income in the 1990s, compared to 2 percent in rich countries. Many—such as China, Hungary and Mexico—adopted domestic policies and institutions that have enabled people to take advantage of global markets and thus sharply increased the share of trade in their GDP. People in these integrating countries saw their wages rise, and the number of people in poverty decline.[2] Crucially, the past two decades of weakening protectionism have seen the biggest decline in poverty in history, mainly in those countries that understand this reality. The highlight of my time at the WTO was China's accession to the organization and there can be no doubting the remarkable impact this has had on both China's domestic economy and the global economy. And others, like Russia and Vietnam (which became a member of WTO in 2007), will ultimately add the impact of their own full economic potential from within the multilateral system.

Big corporations are an essential element of this welcome expansion and, contrary to popular myth, most foreign companies investing in developing nations behave responsibly. ILO research concludes that multinationals are more likely to be better employers than smaller, local companies because they are vulnerable to public opinion and to scrutiny by aggressive NGOs, analysts and journalists. In short, their reputations are at stake. They tend to import safer, more-efficient production processes. They pay more attention to the environment. They often invest strongly in local communities. Their governance standards are usually high, and they tend to stick around in troubled times.

Even the nature of multinationals has changed. In the old days they visited countries with a deal: "I will build a tire factory, if you promise me your domestic market." The allure for the government was instant jobs that, in the absence of global competition, meant they could pass on any cost to consumers in a trapped, closed market. This is, effectively, a flat tax that hits the poorest. Governments are mostly wiser now and seek investment where it adds real value in the global supply chain.

In the period between 1990 and 2001, developing countries began to grow their shares in world trade, their share in global merchandise exports and imports jumping by 6 percent and 5 percent respectively.[3] Trade between developing countries also mushroomed by 12 percent a year, twice as fast as global commerce generally. Although the biggest success stories come from just a handful of countries, only the Middle East and Africa among developing regions failed to boost their exports more strongly than industrial countries in that period.

Poorer countries also secured more investment. The share of developing nations in world foreign direct investment flows moved from an average of 17.5 percent in 1986–1990 to 27.9 percent in 2001.[4]

While we can alleviate some of the impact on the developing world of increasingly free trade in goods and services, we cannot shield poorer countries from the fact that the wealth of nations is increasingly based on knowledge, and knowledge is limitless and mobile, the most sustainable of all resources. The challenge for a developing country is to establish the infrastructure that will allow it to attract investment, redirect resources from uncompetitive industries, and put more into education and healthcare, giving current and future generations a better chance of competing globally.

Western subsidies on products such as cotton and sugar are obscene and must change. Anti-globalization activists do poor countries no favors by demanding that they get market access for their products without acknowledging the need for domestic reform, openness and competition within those countries. While calling for the first but ignoring the latter, the activists are simply ensuring that the corrupting influence of protectionist crony policies is kept in place. Africa's problems do not stem from globalization but from not enough globalization, not enough investment, and not enough trade.

Trade creates friends and is a key factor in development. Control breeds enemies. That's why new opportunities for trade between India and Pakistan, China and Taiwan are so important, and is yet another reason why the global community needs to continue its efforts to accommodate and integrate nations such as Myanmar, North Korea and Iran into the wider trading community. If Russia were a member of the WTO, it would be very difficult and costly for it to stop imports from the Ukraine, Georgia or Poland. Multinational agreements, ratified by their parliaments, take a dangerous lever from the hands of politicians, which is why the WTO is so important for peace, security and development.

The open economy

We need to remind governments why our parents created an open, worldwide, rules-based trading system. Mill, Hume and Adam Smith all argued that expanded commerce produced good government, reduced the propensity for conflict, enhanced individual liberty and security, and promoted equality by lessening the servile dependence of individuals on their superiors. The effect of increased commerce on individual freedom was, according to Smith, the least-observed advantage of commerce.

The trading system has promoted more than prosperity. Its treaty-bound commitments help secure peaceful, predictable relations among states. Governments have neither the need nor the opportunity to raise armies solely to secure access to land, raw materials and labor. What matters for prosperity is productivity and peaceful commerce. It is the multilateral trading system that provides the rules and commitments that are the essential bulwark against commercial confrontation pursued through military means.

Not all countries with market economies have been democracies, but all modern democracies, without exception, have had market economies.[5] The experience of the countries of southern Europe in the 1970s and of Latin America in the 1980s suggests that those that combined market economies with undemocratic governance made the transition to political democracy more easily than did the formerly communist countries of Eastern Europe and Central Asia in the 1990s. There is both an affinity and an overlap between the design and the procedures of liberal economics on the one hand and those of liberal politics on the other. The defining features of liberal politics have counterparts in market economies. First, individual choices are paramount. Popular sovereignty corresponds to consumer sovereignty in the market. Second, the reach of the state is limited, with certain areas—political rights in the case of democracy, private property in a market economy—fenced off from government control. Third, they are both underpinned by the rule of law—the impartial, consistent and equal application of clear and well-known rules across society.[6]

Political and economic freedom does not require pure, laissez-faire market capitalism of the style that operated in the nineteenth century. Western democracies, by trial and error, have learned that the state can play a beneficial role in curbing market excesses and regulating in the interests of consumers to maintain social mobility and to create a floor under which no citizen should fall. But attempts to usurp the role of the market entirely, or even largely, have almost universally led to a loss of economic vitality.

Competition is the key to innovation. Choice drives better results, and the removal of barriers and regulations exposes crony capitalists to healthy competition. This always favors small business and the start-up companies who have the initiative to challenge and out-think and out-compete their bigger rivals. Competition is a great cleansing agent, and is the least-acknowledged development advantage brought to international trade by the WTO agreements. Lowering entry costs for new business is one of the noble by-products of opening trade. This is the "bubble up" theory, as opposed to the "trickle down" theory that privilege frequently uses as the rationale for its self-serving policies.

Where freedom and individual action are cherished, ultimately a large measure of economic freedom must be preserved; otherwise, the results are sadly predictable: low growth; corruption at worst; inefficiencies and poverty at best.

Migration

Mobility has been a defining trait of humankind. The history of our species is the history of the movement of people. And they move now for the same reasons as always: seeking more from life, a better opportunity for their children, a safer existence. Hope drives them on. People move more within nations for the same reason. In an ideal world, this would be from choice, not fear. Increasingly, this is becoming the case; countries that welcome diversity are attracting talented and creative people, which improves their competitive advantage.

In 2005, after two years of submissions, visits to most regions, and public hearings, the Global Commission on International Migration, on which I served, released its findings. The report highlighted the significance of what has become an issue of intense public and political controversy throughout the world. As of 2005, nearly 200 million people were living in countries in which they were not born, counting only those who had lived outside their own country for more than one year.

This figure included 9.2 million refugees. Recent migration toward open societies across the world over the past half-century has highlighted the extent to which authoritarian failed states are falling behind. The anti-globalization, anti-America, anti-capitalism mantra of some NGOs misses the point. The reality is that people are migrating to the most successful, fastest-growing, most globalized parts of the world; not the other way around. To paraphrase the cliché of the service industry, the customer is always right.

The key factor driving current migration flows is the desire to flee repression and poverty. Where there is the greatest outward movement of people you generally find the biggest tyrants, the weakest economic conditions, the worst human rights, and the most-closed economies and societies.

And we must not forget that migration is the oldest form of technology transfer. When the French expelled the Huguenots in the seventeenth century, 200,000 of them took their glass and clothing techniques to other cities all over Europe. Hitler expelled Jewish scientists from Nazi Germany, probably denying himself the atomic bomb that could have given him global dominance. Each group of migrants brings skills, enterprise, sweat and ideas. Over a period of just 30 years, 20 million migrants arrived in the United States, catapulting it to the front rank of nations. The initiatives they founded eventually outshone many industries in their homelands. Germany led the cinematic world until it exiled its Jewish expertise, which regrouped in Hollywood. The Kodak empire was established by German immigrants. Switzerland prospered through the banking and watch-making skills of refugees. Refugees, from Albert Einstein to Madeleine Albright, have filled universities and provided much of the stimulus for the United States' spectacular success. The history of United States economic success is the history of migrants: take Andrew Carnegie (steel), Samuel Goldwyn (movies), Helena Rubenstein (cosmetics). As well as Kodak, think of Atlantic Records, RCA, NBC, Google, Intel, Hotmail, Sun Microsystems, Microsoft, Yahoo and eBay. All were started or co-founded by migrants. One-third of the Fortune 500 companies have migrants as CEOs. Half the richest Americans ever have been migrants—that is the genius of America.

Migration is useful also to countries with aging populations. The populations of Ukraine and Bulgaria are predicted to drop by one-third over the next 40 years. Italy's population will drop by 30 percent in 20 years. Migration can help ease the burden on younger generations.

Neither should we forget the importance of the remittances back home made by the migrants.

However, the sheer volume of migrants does impose strains on some host countries, striking at the very identity of the nation-state. Social cohesion is a fundamental responsibility of the state and the nation-state reserves a legitimate right to determine who and under what terms migrants can become residents or citizens.

Migrants, too, have rights, but they also have obligations. Unless they are forced to live in unacceptable ghettos, they should accept local culture and respect local values. Integration is not assimilation. They need to accept and appreciate the standards, laws and values of their new home states. One of the most difficult questions policymakers face is how to respond when a tiny minority of migrants—and, in particular, their children, frequently born in the new land—hate the societies they are in. The consequences of failing to address this are catastrophic.

Prejudice is emotional. Racial and religious hate has to be taught, normally at the breakfast table, which is why immigration is frequently an election issue everywhere in the world, producing the worst kind of politics and politicians. One in 10 Europeans and one in eight Americans, a fifth of Canadians and nearly a quarter of all Australians are foreign-born. Three-quarters of America's population growth in the second half of the 1990s was due to migration, and Europe's population would have fallen by 4.4 million over that time had it not been for migrants.

The average wage of US-born workers rose by 2–2.5 percent in response to the inflow of foreign-born workers between 1990 and 2000. Immigrants lowered the wages of local workers without a high school diploma by 1 percent, but increased the wages of those with qualifications by as much as 3–4 percent. One study showed that a 10 percent rise in the number of foreign students increased total US patent applications by 4.8 percent. For every 1 percent increase in the number of first-generation immigrants from a given country into California, Californian exports to that country rose by nearly 0.5 percent. In 2005, the official value of remittances sent home by migrants, $167 billion, was twice the value received by developing countries in aid from wealthy countries.

Economists can prove that a more open labor market would bring great gains in global wealth, as trade and investment have done. But a world completely without walls is not going to happen. Though diversity has been quantified as both an economic good and a generator of innovation and business, prejudice trumps logic when people feel their well-being is threatened. Perhaps it's a defensive part of our makeup, our DNA. The truth of it is that the battle for economic success will most likely go to those countries that can attract the smartest migrants. Several hundred thousand overseas-educated graduates now live, produce and pay tax in America: a direct subsidy by taxpayers in other countries to America!

Diversity does create headaches and new sets of challenges, but it also makes life more interesting and societies more dynamic. One need only visit Toronto, Rio, Dublin, London, New York, Hong Kong, Sydney, Auckland, or Cape Town to experience the truth of this.

Tolerance is good economics

In the new economy, competitive advantage lies in the creativity of people. This, underpinned by open communication systems, property rights and the predictable rule of law, is what matters now. Skilled entrepreneurs are highly sought after and highly mobile, choosing to work where there is respect for diversity, cultural dialogue, the arts, openness, tolerance, free information, food, and entertainment.[7]

Inward-looking societies, where diversity is feared and scorned, are damaging for growth and jobs as well as for their international reputation as a nation. Political and religious bigots and zealots are costly, whether they reside in Australia, India, the Middle East or Africa.

When I was a boy, the church sent me door to door to collect old clothes to be sent to the poor in Singapore. (I always wondered what they would do with woolly jerseys.) Now Singapore has a higher per-capita income, and its people live longer and enjoy a lower infant mortality rate than we do in New Zealand. This came about through the hard work of its people, enabled by good governance, an outward-looking attitude and farsighted leadership. But the present leadership knows that Singapore must reinvent itself if it is to maintain its position in the face of competition from China for investment. The policies that built its present success—hard work and a puritanical no-nonsense nanny state—are now losing some of their former appeal and Singapore is losing out to Hong Kong in attracting investors and managers. Singapore has to create a new, more sophisticated economy based on services, information, healthcare and education. A state committee, Remaking Singapore, is looking into ending strict censorship laws, abolishing petty laws governing individual behavior and allowing pubs to open all night. In a complete reversal of its policies on "degenerate behavior," the government is now hiring gays and lesbians in the civil service. In the 1960s, I was stopped by the police in Singapore and told to get a haircut within 24 hours or leave. How things are changing (and time has solved my hair problem.) While Singapore scores high on economic freedom and the sanctity of law, it has been strangely reluctant to be more open politically.

Globalization is forcing change. Societies must adapt, or stagnate and perish. I've always thought tolerance was a good thing in itself, and now economists have quantified it. Politicians who play to the future, rather than to the gallery, must implement change if they want the best outcome.

Education and freedom of religion

Education makes a people easy to lead, but difficult to drive; easy to govern but impossible to enslave.[8]

The fundamental decision to separate church and state was an important factor that gave an edge to countries that built on the Enlightenment experience. The principles that evolved from the Reformation and the Enlightenment—freedom of and from religion, freedom of conscience, tolerance of difference, and equality—imperfectly practiced though they are, were revolutionary. In their time, they were big ideas that had to be asserted.

A message from that era was that we are all the children of God, and thus equal. This profound principle advanced the idea of equality, and provided the moral base to fight slavery, treat women and minorities equally, and drive children out of coal mines. It was also a spur to universal education. In Scotland, each reformed church became a school. Education was established as a basic principle of citizenship, a basic responsibility of society. Countries that give no rights or education to women, meanwhile, deny themselves so much potential and are doomed to stagnation or worse.

Before the Reformation, the church and priests had a monopoly on information, mainly because only they could read and write. The arrival of the printing press empowered ordinary people to challenge these assumptions and Calvin was able to turn out hundreds of books and pamphlets. The genie, once out of the bottle, could not be put back, despite the attempts of oppressive leaders from both church and state. Education and literacy remain key weapons in the fight for freedom, development and opportunity for all.

I once attended an international student conference on "Education Without Borders" in Abu Dhabi. Other guests included Nobel Prize-winners, an astronaut and various state ministers, and we all gave speeches and presented papers. I reflected that all those attributes of learning and literacy which were fought so hard for centuries ago are now accessible across entire regions and are just a mouse click away. The students compared papers, networked, and suggested projects about how to assist the poor and how to drive up equality and opportunity. The prize for best paper was won by a young South African who has no electricity in his home village. A previous winner was a blind Austrian girl with a paper on how to empower disabled people.

It was around that same time that I had a conversation with a wealthy Saudi businessman who explained how he judged a country's economy and made investment decisions based on how its communications system worked. It took me 10 years to understand how smart that was.

The Enlightenment's ideas of freedom, tolerance, individual conscience and dissent would not have spread as far or as quickly without the printing press. Now the internet provides an even more revolutionary opportunity to build understanding and solidarity between people. The artificial walls that separate people and cultures are crashing down and the new information age is destroying the hold of tyrants everywhere.

Reports on the US War of Independence took weeks to appear in London newspapers; news from the Crimean and Boer wars took days. Now hot issues can hit websites well before cabinets have been briefed. The Vietnam War was fought out on the public's television screens, which exerted a huge influence on government policy. The 9/11 terror attacks were seen live by millions worldwide. The instantaneous availability of information from many sources is democratizing policy-making.

Civil society

Without an active civil society—media, intelligentsia, artists, voluntary groups, independent social organizations, churches, trade unions—pushing for better outcomes, creating public opinion that politicians and bureaucrats must respond to, the worst happens. It is no coincidence that the aim of Nazi and Soviet states was to eliminate all social groupings that the ruling party did not control. Dick Howard, in his book *The Spectre of Democracy*, wrote of how students in Prague in 1967 had got into trouble for organizing a demonstration against the Vietnam War, even though their government was opposed to the war.[9] To such regimes, independent activity is always a threat, autonomy a danger, and self-organized groups a menace.

Tyrants fear information most. Because knowledge is power, independent sources of information, such as a free media, are the first to be muzzled. Whether in politics or commerce, ambition makes cowards of many and they are happy to repeat what those in authority want to hear. For others, the risk of being out of step makes them hold their tongues and surrender their judgment when it's necessary to point out that the king has no clothes. This all reached hideous heights during the reigns of Hitler, Stalin and Mao.

Novelists and writers are also prime targets of repressive regimes because of the power they wield in molding public opinion. In their day, the novels of Charles Dickens and Upton Sinclair mocked and challenged the manners and patterns of their respective societies. Aleksandr Solzhenitsyn's *The Gulag Archipelago*, released in the West in 1973, exposed Soviet Socialism as a totalitarian dictatorship resting upon a foundation of slave labor and mass murder. Solzhenitsyn could probably count himself lucky to be deported the following year; millions not so articulate perished. (It is interesting to note how in subsequent years Solzhenitsyn was rehabilitated, being given a State Award for his humanitarian achievements.)

In the new information age, grassroots pressure groups and the media have more power than many politicians. A few minutes' affectionate attention from Larry King can be more politically rewarding than visiting a town to meet voters in person.

The institutions of a free civil society provide a powerful check on oppression, privilege and inefficiency. When democratic governments make bad decisions, they are answerable not only to parliamentary scrutiny, but also to every news network and every journalist who dreams of a Pulitzer Prize. If there was deliberate deceit involved in the presentation of the reasons for war in Iraq, it will come out, as has the grotesque failure to plan for a post-war Iraq.

When democracies carry evil traditions, such as segregation and racism in the southern United States, artists, social commentators and popular media contribute significantly to changing attitudes. *Uncle Tom's Cabin* did more to expose the evils of slavery in America than most politicians' speeches at the time. "The Lonesome Death of Hattie Carroll" and other songs by Bob Dylan and his contemporaries pricked the conscience of a nation and helped build the constituency for change, as the works of poets and writers have done throughout the ages.

The capacity for effective and fearless self-criticism is one of the West's greatest strengths, exposing mistakes and helping to weed out the bad and the incompetent. In dictatorships, the critics disappear; self-criticism is absent, allowing the likes of Kim Jong Il to hide their shortcomings from themselves and their people.

China's handling of the SARS epidemic in late 2002 showed how far the country has arrived in the past two decades. International pressure from the World Health Organization and the media forced the Beijing leadership to admit that the problem was worse than initially suspected. Equally important, the authorities began a mass-education campaign to alert their own public to the dangers and possible precautions. And in a move that would have been unthinkable a decade before, the Health Minister was sacked.

The global market—guided by global media, bloggers and NGOs—rewards reputation more than anything. The belated but transparent accountability over SARS reflects China's enhanced understanding of the importance of its international image. (Its dependence on exports makes China vulnerable to the whims of its customers.) That understanding was clearly evident in the open and prompt response to the Sichuan earthquake in May 2008.

An exporting country's reputation can only be safeguarded in the long term by the development of trusted institutions—checks and balances of the sort inimical to autocratic government. This is not to suggest that China is about to embrace "one person, one vote," but it's a long way from Mao's Great Leap Forward. Protestors in Hong Kong recently forced changes in proposed anti-subversion legislation—a far cry from the reaction that saw tanks in Tiananmen Square just two decades ago.

Nations, like individuals and businesses, seek respect from their peers. Winning the Olympics for Beijing, and the international spotlight and transparency inherent in running the games, is a further indication of Chinese progress. Sending a man into outer space (only the third country to do so) is a matter of national pride for China, a test of the nation's scientific virility. Ambitious nations seek respect from the global, political and commercial marketplace. There is now a global jury, a global market that rewards and punishes good and bad behavior.

Though in Western societies today trade unions are sometimes regarded as forces of conservatism and privilege, after the excesses of militant factions in earlier decades, free trade unions are a basic component of a democratic economy. Historically, trade unions have played a crucial role in the development of freedom. Freedom to organize in the workplace was, along with collective bargaining, a big idea that improved the lives of millions. Unions are a manifestation of the great and powerful tradition of dissent and criticism. Throughout the world, they led the march for freedom, from the Philippines to Chile and South Africa. The pivotal role of Solidarity in Poland is well known and it was union leader Morgan Tsvangirai who led the opposition to Mugabe in Zimbabwe. When a Chinese ship full of weapons bound for Zimbabwe sought to berth at Durban in April 2008, South African watersiders refused to allow it in, just as workers in Australasia boycotted ships loading pig iron for fascist Japan in the 1930s.

While many have a record of selfless public service, when trade unions conspire too closely with government and business, the result can be Peron's "corporate state."

An active, constructive civil society is vital to ensure further progress in building successful states. As freedoms develop in societies, the political market acts like any other in correcting itself in response to public pressure.

CHAPTER 16

A New Democracy

The democracy of the market has been the most effective economic mechanism yet devised to create growth and jobs. But its purpose is to create opportunity and wealth, not share it. The market, when left to itself, is essentially anti-competitive.

Business cannot succeed in societies that fail. Where ownership is diverse and works to hold businesses and managers accountable, shareholder democracy is a cleansing and correcting agent against the excesses of the powerful. It is a healthy and growing phenomenon but, like all freedoms, it is open to abuse.

Investor democracy and choice have created a demand for ethical investing, forcing investment houses to keep away from products such as tobacco that are deemed inappropriate, or products from countries with poor human rights or labor and health standards. Soon consumer democracy will demand public exposure of carbon footprints on products and in company reports. In the main this is healthy, making commercial adjustment for long-term sustainability. It is putting pressure on nations that don't respect consumer values and is influencing governments to consider these issues when negotiating trade deals. Consumers will want more fuel-efficient cars; they will want to know the conditions in which products are made and what's in them.

Public engagement is vital to healthy communities. Margaret Thatcher infamously declared, "There is no such thing as society." She was wrong: visit any football club, trade union meeting or Rotary club; or watch concerned neighbors and volunteers run neighborhood groups, flock to beaches to save stranded whales, or just bake scones and look after friends. They are society at work and can never be replaced by government officials or corporate sponsors. Volunteers are the civic strength of community. They are the community. This impulse to improve the community through personal involvement is a great civilizer. It rewards those who give and the community that receives, and makes life better.

Time and again we have seen how voter and consumer decision-making is enhanced by information. The phrase "the democracy of information" is now something of a cliché but I saw at first-hand how it assists in development around the world in a study by the Panos Institute in London, to which I made a modest contribution. The compelling evidence of this included:

Media and accountability: In 2001, an Indian online newspaper, Tehlka.com, taped secret video footage of senior politicians, bureaucrats and army officers apparently receiving money in connection with a defense deal. The subsequent public outrage led to the resignation of the president of the BJP, the ruling party.[1]

Participation promotes efficiency: In Bolivia, citizen participation in annual planning, budgeting and oversight on municipal hospital health boards was effective in reducing corruption[2] to a greater extent than previous anti-corruption administrative interventions.[3]

Indian conglomerate ITC, which manages an agricultural trading company, created a network of e-Choupals (internet-connected computers) in rural communities to eliminate the inefficiencies in its supply chain caused by corrupt middlemen. Since June 2000, more than 5,200 e-Choupal kiosks have been established to serve 3.5 million farmers in 31,000 villages. Through these, individual farmers have been able to check the market trading price of their produce and sell it to the best-paying market, resulting in an increase of up to 20 percent in farmers' earnings.[4]

A similar scheme in Senegal, set up through a partnership of telecommunications companies, fishing unions and the Canadian International Development Research Center (IDRC), has produced equally impressive results. The IDRC has reported that food producers using this service have seen their incomes increase by an average of 15 percent. In 2005, more than 3,500 Senegalese producers were using the service.[5] Similar initiatives have also been developed in Burkina Faso, Ghana, Mali, Uganda and Zambia.

Mobile banking: South Africans send the equivalent of $1.5 billion each year to their relatives in other parts of the country. The money is usually sent informally because 16 million South Africans don't have a bank account. But at least 30 percent of them do have mobile phones, which makes it possible for mobile-phone companies such as Wizzit to offer secure banking services via text message. In 2006 Wizzit had half a million customers—80 percent of whom had no bank account.[6]

This is a growing market. Prior to 2006, only 10 percent of the sub-Saharan population had mobile network coverage; by the beginning of 2007 this had expanded to more than 60 percent and is expected to reach 85 percent by 2010.[7]

Regrettably, some governments still resist the new technology that investment can bring from the world's best companies. As we saw earlier, trust builds confidence and reciprocity and where there are low levels of trust in government and business institutions, people work and live outside society's legal structures.

Democracy provides the collective organization that gives life to individual ambition and liberty. I sense that people subscribe to the socialist view of equality, fraternity and solidarity but doubt, through grim experience, that bureaucracy can ever really promote liberty. Freedom is cemented and expands when there is ownership, which in turn engenders responsibility and mutual obligation.

Collective responsibility created a social democratic concept of, for instance, social security, free and open public education, social cohesion, and social responsibility to neighbors as well as ourselves. Yet, unless held to proper account, institutions invariably end up serving themselves rather than their membership and the wider public. They frequently do the opposite of what they intended by creating new privileges and a new ruling class. The interests of bureaucracies often outweigh the needs of parents, the ill, and the public. Choice and competition are largely absent from the great public institutions in modern welfare states, despite massive increases in public expenditure.

Better outcomes will not come from cutting expenditure on public goods such as health and education, as conservatives advocate. We need to face the unpalatable truth that when governments assume too much collective responsibility this weakens the traditional institutions of family, society, and individual obligations and responsibilities. Why work if there's more money to be made on a welfare benefit? Why respect the system when there are loopholes that enable large corporations and rich, more mobile individuals to pay as little tax as possible?

We need to attack both the narrowing of the tax base by the mobile rich and the widening of dependency through state-owned social systems.

I still don't accept that government is the whole problem, any more than I accept the Marxist analysis that capitalism alone is the problem. The Marxists argued that you could abolish theft by abolishing property; the extreme "right" suggests you can abolish poverty by abolishing welfare. I remain a militant moderate.

Yet new levers have appeared that offer us a fresh opportunity to democratize, individualize, personalize and provide new ownership to reform our welfare state and the way we manage public programs. As we have seen, putting government services online in some developing countries promotes efficiencies and reduces the opportunity for the corruption and arrogance that government agencies so often display.

Technology presents a revolutionary path to reform, offering the possibility of storing health records, pension and educational entitlements on a computer chip via a personalized "citizen's card," and a new way of managing personal ownership of the taxes devoted to public welfare policies. This is a big idea. The welfare state has, alas, created an unhealthy dependency and has become slave to its own bureaucracies. Like all good revolutions, it started with the best of intentions and helped liberate people from want by catering for their most basic needs. However, what started as a platform has become a ceiling, trapping and limiting many.

Today, even to attempt to discuss what has become a multi-generational reliance on welfare is to invite accusations from the liberal establishment, who portray such talk as insensitive, right-wing, even cruel. Thus progressive thinkers are often paralyzed politically.

While people fall through the cracks in our education system and somehow come out of school without the basic ability to read or write and the skills to be gainfully employed, few seem to fall through the cracks in our welfare system. People are smart and will seek out advantages in any system.

All this is not an argument against society giving the poor a hand up; it's about changing the welfare state to look after the welfare of the individual. We now have the tools to do this.

Individual freedom

With the technologies now available to us, power can shift from institutions to individuals. We can now more easily individualize pension and welfare schemes. Needs-based individual accounts created by tax and levies topped up by savings, and with personal decision-making mechanisms, could abolish welfare and public programs as we know them. Citizenship can now be made more personal.

The impulse to collectively insure ourselves against old age, illness and accident, to provide justice and social mobility by providing a safety net, has been the dream of liberals, progressives and social democrats for generations. We have achieved much but our instruments were unwieldy, blunt and prone to exploitation, and are now outmoded. Our once-proud pay-as-you-go pension plans are no longer viable. Essentially, they have become pyramid-selling projects, elaborate hoaxes, Ponzi schemes, which are outlawed in most countries when done for private gain but not when done for votes by politicians. While many OECD countries are now, belatedly, recognizing this and dedicating some modest investments for future retirement costs, few mature democracies have invested in funds that can be drawn down for healthcare as our population ages.

Compulsory savings for retirement and public responsibility for health and education are good concepts. But there's no reason that governments should have sole responsibility for this. Competition between delivery agencies, allowing individuals to direct how their "social wage" is spent, and rewards for good choices in expenditure and lifestyles, are not currently possible. People's social wage represents how public expenditures are spent on their behalf and is inherently based on need. Thus, a wealthy person with a child in school or a parent in hospital finds his social wage is smaller than the social wage of a person on a modest income in a similar situation.

If we can close our eyes to ideology and open our minds to possibilities, this has in it the germ of an idea that can satisfy our distrust of wasteful government expenditure, provide choice, and yet keep in place the essential good that the welfare state can provide. It is about trusting people to make choices for themselves, so that individuals need not be clients of governments but real citizens and consumers who will hold their systems and expenditures accountable. Ownership builds responsibility, makes spending effective and accountable, and would help break depressing cycles of dependency. Progressive governments broke the dependency of protected industry on taxpayer handouts. Now we can liberate people from the bureaucracy but still provide, and improve on, traditional social democracy.

In advocating this, I will probably be assaulted from both the "left," who will automatically think I'm writing about privatization, and from the "right," who think we should abolish the welfare state but never get around to it because it's still basically good and popular. The latter say government is bad, and then run it badly to prove their point.

Ideology becomes theology after a time. TV naturally turns the cameras on to the doctors or teachers or the representatives of those who have the power to seek their "unbiased" view. To no-one's surprise, they like the status quo: they just need more money. Strangely enough, in countries like mine where those who control the levers of power in social policy oppose contracting out except to themselves and their supporters through NGOs, contracting out to social organizations seems acceptable. They argue that a private company, which has to make itself and its shareholders a return by taxable profits, is automatically inferior to a government agency, or to a so-called non-profit organization—even when the evidence shows that private companies can provide some services better and cheaper. Such suggestions are rejected for purely ideological reasons. As Mao once said, "Rather socialist weeds than capitalist crops," while millions died and hungry children couldn't taste the difference.

Public services and individual choice

When Tony Blair advocated "academy schools" to try to break the bureaucratic cycle of underachievement in the United Kingdom, this caused great resentment among traditional labor activists, who saw this as selling out a socialist principle of state control. The evidence on the results of academy schools is mixed, but look carefully at the critics and their motives. The welfare state is now the status quo, and its employed beneficiaries are often the most vocal in opposition to change or measurement. What was radical becomes, after a time, conservative.

A US study of 4,000 charter schools showed that every one outperformed its nearest public school. They were more cost-effective, and minorities at charter schools did better academically. The schools also did better at fostering tolerance, civic participation and social integration. These findings were confirmed by results of similar research in Ireland, Denmark and Australia.[8]

In 1993, socialist Sweden created a voucher system which opened up a national education market by funding all schools on a similar basis. This led to improved student achievement, greater parental satisfaction, and a fivefold increase in the number of independent schools across a broad cross-section of neighborhoods. A voucher system was established in the Netherlands as long ago as 1917, and the private sector now enrolls 76 percent of all primary and secondary students. The country performs well in international test scores and parents report high satisfaction in finding schools that meet their children's needs.

Both Sweden and the Netherlands are social democratic countries. The kneejerk reaction by some governments against more private-sector involvement in education thus seems more ideological than evidence-based. Customer-satisfaction studies demonstrate that when parents have a choice they are more positive about their school of choice. As a pastoral letter by the Catholic bishops of New York State put it: "The freedom to choose the education best suited for one's children is a basic right of all parents, regardless of income."

While the evidence regarding choice and private schools may make for uncomfortable reading for those of us who believe in education as the great equalizer and the state as the mechanism to deliver it, the notion of people owning and being able to direct how their taxes are spent on education is a big idea whose time is coming.

Education has never been equal: the wealthy have always been able to buy special tuition; employers have always respected a B grade from a "good" school more than an A from a "poor" school.

The most uncomfortable research is emerging in developing countries where, in early post-colonial days, strong governments with enormous goodwill introduced education systems that monopolized the market for the poor, who had no choice. In Africa, India and China, a huge, vibrant black market has emerged in the education of the poor. In Ghana, for example, more than 65 percent of children—children from slums—now go to private schools. This is a global trend among the very poor. In rich countries such as mine, we have an epidemic of school absenteeism. In poor countries, where they are allowed to attend school, the kids get it. They appreciate school. It's the teachers who frequently don't go to school, except on pay day. That's the sorry experience of corrupt, unaccountable school systems.

In Russia, three out of four students go to private schools; the number in China has doubled since 2003; and in India 30 percent of students go to private schools;[9] in Hyderabad, 80 percent of the schools serving the poor are now private (red tape, corruption, and teachers who don't turn up in the state system are common reasons given in research, and the cost to ambitious poor parents can be as low as a few dollars a month.) In one remote area in China in which, officially, there was no private education for the poor, researchers discovered 600 private schools, which were twice as cost-effective as government schools, had better results and little teacher absenteeism.

While it's education at primary level that has seen the most dramatic evidence of parents taking control and opting out of corrupt, inadequate systems, one study in 2005 found that fewer than 10 percent of Chinese graduates were considered suitably qualified to work in a multinational company. While this is changing rapidly, it explains why ambitious parents by the hundreds of thousands are sending their young to get educated overseas.

Even in developed countries such as the UK, studies have shown that children from poor backgrounds who were lucky enough to get scholarships to fee-paying schools did better than their peers in state schools, both academically and in their career earnings.

All of this points to the fact that choice drives better results. Governments must insist that the needs of the children come before all considerations. The state needs to do a better job in providing public services through proper leadership, accountability, funding and some competition.

In the end, I'd trust the parents and the children first about schooling decisions. In just about any other facet of life people can choose and have control over what happens. If they don't like the work of their hairdresser or service at their local shops, they don't go back. Education and health, so much more important, remain areas where people of limited means just have to take what's offered. Teachers are vitally important but are often poorly paid and not respected. Global research indicates that the most effective way to improve student achievement is to invest in good teachers.

Good teachers should be rewarded. Too often good teachers have to leave the classroom, in order to earn more and gain more respect as administrators or headmasters. While this may work, too often the skill mix is wrong and we lose good teachers and get poor administrators. (Sadly, this is also true of how we manage our police systems, where good officers are promoted out of policing.)

We should not tolerate market failure when it means a child leaves school unable to read, or if a sick person gets inferior medical treatment. There is market failure now in many of the things government pretends to deliver, but government departments cannot go broke and don't have to do better; they just ask for more money. This will only be corrected if people are redirected by choice to better-performing schools and hospitals. True participation comes through choice, but the poor everywhere are always those with the least choice. Dignity through ownership is an added value of this mechanism that could change the way government does business. This goes beyond ideological differences. We must as a matter of urgency save the welfare state or others will use its inefficiencies, queues and insensitivities to sell it and destroy it.

Knowing the present model doesn't work, the response of many politicians has been to hire expensive consultants to check on their bureaucrats. Nye Bevan, the great Welsh socialist who established the National Health System in Britain, warned in his day that "the bugle call of revolution was being drowned by the rattle of the civil service tea trolley." It would be interesting to know, then, what he would have made of the situation in 2003/04 when spending on management consultants in the NHS more than tripled in a year, to £85 million. For Bevan, the first function of a political leader was "advocacy. ... [H]e... must articulate the wants, frustrations and the aspirations of the masses. ... [H]is words must be attuned to their realities. ... [H]e should share their values, that is, be in touch with their realities."[10]

Now Bevan's iconic achievement, the jewel in the crown of the best-ever British Labor government, needs resetting and polishing, as it does in other countries with this experience.

It's very hard to even have this debate in many social democratic circles. Any questioning of the status quo immediately brings out the accusation that what is being advocated is just the Americanization of health. This is not the real choice. While the US system undoubtedly combines the worst of all systems, except for the rich and those with good insurance cover, public expenditure on health is exactly the same in the United States and Britain, at 6.2 percent of GDP. In fact, America's Medicaid program alone spends more on caring for 40 million poor Americans than the UK's NHS does on looking after the country's 60 million people.[11]

Overall, I'd rather be poor and sick where there's a socialized health system, as in Canada or Britain, but that's not a good enough answer. The answer has to lie in a mixed response: public, private and choice.

Progressives need to have the courage to address and reform their earlier achievements, with the same objectives in mind. I'm not opposed to the state running things—in many cases, it's desirable and necessary—but I've come to the conclusion that there must be competition and choice. This drives up better outcomes, and a dominant state provision of services is necessary to keep the private sector honest and competitive. We should not fear the state or private delivery systems; we should fear monopolies. We need to focus on the needs of the patients and those who require skills for the future, and should seek accountability from those charged with responsibility for ensuring that such needs are met.

CHAPTER

17

Mobility and the Decent Society

Social mobility, another big idea, works because it widens the base of economic and social participation. Equality of opportunity is not just a moral good, it's an economic good. Most agree that patronage based on tribal affiliation or dubious loyalty in politics, business and the bureaucracy lowers standards and leads to decay. Most now accept the value of a merit-based society, where those with talent, drive and enterprise can rise. This must give us even more reason to be tolerant of differences and seek out ways to provide a ladder of opportunity for those currently locked out. A successful, growing middle class is vital to progress everywhere, as Aristotle recognized more than 2,000 years ago: "Where democracies have no middle class and the poor are greatly superior in number, trouble ensues, and they are speedily ruined."

"Middle class" and "bourgeois" are words of contempt for some intellectual radicals who don't understand the aspirations of the poor for themselves and their children. And unless there is widespread confidence that hard work gets rewards, people will not move forward, take risks, invest or try harder. Tax and social-benefit systems that do not recognize this penalize initiative and eventually militate against social mobility. In a free-market system, social mobility goes both ways. Those at the top seldom welcome competition and often seek government protection or introduce procedures, rules, and heavy compliance costs to protect their privileges.

As we have seen, modern technology has facilitated the entry of new businesses and created more-open markets that are less susceptible

200

to pressures from established elites—a seldom-reported advantage of globalization. Mobility of capital and consumers, outside localities where production is based, provides more choice and thus competition.

While capital and production have undoubtedly become more mobile, we need to look more closely at social mobility as an important principle of economics, social justice and progress. The ultimate in social mobility, of course, is when people migrate; leave their homes to seek a better life in another country. Within successful countries, people move to where there are better employment prospects, better schools and a better life. The search for social mobility and a merit-based society brought us face to face with the prejudices of the "class" war. These impulses may be traced back to the Levelers and Chartists who, at different times, fought for greater opportunity and a wider franchise. The more romantic Labor types dismiss the tragic Marxist aberration of this proud tradition, just as we dismiss the Luddites as primitive protectionists.

In many societies class membership—which was once a life sentence—has been broken down to some extent. However, in places like India, where the caste system is reinforced by religious rationalization, the old social rigidities have been maintained. For a long time, the capacity for an individual to move from poverty to wealth did not automatically mean social mobility. In feudal France, Japan, and Confucian China, wealthy merchants were in the lower ranks of society. Inherited status was often socially superior. Echoes of this still exist even in the New World which, in part, gained its present success by providing wider opportunity for many (as long as they were white and not female, that is).

It's accepted now that a successful development agenda is promoted by creating a meritocracy in the public service, universities and business. But even in mature democracies, the class war is not over. Despite record increases in public expenditure and the lowest unemployment over an extended period for generations in the United Kingdom, social mobility has stalled.[1]

Social mobility—the way in which someone's adult outcomes are related to their circumstances as a child—is lower in Britain than in Canada, Germany, Sweden, Norway, Denmark or Finland. And while the gap in opportunities between rich and poor is similar in Britain and the United States, in Britain it is getting wider.

Norway has the greatest social mobility, followed by Denmark, Sweden and Finland. Germany is around the middle of the two extremes, and Canada was found to be much more mobile than the

United Kingdom which, along with the United States, has the lowest level of social mobility. School choice—or lack of it—is often destiny.[2]

The genius and hope of the United States was that it was created with an idea that birth ought not to determine destiny. Lincoln declared, "I hold the value of life is to improve one's condition." It was respect for the work ethic that gave rise to the American Dream—from log cabin to the White House. Social mobility in the United States was for a long time a matter of inspirational equality, not a desire to legislate for equality.

The Obama presidency shows a seismic change in the role of the government and society. Social activism is back in fashion. The global economic crisis has given these principles traction. US business is at a disadvantage vis-à-vis its international competition. For example, 46 million Americans don't have health insurance and, in February 2009, it was reported that health costs were a major factor in one-third of US bankruptcies. For 100,000 Americans annually, illness means a loss of their jobs, their homes and their retirement hopes. No other Western modern democracy would accept this. Although the United States is an overall winner in trade liberalization, many Americans are wary of new trade deals precisely because the safety net to cover workers whose businesses suffer is weak, and re-training programs are poor. This made it difficult for Obama to stop a "Buy America first" legislative initiative. He succeeded, though—mindful perhaps that President Herbert Hoover had signed just such a bill during the Great Depression.

When the top 1 percent of a society is responsible for 23 percent of all spending, something will break. The genius of economic freedom is that, underpinned by social policies, it widens the economic and social base of society. But in the US, for a generation special interests have succeeded in killing reform, which is seen by many as creeping socialism. Not for the first time, the economic case for social justice, equity and opportunity converges. Most democratic capitalist economies have the state or some other instrument that makes health and retirement a wider social responsibility, rather than the responsibility of the company. Big US auto companies, however, can now carry more costs in their benefits to retired workers than to existing workers. To do this, of course, reeks of socialism, something US society cannot handle. Don't be surprised to see GM, the *Wall Street Journal*, and conservative think-tanks arguing to remove health and retirement costs from business' balance sheets.

Getting up from being down

The welfare state was created out of class struggle. While I still support its objectives, we have to find more effective mechanisms to achieve them, because we have institutionalized failure and made it a permanent paid option. The welfare state was created to liberate people, not imprison them within strict rules and preconditioning.

Evidence abounds showing how education is the best way forward. Doctors marry doctors and produce more university graduates. Upper-middle class, highly educated people are attracted to areas with good schools and like-minded parents. Their children do well and the cycle is repeated, creating a hereditary meritocratic class. The choice of a school often dictates a child's destiny. What chance, then, for kids from outside of these areas, from suburbs where more go to jail than to university? As some see it, the upper class doesn't so much oppress the lower class as outperform it generation after generation. The crucial inequality now is not only finance capital, it's social capital, so that it is silly to make a distinction between economic policy and social policy.

Poor children, too, inherit their parents' attitudes and expectations—in this case, though, they revolve around failure. Anyone who's been a social worker or an MP, and I've been both, knows those families whose kids are not going to make it. Growing up in a one-parent home without books, plagued by violence, drugs and booze, children learn to perpetuate this vicious cycle.

There has to be total focus on these children at risk. Why not insist on conditions before the parents get state payments, to ensure their kids go to school, and that schools are held accountable for results? Why do we make kids pass examinations, but not teachers and schools? In both the United Kingdom and New Zealand, the government refuses to make public the ratings and results of individual schools because it may give parents and children the wrong idea. What does this tell us about bureaucrats who fear transparency? By contrast, the biggest-selling editions of newspapers in Ireland are those that report annually on school grading.

The opportunity cost of failing to develop human capital is now much higher than it was a quarter-century ago. The wage premium associated with a college degree has jumped to around 70 percent in recent years from around 30 percent in 1980; the graduate degree premium has soared to over 100 percent from 50 percent. Dropping out of high school now all but guarantees socioeconomic failure. We can spend all we want on schools, but if families are disrupted, the social environment becomes dysfunctional, and the families' culture and history is one of failure. Bigger budgets won't always help, but lower budgets certainly won't.

It is good news that economic signals now so strongly encourage the development of human talent. Yet the supply of skilled people is responding sluggishly to the increased demand—which brings us back to the real issue: the human capital gap, and the culture gap that impedes its closure. The most obvious cultural deficits are those that produce and perpetuate the inner-city underclass.

While the poverty rate nationwide in the United States is 13 percent, only 3 percent of adults with full-time, year-round jobs fall below the poverty line. Poverty in America today is thus largely about failing to get and hold a job, any job. The problem is not lack of opportunity. If it were, the country wouldn't be a magnet for illegal immigrants. The problem is a lack of elementary self-discipline: failing to stay in school, failing to live within the law, failing to get and stay married to the mother or father of your children. The prevalence of these conditions reflects a dysfunctional culture that fails to invest in human capital; one in which its productive capacity has now outstripped its cultural capacity.[3]

The OECD tells us that if a child is an enthusiastic and regular reader, this alone can have a bigger impact than having well-educated and wealthy parents. In the United Kingdom a national reading recovery program to provide individualized assistance to six-year-olds in most need reported that children in the scheme made 20 months' progress in one year. This compared with just five months' progress made by those outside the scheme.[4]

Reading recovery costs nearly $4,000 per pupil, but the cost to taxpayers of a child who leaves primary school unable to read is nearer to $140,000 when problems relating to truancy, sickness, unemployment, and involvement in drugs and crime are taken into account.[5]

In the main, parents define what is going to happen to their children. It's too easy to blame society for poor results, but it's not society that forces parents to leave their partners or hit them, or drink, steal and take or sell drugs.

It is a question of ownership; about how we can take power from the institutions that were created to help the poor and give that power to the poor. But this is no easy matter. In many inner-city schools and hospitals in the US, for example, oligarchies of activists, unions and opportunist politicians have become embedded, providing "a way for people with political connections in the black community to get high paying jobs."[6]

When individual responsibility is taken away this is predictable. Perhaps this is why so many break so readily what used to be community norms of behavior. Where once there was shame and embarrassment if a family member went to prison, had children out of wedlock, was unemployed or neglected their children, these days offenders can be seen outside court giving a defiant finger to the cameras. Gang membership is often a bewildering reversal of community values: bad behavior is often rewarded by a promotion and a rise in station. It is difficult to get politicians to focus on these problems: if they are from the left (which was created as a political force to attack the problems of poverty and alienation), they will be accused of blaming the victims, being racist or against human rights; while those on the right are not motivated because these people are never going to vote for them.

Perhaps it is inevitable that so many modern liberals don't understand the poor and are overly romantic about them. Even if many have come from poor backgrounds most no longer adhere to the values of their blue-collar parents. These days, they tend to spend more time with lobby groups representing the poor than with the poor themselves. Lacking the everyday experience of poverty's humiliations and corrosiveness, they may have sympathy, but not empathy. The elite are even less understanding, but we don't expect them to be.

It is the very young and the old who pay the highest price of failure in modern societies.

Promisingly, Britain's prime minister, Gordon Brown, has spoken of the need to "personalize" public health and education, but the groundwork must be done, the issues explained, the options made clear before change can be effective.

Social spending to achieve different social outcomes is good except when shallow, mean-spirited policies create even more disincentives to work. For example, the withdrawal of benefits when people move back to work and their conditions improve creates even more disincentives to get ahead. My weary experience is that poverty traps exist in blunt and inflexible welfare states, perpetuating a cycle of dependency in many of our countries. It is noticeable in nearly all welfare states how, as unemployment has gone down, there's been a dramatic rise in the number of those on sickness and disability benefits. The impatient "right" will advocate cutting or abolishing benefits to encourage people to work. (It's funny how the poor need less money to encourage them to work more, but the rich need tax cuts and even more money to make them work harder.) Targeted correctly, social spending is a prerequisite for building a stronger economy by increasing social mobility and providing social confidence to ride out the disruptive effects of change.

Rather than being a ball and chain on the economy, social spending has positive economic consequences. It enables a steady growth in consumption by the poor, and it has a strong counter-cyclical stabilizing influence during recessions. It can also have an amazing effect on employment participation rates and skill levels. Denmark's universal childcare system, for example, has produced two economic wins. It allows young mothers to re-enter the labor market quickly, and it also ensures that young children from low-income homes have the kind of emotional, social and intellectual engagement that supports the development of their cognitive skills at a crucial age. All the Nordic countries, with similarly high levels of social spending, report high employment participation rates for both men and women, high levels of educational attainment and a general readiness—because their living standards are ensured—to take risks, retrain and change jobs. The Nordic economies enjoy all the benefits of a market-based system of incentives for their dynamic, high-productivity private sectors and the benefits of high social spending, which makes it easier for workers to accept economic change.

These are pluralist market economies with strong public realms and a commitment to justification; they also enable ordinary people to develop their individual capabilities. In short, they embody contemporary Enlightenment values—as powerful now as they were 200 years ago—in sustaining the West's economic advantages.[7]

If anger about failure gets loud enough, opinion leaders and politicians respond. A government can't claim to be open if it is deaf to popular opinion. The crowning achievement of progress towards freedom is freely held and regular elections which impose the will of a free, educated and informed people.

The best democracies have entrenched the concept of a loyal opposition, which formalizes the tradition of self-criticism that is so important to successful societies. Opposition to the country's government is not seen as an act of treachery, a concept that is difficult to explain, let alone implement, in nations with no tradition of parliamentary democracy.

Regular, free, robust and fair elections are a critical part of the success of the liberal democracy. They are the best means to maintain the other elements of the equation. In their absence, the temptation for governments to weaken the power and independence of the courts, or to erect trade barriers to create privileges for their mates, or to undermine the influence of civil society, often proves too great. Each part of the equation—good governance, openness, civil society and elections—reinforces the others. If nations want first-world results, they need to adopt first-world mechanisms and standards.

PART 4

ENEMIES OF THE OPEN SOCIETY

The philosopher Karl Popper began life as a social democrat. His most important work—*The Open Society and Its Enemies*—was, like so many of the best books, written in exile (in New Zealand, in fact). Toward the end of his fruitful life, he confessed that perhaps he was still a socialist but he could not get over the power problem of bureaucracy.

Western democracies always struggle with the conflict between liberty and equality—the left wants more equality (generally secured by government support), the right more freedom—and the intense struggle of how to maintain order and liberty in a free society. Done badly, one can contradict the other.

CHAPTER 18

Power and Manipulation

Road fatalities are costly. We could reduce the death toll by 90 percent, if no-one was allowed to drive faster than 20 miles per hour and everyone had to drive an armored car. That would be unacceptable, but compulsory car seatbelts and helmets for motor cyclists are acceptable. Politics and policies are about the possible, what is acceptable, and what will work.

At first glance, it may seem a stretch to compare the inanities of busybody politicians and overactive bureaucrats in open societies with the most insane cruelties of those who seek to impose their will by terror on the people, but the instinct is the same. It's about power and control, about the urge to tell people what to believe and how to live. Rigging party ballots is just a step away from abolishing voting altogether; the result is the same. Power, combined with a total conviction that one is right and all others are wrong, corrupts; and absolute power even more so. Unless power is checked and held accountable by the law, civil engagement, a free and competitive media, and a parliamentary opposition, eventually almost anyone in power tends to misuse that power. A classic case in point was that of President Richard Nixon, but democracy worked and Nixon was forced to resign. The constitution allowed for it, Congress did its job, and so did the media and public opinion. We've seen it with the resignations of ministers in Westminster democracies: erring politicians are not always easy to catch, but the system has been proven to work.

A key factor that produces good governance and sustainable development is the quality and professionalism of the public service. Research in developing countries has discovered that the quality of the public service lifts living standards by exposing corruption, delivering services, and providing free, fair and fearless advice. Closed economies and the leaders produced within them never seek or get fair advice. Scared and ambitious people tell them what they want to hear.

Even in the most mature of democracies, it is not always possible to see through those who seek favors and promotion; in non-democratic societies, it is almost impossible. In the small nations in the Middle East, however, some enlightened monarchs are beginning to seek more democratic results—to the concern of their wealthy "nobles." But they face a struggle in their own privileged circles, and with their families and neighbors, because this could be contagious.

It has been proved that a country that is able to lift the quality of its public service can double its annual incomes in a decade, but could the reverse be true? Could a developed, open society go backward if its public service becomes politicized and corrupt? Yes, partially, but there would be a political correction, a change of government. The people would reject it, eventually, because it lowers living standards and goes against the grain of ethics in public life.

However, there is an insidious, slippery side to many democracies. Just as the share market, the exchange rate, and inflation and employment figures are indicators of the success or otherwise of a government's economic policies, so opinion polls are an instant referendum on politicians. Speaking as a former politician, opinion polls (to misquote Shakespeare) "make cowards of us all." A real moral hazard exists in democracies when ruthless politicians will do and spend anything to retain power. Money doesn't talk in politics anymore; it screams. The first billion-dollar electoral campaign in the United States is within sight. Politicians are today caught up in an age of perpetual campaigning, obliged to maintain a high media profile as they go about the endless pursuit of funds to keep them in business and in the public eye. In such circumstances, bureaucracies increasingly assume power from their political masters.

Power doesn't always corrupt; it's what has to be done to get power and keep it that corrupts. An oligarchic elite hovers and hoovers around democratic capitals. In the eight years from 1998 to 2006, the number of professional lobbyists registered at the US Congress—many of them former Senators and members of the House of Representatives—doubled to 35,000 (there are said to be four healthcare lobbyists for every member of Congress). This is now a $5 billion per annum industry.[1]

The migration from representative politics to the manipulation of constituencies by highly financed influence groups is dangerous, and growing. Self-interest is the basis of capitalism, but what happens when it's turbo-charged and unaccountable, within many levels of government, where it can serve its own interests without the sanction of scrutiny? What happens when an "oil lobbyist" is appointed to a senior bureaucratic position inside a government agency that has responsibility for environmental issues?

Lobbyists are legal and proper, but to appoint them to positions of political power inside the bureaucracy which gives advice to cabinet ministers, or to allow them to enjoy delegated authority, is wrong and dangerous. A professional, independent public service should be separated from politicians and the influence of political parties and their legions of fundraisers and hangers-on. Otherwise those elected to represent the people will simply hear what they want to hear and standards will fall.

Spinning deceit

Ever-tightening news cycles, combined with a lack of space for clear thinking, and the need to be seen to be on top of the issues, often lead to reflex decisions that attack symptoms rather than substance. In my own country, for example, grotesque child abuse and baby murder quickly led to TV campaigns proving the government "cares." Activity becomes a substitute for direction. The favorite expression at many cabinet meetings when problems appear is, "Get it off the front page." That is spin, not substance.

The diaries of Alastair Campbell, Tony Blair's "spinmeister," make fascinating reading for political junkies, especially in relation to how he manipulated the media. For politicians reading the book this merely confirms their prejudices about how ill-read, superficial, and self-important political journalists become. But the politicians have only themselves to blame for this, as they fawn over key journalists and court the media magnates and commentators.

In a climate of manipulation, trust evaporates and the worst motives are imputed to all sides. Remember the security reports in Britain which formed part of the rationale for the Iraq War? While

Campbell was exonerated from the BBC's claim of cynical, possibly even illegal and immoral, indifference in the intelligence assessments on Iraq, the system worked in the end, with both the BBC's director-general and chairman being forced to resign, and Campbell and Blair's image being irreparably tarnished.

Even at the greatest of political summits, political staffers rush about claiming the credit for their bosses or blaming others for failure and more time is spent on writing the communiqué, the statement from the conference, than on the substance of the meetings. Establishing a commission of inquiry is another age-old method of giving the appearance of action. While this can sometimes be a good response when calm, distance and information are required, too often it's a tired technique to defuse and deflect attention from an issue. The best political managers understand this to the point where, in some countries, it has become a way of political life.

Traditionally, the public press gallery has performed an important function within parliaments. Here, it is the job of the specialist political journalists of the "fourth estate" to report on the workings of the legislature. Many of these "political specialists" move on to become advisers to ministers or to more highly paid consultancies. This is the moral hazard faced by journalists who cover politics. Perhaps, as an ex-politician, I should be the last person to suggest that journalists should be better paid and on longer contracts, and that there should be a stand-down period before they can work for the interests they were earlier paid to scrutinize.

As political parties shrink, which is happening in all democracies, there has been an inexorable rise in the number of political consultants, pollsters and speechwriters—many of whom are former members of the press gallery. The consultants are taken on because politicians have become increasingly poll-driven. Their role is to manufacture new ways to present their candidates as authentic—a classic oxymoron if ever there was one. Perhaps sensing this "spin," many don't bother to vote.

Politics and the media throw up saints and sinners, the courageous and the cowardly. For every Senator Joseph McCarthy there is (or should be) an Ed Murrow to expose him. Media magnates and the likes of the celebrity activist who shares my name still manufacture headlines and a great deal of money out of often dubious partisan comment. The line between opinion pieces and news reporting has become increasingly blurred.

There is a plague of extreme commentators in media outlets such as Fox News, which can carry the most partisan of comments and follow it up with the inadvertently humorous byline: "We report, you decide … fair and balanced." Nevertheless, I advise people to watch it occasionally, the better to understand the minority of angry rightwing Americans. None of this is new, of course. In the 1930s the populist priest Father Coughlin thundered away on radio in anti-Semitic, pro-Nazi rants.

In the absence of political parties with a large, involved membership, we have seen power increasing at the extremes of the political spectrum where funds and highly motivated individuals tend to gather. The center collapses as strong Christian groups on the right get their true believers out to vote; ditto for the left, with new organizations such as MoveOn.org playing an ever-larger role in policy-making, fund raising and organizing to motivate their true believers.

All's fair in politics and war. In democratic nations, there is the fundamental right to free speech and anonymous bloggers can attack at will, without the need to check facts. Equally, though, people should have the right to know who the authors are and who funds them. Through the anonymity of the internet, smear campaigns can run free. Small disagreements are exaggerated and policy takes second place to crude personal attacks. Even in the mainstream media, a comment taken out of context or (as I know to my cost) footage of a politician scratching his head can be manipulated into something seemingly sinister.

Personal experience has shown that the media often prints what is said, rather than what is meant. If respect for politicians is at an all-time low, trust in the "commentariat" is even lower. The values represented by political commentators in capital cities are often not those of ordinary people. They are now, in the main, socially liberal, and their power and self-importance are irritating to those who don't share their values, causing cynicism and an opportunity for backlash.

Such a hostile climate is often inimical to openness because politicians have to be disciplined and bland, which restricts debate and access. Access denied is information restricted. Information is the lifeblood of politics and democracy; humor and a sense of proportion its oxygen. Bubble politics, where no-one dares say what they think without testing it in focus groups or opinion polls, is an appalling prospect.

A competitive media, strong civil society and democracy can stop the McCarthys of this world, and laws, customs and habits should protect courageous journalists who apply pressure to the powerful who hope to prosper in the dark, away from scrutiny. But it is not all bad, however: the internet has also opened up a whole new range of opportunities for others to poke fun at and holes in the arguments and armor of all those who seek to tell us what to do and think.

But these days our democratic institutions are also open to a different line of attack which has the effect of concentrating power in the hands of the few. Economic jargon, like Latin in the church of old, has given rise to a new priesthood in the upper realms of government social-service organizations. Many social democracies have fallen victim to a new form of social control by earnest advocates who, enraged that politics of equal opportunity have not made people equal, have turned the system on its head by demanding equality of outcome. This, inevitably, takes us down the slippery road of quotas, rigged examination results and social conditioning to make us better people, just like the advocates of such policies, who refuse to consider evidence that many affirmative-action policies are captured by second-generation middle-class people, rather than the poor. Such policies do work for a time but then become the property of the new elite. This is not an argument against intervention, but a case for a regular refocusing of operational objectives.

Enforcing shared values is dangerous and erodes diversity, even in democracies. People have a right to be bigots, to have appalling views of society, so long as they don't hurt anyone in the process. Government is about protecting people from each other, not protecting us from ourselves. Idealism, an absolute view of life, has in it the stuff of tyrants or the appeasement of tyrants by over-embracing simplistic worthy causes. Too often we think the people we deal with enjoy the same values and, being polite, find it hard to say no. During the early 1990s I had great sport teasing the over-earnest proponents of political correctness who wanted, for example, to ban toy guns, hot-cross buns, and the word "manhole" in municipal planning. The word "Christmas" is under attack in many countries under the guise of secularism. The proponents of such ideas are a dim, humorless group who never argue on substance or evidence: from behind the safety of a collective position, they feel no need to convince anyone but, rather, accuse opponents of not sticking to the correct party line. Labeling someone a "right winger" is enough to win an argument these days, it seems, just as in earlier times calling someone "communist" would do. But what may start out as being simply fashionable and silly can become sinister.

Depending on one's perspective, society is run either by science, reason, evidence and logic, or the modern equivalent of mob rule,—opinion polls and radio talkback. Politics, however, works best through the rigor and vigor of open debate of differences. But it's tough to argue when government institutions have a collective view of life and seek to enforce it.

The term "political correctness" may have been introduced into the language by Nikita Khrushchev who, in exposing the crimes of Stalin, also accused him of originating "the concept of 'enemy of the people'," a term which "automatically rendered it unnecessary that the ideological errors of a man or men engaged in a controversy be proven." This certainly has echoes today when, if you don't happen to agree with the views of unelected human rights commissions, you are deemed to oppose human rights.

Society advanced when it was evidence-based (particularly in medicine). The rule of law and equality before the law gave Western civilization—with its commitment to tolerance, public scrutiny and property rights, even humor and democracy—its edge. The post-modernist view that all cultures are equal is a dangerous proposition. Cultural sensitivity has evolved into cultural vetoes. Is female genital mutilation acceptable because it is culturally based? The herd mentality that attends upon the prevailing orthodoxy is a form of censorship, a rejection of evidence and even common sense. The tyranny of the majority has been replaced by the tyranny of the minorities and their state-sponsored advocates and special-interest supporters, who have taken unto themselves powers that were once the preserve of individuals, courts and parliament. It takes guts to oppose the prevailing orthodoxy. Skepticism is healthy; cynical appeasement is cowardly.

A level playing field

Competition, the struggle of ideas, is the lifeblood of politics. The prevailing orthodoxy censors this. Perhaps that's why there is an increasing tendency to take competition out of sports or education (as one teachers' union put it, "Examinations are bad because they discriminate against the less able"). But competition entails disagreeing with the prevailing orthodoxies of the day, and that takes moral courage. As George Bernard Shaw said: "Reasonable people don't make change; thus all human progress is based on the unreasonable person." We need more unreasonable, questioning, skeptical people in our parliaments, in all our political parties, in our media, and, especially, in the general body politic.

In economics the concept of "moral hazard" is often linked to the insurance industry where it is used to explain, for instance, the theory that fire insurance increases the incentive to commit arson. Economic literature is full of studies explaining how the International Monetary Fund's loans to some countries create a moral hazard and perverse incentives where governments are bailed out, and that this actually works against reform. A moral hazard always exists where public servants and governments can graze in an unaccountable, non-transparent manner on the taxpayer. It is rampant in the private sector even when there are controls, licensing and monopolies. Competition and transparency are the cleansing air against the possibility of corruption.

There is a real danger of moral hazard in democracies where the government uses taxpayers' money to promote its own interests. Every government has done it, with each successive government being a little more eager and better at it than its predecessor. Technology and the proliferation in political advisers, whose job it is to get their masters re-elected and their policies marketed, have increased this moral hazard. Information and advice about government policies is proper, but did Australian voters, for instance, really need a fridge magnet before an election to advise them what to do if terrorists attack?

Expensive TV advertising is used extensively by governments to show how much they care. Millions of dollars are spent on worthy issues such as anti-smoking campaigns, alcohol abuse, dangerous driving, eating correctly, exercising, and so on. Though much of this expenditure is hard to justify, it is equally hard to refuse, especially when the precedent has been set by others.

All such expenditure should be subjected to public scrutiny since ultimately it is the public that pays for it. There needs, too, to be public disclosure of incomes earned by members of the parliamentary press gallery outside their jobs; registration of lobbyists; and compulsory disclosure of political donations by companies and individuals. Unless people are given such information this incremental slide into sleaze will continue and moral hazard will simply expand.

Most people these days would agree with Pierre Trudeau's assertion that "the state has no business in the bedrooms of the nation" and few would argue against the advances made in women's rights over the past 30 years. But when states step in to redress clear imbalances in certain sections of society—through anti-hate legislation or to enable gay marriages or civil unions, for example—this opens up a whole new range of possibilities that may not be so acceptable to many. When backed by over-zealous enforcement agencies such as human rights commissions and broadcasting standards authorities, something else begins to happen. Reports from Canada suggest that churches have been brought before the bureaucratic authorities to force them to perform gay marriages. To refuse to do so is discrimination. Does a right now exist to, say, sue the Catholic Church or the mosque to enforce having women clergy or gay priests?

While it is fair enough that people should not discriminate in employment, housing, or in opportunities for education, it is hard, even dangerous, to force people to be tolerant or respectful under threat of legal punishment. There were once laws against mocking the sovereign. If that law was still in force today, English prisons would be full. It's all a matter of degree of implementation, balance and common sense.

Steering a sensible course between the conflicting and often dangerous orthodoxies of the extremes, left and right, is never more necessary than in the realm of religious belief, where extreme claims are made to justify the extreme measures they promote. Every society will face these issues. How to navigate through them while keeping a sense of justice, balance and good humor will be the challenge.

Excessive bureaucracy is by no means a problem peculiar to socialism. Bureaucrats everywhere are often more interested in preserving their own power and promoting their own advancement than in helping others. They can be found in almost every state system and in almost every large organization as well. While bureaucracies may be necessary in large organizations of any kind, they are not necessarily efficient and they do not promote open society. Their strict hierarchical structures and rigid procedural rules treat human beings as automatons, incapable of thinking for themselves or of distinguishing between the rules and the ends which they are intended to serve. This has the effect of transforming civil servants into civil masters, and leads to what Popper referred to as the tyranny of power in the hands of an oligarchic elite.

Twenty years ago, the television series "Yes, Minister" gave birth to a whole new generation of political comedy based on the enduring struggle between elected politicians and the senior bureaucrats who ran things, and always would (politicians of my generation swore it was a documentary). Here, the role of the political advisor, usually planted in the minister's offices by the Prime Minister's department, is to keep the minister "on message." "Spin" is, in advertising terms, selling the sizzle, not the sausage.

Politics, how to sell the politicians, takes up more time at cabinet and caucus meetings than policy substance, which is driven by polling and focus groups and is decided well before a cabinet or party meeting. Here, the communications experts encourage the politicians to announce grand objectives with grander slogans—to halve child poverty within 10 years; to lift economic performance to the top half of the OECD; to achieve the best of work/life balance. If words such as "transformational" or "sustainable" can be slipped in somewhere, so much the better; so long as the actual results (sorry, "outcomes") will only be measurable two or three election cycles down the line. This is a global fashion.

The 1980s and 1990s saw a lot of government services contracted out, and an explosion in the number of commissions, which, we were told, would be independent of politicians and politics, and could deliver honest services and advice. For "independent" read "unaccountable." Unlike politicians, the commissioners are not answerable to public opinion; they are above it, and are answerable to some higher authority. Their mission is to make us better people, more sensitive; a bit like them, in fact. Such attitudes led to absurdities such as a New Zealand commissioner's edict that the rights of property owners not to have their fences defaced by aggressive graffiti had to be balanced against the rights of young people to express themselves; or to the worthies declaring that a TV advertisement, about a young couple who sabotaged each other's attempts to get the car keys in a comedic series of slapstick bombs, encouraged domestic violence; or that another charming TV advertisement featuring two toddlers driving a car and dating and surfing encouraged pedophiles. Such attempts to turn the country into a kind of well-meaning boarding school by social activists who see themselves not as public servants but as the public's conscience tell us more about them than us.

When has any commission, pressure group, or government program ever abolished itself; ever said, "We are not relevant; it doesn't work" or "The job is done"? Never. They just seek more resources to do better. Perhaps the economic downturn will create some financial and intellectual discipline. But prepare to laugh when busybodies and politicians claim the credit for a drop in pollution as industry winds back.

19

The Dangers of Absolute Conviction

We in the West also face the challenge of moral clarity, moral equivalence and moral ambivalence. It is getting harder to say "No." To appease is to please. The slippery slope of populism is a denial of true leadership.

How is it that Amnesty International, a great NGO, and the United Nations' Human Rights Commission so often name Israel as a violator of human rights, but rarely mention other nations in the region? How can the greatest benefactor of globalization, Hollywood, produce so many anti-globalization movies ("Battle in Seattle," for example, portrays the WTO Ministerial Trade conference failure at Seattle as a sinister plot to rape the poor) yet none in favor of it?

When people scream "undemocratic" at the WTO, they frequently mean that they, not the ministers, should be at the table. Parliaments, they say, are not representative of the people, we are; and they point to polls saying how low politicians are in public trust and esteem. Enemies of reason, manipulating and speaking for the poor and oppressed, are a big, age-old enterprise.

Why is it that the world's hyperpower, America, is always portrayed as the hyper-hypocrite? There are votes to be had everywhere by being anti-American at the moment, with some stretching credibility to breaking point in claiming that the United States is the greatest threat to peace in the world.

Anti-globalization books sell well, even when authors such as Joseph Stiglitz, a Nobel Prize winner, and Jeffrey Sachs, an adviser to the Secretary General of the United Nations, actually conclude that we need greater globalization, more trade and better opportunities for poorer countries (which is exactly my position and the agreed agenda for the Doha Development Round). Fashion, it seems, trumps substance; as does slander.

Of course America makes mistakes; few can say that Iraq was well handled. Whether we were lied to about weapons of mass destruction, history and a free society will one day reveal. America is too big to make small mistakes. When most countries get it wrong, they are a danger to only themselves. When America gets it wrong, the impact is felt around the world.

Yet despite all the criticism, unfounded or justified, whenever the blood begins to flow anywhere in the world, from the Balkans to Darfur and the Congo, people turn to the United States to act and show leadership. But how people can argue—and many do—that there is no difference between US excesses and the millions of murders committed by Stalin and Mao should confound any reasonable being. We know of the excesses at Guantanamo Bay and Abu Ghraib precisely because the United States is an open society. While it is true that the Bush Administration's simple explanation of the need for democracy has given the principle a bad name, Barack Obama may help change the rampant anti-Americanism this bred.

It is said that a student of history must adhere to either the cock-up or the conspiracy theory of history. I go more for the former in open societies—there is always a cellphone camera, a journalist on the prowl for a Pulitzer Prize, movie rights, fame and wealth for exposing wrongdoings, or politicians seeking power by alternative policies and exposing their opponents. There is a general rule when dealing with governments: if governments don't trust their people, why should we trust them? By all means, work with them, encourage, advise, trade, try to cooperate, create institutions to channel differences—but don't trust them. History shows that when governments are not accountable to their own public, then bad things happen. Bad governments are frequently bad neighbors. The more closed the neighbor's economy and society, the more likely it will be to profit from everything from drugs to people-smuggling, from selling nuclear secrets to dealing in endangered species and illegal logging.

What puzzles me is the position of many of my fraternal colleagues internationally, who so often appease the most evil of individuals and movements in the name of tolerance or cultural understanding; echoes of cultural relativism at its worst. The "left" in my day taught me that Nasser in Egypt and Ataturk in Turkey were heroes of independence and nation-building. They kicked out the imperialists, came down hard on religious extremists and pushed ruthlessly for modernity, even if too often it was along Soviet/command-economy lines. The "right" fought to maintain imperial privileges and influences that disgusted the activists of the day. Those who seek a totalitarian caliphate have spoken often of their hatred for Nasser and Ataturk and consider the nation-state blasphemous and impious. This is also true of Israel, where a minority of ultra-Orthodox Jews continued to regard the State of Israel as inherently evil, "a pollution that encompasses all other pollutions, a complete heresy that includes all other heresies," wrote Veramiel Domb in the *Neturei Karta* newsletter in 1975. "In its very essence, Zionism utterly denies the essentials of our faith."[1] In both cases, the battle is between secular nationalism and radical religious extremism which, as Mary Kalder puts it in her book *New and Old Wars,* "is a contest between those who support cosmopolitan, inclusive societies based on tolerance and freedom of expression, and those who favor exclusive identities that are characteristics of closed societies."

The extremists on both sides cite scripture to justify their claims, but we see what we want to see; our powers of rationalization are stunning. For example, in a CNN poll conducted in 2002, 61 percent of those polled in Muslim countries did not believe Arabs were responsible for the attacks of September 11, 2001, despite bin Laden claiming the credit. Saddam Hussein, who murdered more Muslims than any other person in living memory, is still regarded as a hero in many parts of the Islamic world.

Bin Laden's video message to the world in August 2007 was a frontal attack on the evils of capitalism and private ownership. He whipped up anti-capitalist, anti-rich fervor with all the skills of the old Marxists, the fascists and the leaders of the French Revolution. Presenting himself as the champion of the poor, he was contemptuous of bourgeois democracy and bourgeois values and society. Yet in reality here was another wealthy fanatic manipulating the poor and, with simple sound-bites, providing the desperate with someone to blame and hate. If he didn't have the resources to serve his ends, he would be just another crackpot dictator, a second-rate thinker in a long line of sordid anti-Enlightenment figures feeding off the failures of present conditions.

It is puzzling to see how many ex-Marxists, who lived on the slogans of the brotherhood of man and were very anti-religious, now find comfort in defending radical Islamism. Perhaps in our modern age some of this can be explained away as the tyranny of the missing alternatives. For example, in his book *The Spirit of Terrorism*, French philosopher Jean Baudrillard, explains 9/11 thus:

> At a pinch we can say they did it but we wished for it … [W]hen global power monopolizes the situation to this extent, when there is such a formidable condemnation of all functions in the technocratic machinery, and when no alternative thinking is allowed, what other way is there but a terroristic situational transfer.

Much quoted by anti-globalizers and anti-American zealots, the best-selling author Noam Chomsky, who 30 years ago found much good in Stalin and, later, in Pol Pot, seems to have subscribed to a similar view when he said of 9/11: "The United States itself is a leading terrorist state … and for the first time in modern history Europe and its offshoots were subjected to, on home soil, the kind of atrocity that they have routinely carried out elsewhere."[2]

Yet such popular moral ambivalence is not new and is symptomatic of a long history of excusing the excesses of power embedded by systems and cultures that prevent analysis and critical review. Indeed, in his book *Terror and Liberalism* Paul Berman observes that Albert Camus noticed "a modern impulse to rebel" which had its roots in the French Revolution and the nineteenth century but which "had very quickly, in the name of an ideal, mutated into a cult of death." He went on:

> [T]he ideal was always the same, though each movement gave it a different name. It was not skepticism and doubt. It was the ideal of submission. It was submission to the kind of authority that liberal civilization had slowly undermined, and which the new movements wished to re-establish on a novel basis. It was the ideal of the one, instead of the many. The ideal of something godlike. The total state, the total doctrine, the total movement. "Totalitarian" was Mussolini's word [for it].

This gradual morphing of youthful idealism into a dangerous absolutism may, as Michael Howard in *The Invention of Peace and the Reinvention of War* explains, have its roots in boredom:

> Western societies may now all be peacefully bourgeois; but bourgeois society is boring. There are certainly more sophisticated ways of expressing this ... but it is a phenomenon too often overlooked by historians. As [Alphonse de] Lamartine pointed out in his explanation of 'les événements' in Paris in 1848–9, it was largely boredom that destroyed the otherwise estimable monarchy of Louis-Philippe. The vast majority of mankind has never had enough leisure to experience boredom; they have had to work too hard, irrespective of age or gender, from dawn to dusk, from cradle to grave. But the medieval church knew all about it: they made "accidie" one of the seven deadly sins. Boredom with the mechanistic rationality of the Enlightenment produced the Romantic Movement and much else.

Those most prone to boredom and, often, to violence are young men with too much time on their hands (whether this be by choice or force of circumstance). History has shown that many of the world's great social upheavals—including the French Revolution in 1789, the Iranian revolution in 1979, and in the United States in 1968, for example—have occurred at times when there has been a significant surge in the numbers of young people. The Arab world is currently undergoing just such a surge and there the upheaval has taken the form of a religious resurgence.[3] Half the Arab world is under the age of 25 and this is expected to increase rapidly in the next few years. The population of the Middle East and North Africa, for example, is projected to reach 600 million by 2025, and 100 million new Muslims in the Middle East alone will come into the labor market by 2020.[4] Globalization has caught the Arab world at a bad demographic moment and it remains to be seen if and how this will fuel the rise in Islamic fundamentalism that we have witnessed in recent years.

If there is one great cause of this rise, Fareed Zakaria believes, "it is the total failure of political institutions in the Arab world."[5] He points out that Islam is actually anti-authoritarian, and that obedience to a ruler is necessary only if he rules in accordance to God's law, and suggests that the emphasis on religious reform is misplaced. As another commentator asserts, "Islam, like any religion, is not what the books make it but what people make it."[6]

Beware intolerance

We should not tolerate intolerance. There is a world of difference between marching on parliaments, and shutting parliaments down. In Genoa and Seattle, as elsewhere, rioters crossed that line. The masked stone-throwers who call for more transparency, the anti-globalization protestors who claim to speak for "the people" even as they attempt to sabotage international meetings of ministers and parliamentarians, are not the new foot-soldiers for democracy. They are its antithesis. The new international order they say they want looks suspiciously like a much older disorder—intolerant, illiberal and reactionary.

The wilder elements of the NGO world seem more concerned with being fashionably antagonistic than seriously analytical; simplistic slogans and the unthinking iconography of rebellion—epitomized by photo-spreads of the Baader-Meinhof Gang or T-shirts commemorating the exploits of the Red Army Faction—too often prevail.

There's nothing new here: the United Kingdom Labor Party chairman and leading leftist intellectuals lavished praise on the Soviet Union at the height of Stalin's reign of terror. The same kind of fashionable wooly thinking meant that when millions were dying during China's Cultural Revolution, fashion-conscious, politically correct leftists around the world wore their Mao badges and caps, and quoted from his Little Red Book.

These days, however, there can be no excuse for such behavior. The information age has made it much harder for murderers to conceal their evils, and public outrage forces politicians to respond. Nevertheless, the continuing level of willful amnesia and ignorance is puzzling. Mao Zedong, Che Guevara, Fidel Castro and the like long ago assumed poster-hero status for a generation that seems to have only the vaguest grasp of either their accomplishments or their excesses. When Castro attended the GATT/WTO fiftieth anniversary ceremony in Geneva in 1998, he was applauded longer and louder than Bill Clinton.

At the inauguration of Mexico's president Vicente Fox in 2001, Castro was a star attraction among young students because, they said, "he has done so much for the poor." Yet this assertion ignores the fact that

Cuba is still among the poorest countries in the region and imprisons journalists and homosexuals. Civil society is absent and fearful. If it was logical to oppose Batista, surely it is equally logical to oppose Castro now.

Does this sort of blind hero-worship of those who ruthlessly maintain absolute power while impoverishing their people really matter? I think it does. Especially when, by contrast, enlightened leaders such as Václav Havel or Ernesto Zedillo are held in contempt by the ignorant and especially by those who lost power through democratic change and don't like it.

Self-proclaimed intellectuals, from the time of the French Revolution through the periods when fascism and Marxism prevailed, have always found ways of rationalizing their support for tyrannical systems. Utopian idealism can be blind and dangerous. This is true of most revolutions and curiously true of the ethical blindness to the excesses and failures of Marxism. Apologists have even tried to rationalize the horrors of North Korea.

Socrates understood this, suggesting that intellectuals play an important role in driving democracies toward tyranny by whipping the minds of the young into a frenzy, until some of them, perhaps the most brilliant and courageous, translate thought to action and try to realize their tyrannical ambitions in politics. Then, gratified to see their own ideas take effect, these intellectuals become the tyrant's servile flatterers, composing "hymns to tyranny."[7]

In his essay "Catastrophic Gradualism" George Orwell warned of the dangers of such "intellectuals in whom acceptance of power politics has killed first the moral sense and then the sense of reality." In societies where these prevail, he said, people have "allowed the state to strip them systematically of their right to be sentimental and trivial, taking away their rich language and replacing it with an ugly, utilitarian one, and denying them the ordinary pleasures of a private life."[8]

This loss of sense of both morality and reality was evident during the Cold War when people attempted to make the case for moral equivalence between Western and Eastern Europe. How there could ever have been debate about this puzzled me. Anyone who pointed this out during the days of the uprising of Solidarity in Poland earned the tag "right-winger."

But absolute tolerance has its pitfalls. Indeed, as the French philosopher Bernard-Henri Levy argued in *Left in Dark Times*, it could be "the cemetery of democracies." In bending over backward to be tolerant, some Western societies can slip into condoning practices and views that violate human rights and freedom of expression. Reaction can set in, with ugly consequences, when extreme Islamic protestors can hold up signs saying "Kill Rushdie" and "Death to Jews," yet waving a flag with the cross of St. George in the UK can attract the attention of the police as displaying racial hate or being provocative to minorities.

The beauty of democracy and the decent society is that it tolerates and accommodates differences of opinion. It embraces its critics and can often disarm them through the power of argument. That is why it is so important for democracy to guard its public space, not to give ground to those who would curtail the freedom of speech. Free speech in an open society is about discovering error, the critical powers of man, which Popper contrasted with the "closed" or "tribal" society, with its submission to magical powers.

This is likely to become even more difficult to navigate because, in times of economic hardship and competition for jobs and homes, insecurity breeds protectionism, reaction and tribalism. In such times, people become vulnerable to the most appalling of politicians and leaders who play to these fears.

CHAPTER 20

The Enemies of Reason

Throughout history, villains have used the call to answer a "higher" god or "ideal" beyond the bounds of humanity to consolidate their power. People were asked, and many agreed, to suspend their moral judgment to the leadership of the "great man." Vladimir Lenin said citizens should follow their revolutionary conscience rather than their natural conscience. Hitler called on all Germans to obey the "higher law" of the party rather than the traditional moral doctrines they were taught at home and in the church.[1]

In their quest for the ideal civilization and culture, Fabian socialist intellectuals H. G. Wells and George Bernard Shaw kept blind company with European fascists on eugenics and argued for sterilization or outright murder of undesirables such as the "vicious, helpless and pauper masses." "Progressive" Sweden enforced sterilization upon undesirables up to the 1960s. And let's not forget the many rich capitalists who just wanted to do business. They too were in denial—many still are—in regard to human rights in closed economies, and were opposed to even talking about climate change.

Virginia Woolf, another socialist and an appalling snob, was also contemptuous of working people who, she said, "seem to have taken on all the middle class respectabilities" her class had thrown off. This is evident today in the rhetoric of some Greens and ultra-Liberals who, with echoes of Rousseau's "noble savage" ringing in their ears, seek to insist that working people in rich countries and the poor in poor countries must be saved from progress and development. This dewy-eyed nonsense, mixed with cultural relativism, is a potent cocktail and can, at the extremes, find ways of excusing the Pol Pots, Stalins, Saddam Husseins, and bin Ladens of this world.

In fact, it was just such muddled thinking that blinded people for a long time to the threat posed by Hitler in Europe in the 1930s. In Britain, trade union leaders such as Ernest Bevin were among the first to warn of the dangers inherent in Hitler's activities. This placed him at odds with the Labor Party, which at the time was somewhat in thrall to the leader of its pacifist wing, George Lansbury, and his talk of Christian restraint and disarmament. Fortunately, the saner counsel of Bevin and Clement Attlee prevailed.

Echoes of Lansbury's indignant pacifism and moral crusading reappeared in the 1960s, 1970s and 1980s as the "left" sought a policy of unilateral disarmament before the Soviet menace.

The radical Welsh Labor leader Nye Bevan would later say of the romantic left who began to take over the movement, "Once the trade unions were the cream of the working class, now they are an intellectual spittoon for the middle class."

Reactionaries and their shallow certainties

Business and the "right" have often been appeasers, arguing for profits first. This was particularly exposed in the 1930s. The right's excesses gave expression to the strong strand of thinking that was isolationist, protectionist, tribal and anti-enlightenment. Political parties with names such as "Zimbabwe First," "America First" and "New Zealand First" always have unpleasant attitudes to immigrants, foreigners, foreign investment and globalization. They frequently seek outside demons—Asians, Muslims, multinationals, moneylenders, and speculators—and in the name of patriotism invoke primitive nationalism in a crude call to arms. Having established these "demons" in the public consciousness, they ride in on their white horses to slay them on behalf of the disadvantaged and marginalized in their societies, gaining political momentum and publicity along the way.

In times of economic downturn and change, extremists prosper. In times of economic growth, they fail—another reason development is so vital to progress. The most infamous example of economic collapse breeding reactionary political responses was, of course, the Great Depression, made more lethal in the 1930s by governments' anti-trade protectionist measures, from which came the twin tyrannies of fascism and communism.

Modern representatives of these ideas are to be found everywhere; from Jean-Marie Le Pen in France to Pat Buchanan in the United States. Some need to burn crosses on lawns; many invoke the name of the Lord.

In the United States, moral crusader Jerry Falwell proclaimed that the butchery of 9/11 was God's punishment for secularization and the tolerance of homosexuality. Also in the United States, the now-disgraced former House majority leader Tom Delay suggested that "Only Christianity offers a way to live in response to the realities that we find in the world." On this basis, it seems, he attributed the Columbine High School massacre to the fact that schools in Colorado and elsewhere teach the theory of evolution.

In a speech to the Chicago Divinity School, conservative Supreme Court Justice Antonin Scalia stated his belief that "the more Christian a country is the less likely it is to regard the death penalty as immoral" because the "government carries the sword as 'the Minister of God' to 'execute wrath upon the evil-doer.'"[2]

With politicians, too, dumb, populist headline-grabbing, fundrais-ing extremism reinforces intolerance on both sides. For example, one-time presidential aspirant the Reverend Pat Robertson said of Islam in general: "Adolf Hitler was bad but what the Muslims do to the Jews is worse." While he was correct in pointing out the primitive hatred that is taught in a few Muslim schools he—as one of the most powerful American Christian leaders—was branding an entire faith, encompass-ing a billion people. In any event, history is against him, as we saw ear-lier. Today's Jihadists more closely resemble the Christian Crusaders of old than their Islamic, historic, more tolerant past.

The thread I'm trying to weave here is that totalitarian thinking dressed up as theology or philosophy ends up with the burning of books, the killing of sparrows, and the lighting of ovens for non-believers, heretics or enemies of the people. It is only in democratic countries that the common sense, common will of the people can, in their collective wisdom, stop fanatics.

But perhaps the traditional divisions of "left" and "right" are no longer accurate or appropriate. The dichotomy is now more likely between those who accept Enlightenment lessons and those who don't; those who support modernity and those who oppose it; those who favor open societies and those who don't.

Traditionally, it is those with the most to lose who are most threatened by change and the most likely to lash out to protect themselves and their privileges. This often takes the form of attacks on public morality. "What Rome was during the decline of the Republic," warned the Abbé Yvon, canon of Coutances, "Paris is today. Yes Paris, the center of all corruption and of all vices. It is there that *nouvelle philosophie* has established its seat."[3]

Enlightenment ideas were conjured into existence as the specter and source of modernity's ills, reaffirming religion's place in the modern world and prescribing a program to heal it that was both idealistic and radical. This reaffirming process—which generated so much polarized opposition and hate—was then carried into the Revolution, radicalized and accelerated.

There is a broad, bizarre coalition of those who oppose modernity, fear change, believe their lives are beyond their control and need something to blame. And in writing of the enemies of reason, science and the Enlightenment it is necessary to include in this category those who have benefited most from that which they oppose. Remember, for example, the shock of learning that those who tried to car-bomb London and Glasgow airports a couple of years ago were actually doctors of medicine? That educated people, sworn to preserve life, could set out to mutilate and murder with such callous disregard came as a slap in the face to the principles of the Enlightenment and all who strive to uphold them.

However, history has shown that so many of the perpetrators of tyranny—from Madame Guillotine to the Holocaust, to the Killing Fields of Cambodia, to 9/11—were highly educated people. This is not an argument against education; it is an argument for intellectual freedom, which is the antithesis of "groupism" and extremism. Neither is it an argument against faith (I am a person of faith but have always kept that to myself because, in my country, to say so now invites the same contempt and hostility that being "gay" once did. When asked, I always say "I'm not religious, I'm an Anglican"). Smug atheists can be just as sanctimonious, humorless and hypocritical as smug Christians.

A secular society must be tolerant of those who have a religious faith of whatever shade: people are entitled to their private views no matter how obnoxious. Many secular states in the West are bending over backward to accommodate other religions in the name of ultra-sensitivity while becoming more hostile to Christianity, saying it has no place in modern society. Could it be that our openness to differences and our willingness to accommodate them could become our most profound weakness? How do you handle people born into a democracy who despise the very people and society that succors them?

Environmental monotheism

Everyone is for the environment. It is a movement whose time has come. Where in earlier times politicians always made pious references to God and country (some still do), nowadays there is always a nod toward sustainable development and the environment. This is the success of "green" politics, but the danger is that in some quarters, the environment has become almost a simplistic religious mantra and some see green issues as a way of smuggling back old forms of control. For example, the word "nuclear" has acquired unfortunate connotations and is used as something of a bogeyman, regardless of the fact that nuclear medicine has saved thousands of cancer patients (including me).

Opposition to today's orthodoxies inevitably invites wild and irrational accusations of hating trees or loving concrete or wanting the world to melt. In such an environment, business and growth are becoming the new Satan. Greens have seized the high moral ground and in allowing this to happen we are denying ourselves opportunities for scrutiny and dissent, at great cost.

The very fact that we have a Green movement today is a direct product of open, democratic societies, which, on the whole, have a better environmental record than totalitarian or authoritarian societies. Open democratic governments, policed by a rigorous media and pressure groups, force government departments and private enterprise to be accountable to the people.

There is often a feeling that comes from certain sections of the Green movement that conservation and development are incompatible. This need not necessarily be the case. We will get a more efficient light bulb, a more efficient hot-water cylinder, a better steel industry because it makes good business sense. In many ways, efficiency is just another word for conservation. Smart companies anticipate society's environmental ambitions and plan ahead, seeking to appeal to the increasingly powerful, wealthy and discerning Green consumer market. Rising incomes are the best hope for the environment. Increased affluence means people have fewer children, are better educated, and now have higher environmental expectations. This is true of every continent and atoll.

It is true that the last few decades have witnessed an accelerating consumption of national resources—consumption that is often inefficient and ill-planned. The human species is living more off the planet's capital and less off its interest. This is bad for business and for all of us. Without wishing to sound too cynical, however, in seeking to redress this imbalance, we should maintain a healthy open-minded skepticism, looking for effective answers based on science and rational analysis rather than allowing ourselves to be swayed by the increasingly emotive rhetoric which can only cloud the issue.

The doomsayers have always been with us. Some 200 years ago, Thomas Robert Malthus was predicting that rising populations in Britain and throughout the world would lead to mass famines. In 1962, Rachel Carson's *Silent Spring* predicted that manmade chemicals would wipe us all out within 20 years. In 1970, the respected journal *Science Digest* predicted a new ice age. In 1980, acid rain was going to kill all the forests in Europe and North America. In 1991, Carl Sagan suggested that smoke from the torched Kuwaiti oil wells would lower global temperatures, and cause drought and famine in India and massive agricultural failure in the United States.

In 1972, the Club of Rome suggested there would be a great depression—if not the end of the world—because of resource scarcity: gold would be exhausted by 1981, tin by 1987, petroleum by 1992, and copper, lead and natural gas by 1993.

Panic about the potential consequences of Y2K led to the spending of $100 billion in the United States alone. It never happened.

The fact is that we have made vast environmental improvements over the past century, when pollution was far worse than it is today. Seventeenth-century Londoners were breathing what diarist John Evelyn called "impure and thick mist accompanied by filthy vapor corrupting the lungs." In the nineteenth century Prince Albert died of typhoid contracted from a polluted River Thames. Now, for the first time in several generations, fish are being caught in the Thames.

Some of the North American Great Lakes were considered dead 25 years ago, and some rivers often caught fire. Today 70 percent of the area's rivers are considered safe for swimming or fishing, compared with 36 percent in 1972. Ocean dumping of industrial waste has been reduced by 94 percent. The total forested areas in the world's temperate regions actually increased between 1980 and 1990.

Yet despite strong evidence of practical success, the more extreme elements of the Green movement propose more state control to prevent environmental disasters. Conveniently overlooking the fact that some of the most appalling environmental degradation has taken place in tightly controlled and tightly regulated communist economies, they continue to talk of capitalist greed. We need to get beyond the rhetoric and focus on what is good and what will drive further improvements.

Food insecurity

It is in the area of food production that the scare tactics have been employed most, regardless of the fact that the Green Revolution has doubled the output of food over the last 30 years and saved millions of lives. Far fewer people are starving in China and India today.

In the 1960s, the scientist who created the Green Revolution was awarded the Nobel Prize for Peace; nowadays he might well have his laboratories attacked by zealots who oppose such research. There was uproar when the United Nations' World Food Program started sending genetically modified food to starving people in Africa. (A rather too righteous protest from some NGOs was even taken up by Robert Mugabe, who suggested that rich countries were trying to poison the people he had starved and brutalized in the name of self-determination and self-sufficiency.) Biotech food is eaten in the United States, Canada, Argentina, Australia and the European Union.

Every few years there is a sighting of the Loch Ness Monster, and every few years there is a debate on genetically modified foods, normally at election time in my part of the world. As with Nessie, it is hard to prove what is not there. It is embarrassing to see environmentalists being suckered into using dubious European slogans such as the precautionary principle, which the rest of the world realizes is simply sophisticated protectionism for their privileged, subsidized farmers.

Hysteria and anti-science rants about "Frankenfoods" make great headlines—but what about the potential to save millions of lives? How about evidence? This flawed thinking from the "left" is matched by the inane arguments against stem-cell research from the "right." Hundreds of people die every year awaiting organ transplants. Recently the world's first organs grown in a laboratory have heralded a new era in transplant surgery. Regenerative medicine techniques can be used to generate bladders that are durable. A next step will be to grow more complex organs.

What is in essence a promising procedure for cloning embryonic stem cells from patients with incurable diseases without consuming precious human eggs has been made to sound like a horror-film recipe for humanoid hybrids. Sadly, and despite the best efforts of scientists to correct the misconceptions, at present many governments seem to be swayed more by the scary headlines than by the real potential to advance medical research.

If the worst happens and hybrid embryo research is banned in Britain, similar experiments will still take place elsewhere. Indeed, in a vivid illustration of the new vitality of Chinese bio-science, researchers in Shanghai were the first to demonstrate that the procedure worked. American scientists, who can do almost anything if they don't rely on federal funding, are also working on it.[4]

Science without scrutiny and ethics has in it the stuff of a science fiction nightmare. To ensure there is public confidence in such research there needs to be absolute transparency and accepted standards, so that the rabid opponents of stem-cell research, who in the UK in one year were responsible for over 300 attacks on research facilities and staff, or the eco-militants and animal-welfare militants who committed 1,200 crimes in the United States between 1990 and 2004, can gain no further traction.

There seems to be a psychotic commonality between extremists of every persuasion which allows them to rationalize violence to achieve their idealistic ends, whether it be the Dutch-born Muslim who murdered the filmmaker Theo van Gogh, or the fanatical vegan who assassinated anti-immigration politician Pim Fortuyn.

It is hard to have a sensible debate with people like this when the campaigns which ignite their passions are run on car-stickers and glib soundbites, rather than reasoned debate. It is hard to see how we will feed the world and lower the use of dangerous insecticides and fertilizers without enlisting the new forces of science. We in the West may feel we have the luxury of time on our side, but others are not so fortunate.

The kind of muddled thinking of the animal-rights activist who sees what he is doing as being the moral equivalent of the anti-slavery campaign is as bizarre as (and more dangerous than) Michael Jackson likening his court appearances over child abuse to those of Nelson Mandela and Martin Luther King. Science can move faster than our moral, ethical or legal capacity to cope. But those who wish to burn the books and destroy science have as their forefathers those who burned the witches, not those who freed the slaves. These small groups who manipulate and exaggerate the dangers to a gullible media represent pre-Enlightenment thinking; they are the new enemies of reason.

Their talk of "food miles" is merely an argument for a new form of protectionism, and is music to the ears of the agricultural elites protected by subsidies paid for by the poor. By such reasoning it is okay, explained a Green leader on the BBC, for consumers to be forced to buy local flowers, despite the fact that job-poor Africa can fly flowers to European capitals at a lower environmental cost. In 2006, for example, Kenya, which with European Union aid has phased out pesticide use, earned more than $700 million from this trade, employing two million people, 80 percent of whom were small-scale farmers. How moral is it then to take away these jobs? All activity, economic or otherwise, affects the environment. Do these purveyors of fairness realize that peacekeepers burn air miles too?

Contrary to the views of Green propagandists, and despite the food price spike in 2007 and 2008, the long-run trend of food prices relative to income is down, and there are more forests worldwide now than a decade ago.

The argument that the rich are consuming too much of the world's resources and will eventually overpopulate the world is also off target. Indeed, the opposite is true. We need more rich and educated people. The dirtiest cities are the poorest. Wealthier people tend to be better educated, have smaller families, and be more committed to peace and democracy. They have something to lose.

The Kuznets Curve explains why wealth and growth in the end provide for better environmental outcomes. When income reaches a certain level, the unit costs of production begin to fall as industry becomes more efficient, and an empowered middle class emerges which demands better outcomes. This is borne out by results in the Western world and in the more successful and more democratic economies in Asia: Japan, South Korea, Taiwan, and now Malaysia. That is why it is so irritating to keep reading comments by environmentalists that trade, commerce and so-called Western values of democracy are anti-poor, bad for the planet, and a new form of neo-liberal colonialism. The real colonialism lies in the anti-growth, state-control formulas still being driven by extreme NGOs who always know what's best for poor people in poor conditions. I had dozens of meetings with such NGOs when I was at the WTO. Some demanded that the WTO take action to force governments to accept their anti-growth agenda. How they expected the WTO to be able to force governments to accept such an agenda when they had failed to convince even one government in the world of the need for this is beyond me.

Alarmists and extremists are important because through their actions they put issues on the agenda, and overreaction is better than no action at all. The reality, however, is that market economies look after the environment better, and that democracy and the ingenuity of our species know no bounds when freedom unleashes the genius of the people.

This is not to reject alarmism, nor to say that those who campaigned to clean up the Thames and the air of India were wrong; they are not. Alarmism is important: it forces those in power to respond, explain and correct behavior. Alarmists warn us; they make us prove them wrong; they wake us up.

NGOs: The best and worst of us

I was a protester against Vietnam and apartheid; I have been and still am a supporter of good and lost causes. It was only as a besieged Director-General of the WTO that I began to question the motivation of some of the extreme protesters who posed outside the WTO's gates in Geneva. The World Wide Fund for Nature (WWF) and Greenpeace had budgets larger than the WTO. I gave them a voice at the table but not a vote.

It is good that non-governmental organizations (NGOs) are now major actors on the domestic and international stage because they often represent the best of idealism (Doctors Without Borders, Transparency International and Crisis International spring to mind here). But a very few, often the loudest, can also be violent enemies of reason.

The number of NGOs around the world has grown from 1,083 in 1914, to 13,000 in the 1990s, to an estimated 40,000 today. The UK branch of Greenpeace is a slick publicity machine and has more members than all the political parties in Britain. When I was a paid-up member, I was never invited to a meeting, or asked to vote for a board to agree with a proposition. My opinion was never canvassed by the people who grabbed headlines with their declarations that the WTO was somehow undemocratic because it represented governments (parliaments) and not people.

Some NGOs are exactly what they accuse elected politicians of being—poll-driven, headline-grabbing, and fundraising opportunists. The difference is that politicians have to get elected. They are accountable to their electorate, political party and a relentless media.

In essence the lobbyist and activist's critique of representative democracy is fundamentally an anti-democratic one. It is based on the premise that unelected individuals who possess a lofty, moral purpose have a greater right to act on the public's behalf than politicians elected through an imperfect political process.[5]

The media fall for this all the time, often giving them air time without the cynical scrutiny that politicians or business people face. Power without responsibility is great fun. I once tried to get an agreed code of conduct to govern the relationship between NGOs and inter-governmental organizations, with similar rules to those that public companies and political parties in most countries face: the rejection of violence; the transparency of finances, contributions, and decision-making; and a requirement to report to stakeholders at open annual general meetings. I failed.

The world would be a poorer place without NGOs. They represent both the best of Enlightenment thinking and the worst of anti-Enlightenment dogma. The privatization of diplomacy through the new network of NGOs, interest groups and lobbyists can be healthy, but businesses, well-meaning donors and governments should not engage with groups that don't sign up to transparent, democratic rules such as those outlined above.

Defeating the new and old enemies of reason will never be complete, and nor should it be: that too would be dangerous. They are always with us, and should be, because none of us should have the absolute power to determine who is reasonable and who is not. That would be unreasonable. We should have to argue our way to an even better world.

History shows clearly that the democratic impulse is strong and we can drain the swamps of poverty where this disease still infects millions. I call poverty a disease because it is curable. The cure will take deliberate, careful strategies, which much of this book is about. By alleviating poverty we can take away much of the putrid fertilizer that dangerous opportunists need to grow their power bases. Freedom discredits tyranny. Under firm rules of transparency, free trade and markets do a good job of producing wealth, but are not designed to redistribute it or provide the social systems and social security to enable social mobility and to banish the age-old fears of illness, old age, and accident. That is why we have governments.

PART 5

AFTERTHOUGHTS AND RECONSIDERATIONS

We have seen how the democratic impulse, the urge to be free, to look beyond the horizon, to trade, and to care for others are consistent features of the human experience. History shows that successful nations are those that accept the people's will through a democratic process and the rule of law implemented by a competent, honest public service.

Democracy stretches authority beyond the term of any government, safeguarding the people and society from opportunism that, in response to a crisis, fashion or fad, can be dangerous. Democracy's heavy keel keeps the ship stable during storms. It gives people ownership and responsibility. An active civil society, with responsible trade unions, women's groups, and advocates for the environment and civil rights, is a guarantor of solid democracy. To make the system function best, we need the freedom to organize, agitate, and make a case to the people so that they can demand their leaders act or be replaced. The political marketplace works best when there is an educated, involved private and public space.

CHAPTER 21

Information and Reputation

Because information is power, it is to be expected that jealous, powerful interests will try to control, guide and spin information to their advantage. This is as true of the world of commerce as it is the world of politics. Much of the blame for the current global economic crisis can be attributed to the lack of information and transparency in complicated, opaque banking deals that few understood but many subscribed to.

Hubris and a systemic failure by auditors and financial writers resulted in uncontested accounting and business practices which allowed Bernard Madoff to steal up to $50 billion from some of the most sophisticated investors of the world. If the watchdogs had done more than watch and applaud the "profits" that didn't exist, Madoff would have gone to jail years ago. The sophisticated technology available to those entrusted with serving the public interest and to the media should have made oversight easier. In this instance, it failed because those entrusted to use it were as blinded by spin as everyone else.

There is a real cost to business of inept or unethical performance, just as there are big rewards if a company can boost its reputation amongst consumers and investors. In July 2007, *BusinessWeek* considered what would happen to share prices if major corporations were to switch reputations with a rival. It found, for example, that if Coca-Cola had the reputation of Pepsi, its stock would be worth 3.3 percent more, or an increase of $4 billion.

The first—and some say the sole—responsibility of any business is to make a profit. Without profit, there are neither jobs nor revenue to tax. Nobel laureate Milton Friedman was very vocal in his opposition to the idea that "employees are major stakeholders. It is really a movement towards employee-run enterprises." I disagree with Friedman: labor is not just another product, and the wider environment cannot be ignored. Businesspeople must live in a wider world where social and environmental issues impact upon them—business cannot prosper in societies that fail.

Corporate responsibility and shareholder/stakeholder rights are a growth industry for the legal and professional community, given the criminal excesses of Enron and WorldCom, and other examples of corporate and political rot being exposed by the current downturn. Standards, transparency and commercial honesty can improve all outcomes. Good businesses realize that investing in their employees and the broader community pays off, in both productivity and remuneration terms.

The question then is: should governments direct businesses to do what is good for them or should it be left to the market to reward good practices? The state has a role to provide education and training in partnership with business; and in times of economic restructuring, that role limits the social and political costs. On the other hand, business skills play a critical role in making things happen in poor countries, while giving space for the improvement of public services and humanitarian support.

Failed states are a danger to us all in that they are breeding grounds for disorder, crime, drugs and terrorism. And with two million people crossing national borders every day, the potential health and economic implications for neighboring states are enormous.

A study by the London School of Economics found that places with the highest newspaper readership have the best economic and social outcomes in the developing world. An active media exposes corruption and bad policies. The more closed the economy, the lower the number of readers, the less variety of papers and information available. Freedom to challenge orthodoxy must be preserved, and the instant power of the internet can be a stunning force for good in this regard. This was confirmed recently when a school science project conducted by two immigrant children in New Zealand revealed that the level of Vitamin C in an iconic brand of juice, Ribena, did not live up to its advertised claim. The resulting publicity forced one of the world's biggest companies, GlaxoSmithKline, to withdraw its claims, apologize and promise to behave better.

We need to be vigilant. The enemies of reason in all their configurations are always with us. Populists and tyrants, both political and business, always emerge amongst the creative chaos that is the state of perpetual change. Given the wonder of modern communication, though, they should be easier than ever before to expose and depose. The cost of technology, relative to incomes, has collapsed the entry barriers to organizing in the public space, enabling new ways of mobilizing public opinion. Governments have fallen through protests coordinated in capitals around the world by cellphone messaging. To trade in a globalized, integrated world economy, closed societies must take into account the growing number of consumers everywhere who make their opinions known in the marketplace and in polling booths. Policy-making is no longer the isolated privilege of kings and cardinals, meeting away from the public gaze. Although civil society can be uncivil at times, this is a worthy development.

Demands for equality and ownership have increased social mobility, creating an ever-growing circle of virtue. This is the genius of social democracy. Education, civil and human rights and trade union rights are an inherent part of a successful market economy. Governments have to intervene sometimes to make markets work and to preserve the virtues of competition by ensuring that the rules of the competitive system are not circumvented by the unscrupulous.

President Obama has promised to bring in more regulation in business to ensure that the excesses we have witnessed in recent times cannot be repeated. If it helps promote competition and choice, as well as more honest business reporting, this can only be a good thing.

22

Engagement in a Rapidly Changing World

The world has integrated swiftly, in an economic sense, over the past 50 years, arguably quicker than our legal, political and ethical capacity to cope. Our international political architecture has not kept pace. The nation-state is only 500 years old. Our global institutions are, in the main, no more than 80 years old. We are steadily, imperfectly, improving their effectiveness. There is a vast movement of concerned citizens and consumers who are steadily building a global civil society, a cosmopolitan, color-blind coalition that is forcing leaders to respond. Mostly they are pushing on an open door. We know that international problems of climate change, terrorism, nuclear proliferation, and poverty don't recognize lines on a map. Nobody who has viewed the world from outer space has even seen a nation's borders drawn over the land, although there is some distinction at night, when the lights of successful economies shine. From space you can see the electric glare of South Korea but not dark, dangerous North Korea.

We will see more change in the next 10 years than the previous 50. In biotechnology and genetic research, we have just begun, yet some still see success as a bad thing and fear the future. That's not new either. Newspapers report population trends and falling fertility rates that could mean that there will be no Japanese or Italians in 120 years. But people respond, adapt, learn, and correct policies that endanger them and their interests. They can best do this armed with information, where there are the democratic, legal and commercial systems that allow these corrections.

Despite the traditionally cynical view that the super-rich contribute very little to the growing engagement in the wider world, philanthropists are taking on a much greater role in development. Not for the first time, it is the super-rich in the United States who are showing the way in what is an American tradition, from Carnegie to Hewlett Packard, and now Bill Gates to Warren Buffett. George Soros, the billionaire investor and devotee of Karl Popper who for some reason is branded as "left wing" by Fox News, has put hundreds of millions of dollars into an Open Society Foundation, promoting democracy and good governance. In acts of creative anarchy, he gave civil societies, unions, and churches in Eastern and Central Europe dozens of fax machines and photocopying machines, figuring that if people talked and communicated, they could organize, and if they could organize, they would reject centralism and communism. It helped.

In my experience, wealthy philanthropists like to see their projects work and typically promote simple, often low-cost, deliverables that the politicians and bureaucrats can't steal. One, for example, gave half-a-million wheelchairs to disabled people in developing countries. Another smart idea gave merry-go-rounds linked to water pumps to schools. When the kids push the wheel, the pump draws water up to a tank on which advertising is sold to pay for upkeep. One play-pump can provide basic water for a couple of thousand people and is extremely attractive when a permanent supply of water can be provided for only $20,000.

Bill Gates is already spending more money on combating AIDS in Africa than the United Nations agencies. Ted Turner bailed the United Nations out with several hundred million dollars' worth of donations. Bill Clinton's initiative on global giving has already secured $10 billion.

Private philanthropy from the US to poor nations totaled US$34.8 billion in 2006—almost half as much again as the US government provided—and following the Sichuan earthquake in May 2008, US corporations alone donated US$90 million, as compared with the US$3.1 million in official US government aid. These shifts offer a democratic way for peoples to build cooperative responses without the need for an intervening bureaucracy.

While progress is undoubtedly being made on several fronts, big mistakes and historic follies, have still to be resolved and new ones are still being enacted. One such folly is the failure to agree on the terms of the Russian membership of the WTO that would have brought it into a transparent, predictable, rules-based system, with binding dispute-settlement mechanisms. This is about more than commerce and wealth creation. There are now more than 140 million Russians; but by 2050, there could be fewer than 100 million, as poor health systems, alcohol abuse, and declining birth rates (there are now more abortions than live births in Russia) take their toll. Oil-dependent economies such as Russia's seldom flourish unless their oil wealth is shared. Integrating Russia into the global economy ought to be a top economic and political objective for policy-makers. The longer this problem remains unresolved, the stronger will be the dangerous paranoia and the power of Russia's ultra-nationalists, who make great play of being surrounded by half-a-billion NATO members and over a billion Chinese.

Owning up to the past

Other nations, too, continue to be haunted by their past. Japan is in many ways a model global citizen: the world's second-largest economy, the single largest aid donor, and an important investor and trading nation. From the rubble of 1945, it has built a mobile, wealthy, free society that is an example to the developing world. Yet, in the view of many, Japan has yet to come to terms with some historic ghosts, and even the most progressive political leaders are forced by nationalist sentiment to be very sensitive to war veterans. Japan, it should be said, insists that it has indeed apologized for its conduct during the Second World War and that the states that claim otherwise do so to manipulate their domestic constituencies for nationalistic propaganda purposes.

Germany, on the other hand, has made great efforts to accept its responsibilities in this regard, not least when former chancellor Willy Brandt was overwhelmed with remorse and emotion while laying a wreath at a war memorial in Poland. This was no stunt; it was raw emotion, a transcending moment of moral leadership. The act itself and its attendant symbolism echoed far beyond the gates of Warsaw.

The Japanese are smart, hardworking, and sophisticated. Their dedication, capacity to sacrifice, and sense of duty are commendable. Yet their seeming determination not to resolve such matters is a dangerous thing where there are still votes to be had by not putting this history behind them with dignity, respect and humility.

CHAPTER 23

American Engagement

At the time of writing, anti-Americanism is widespread; we have yet to learn if this is simply the residue of the virulent anti-Bush sentiments that have prevailed during the past few years. In 2007, the Pew Global Attitudes survey, covering 38,000 people in 44 nations, showed that anti-Americanism is not restricted to the Muslim world and is growing. When America is seen as a bigger threat to world peace than Iran or North Korea in many Western countries, policymakers in Washington take notice.

Unthinking anti-Americanism is another folly of our times and those who march and protest about American imperialism should equally fear American isolationism. It was the shared values of America and Europe that overcame German imperialism in the First World War, fascism in the Second World War, and Marxism during the Cold War. The US economic model has inspired Japan, India and China. Nobody should seriously think that terrorism, poverty and global warming can be defeated without US leadership. Madeleine Albright famously dubbed the United States "the indispensable nation." What happens in the United States has an impact upon us all.

Everyone has an opinion on US elections or the actions of its government and President Obama's election was greeted with euphoria around the world. Like hundreds of millions of others, I tuned in to watch his inauguration speech and was misty-eyed. This was the America we all loved, the America of my generation's heroes, JFK, RFK and Martin Luther King, Jr. To see a new generation of young people with tears in their eyes and hope in their hearts was uplifting. A subsequent poll of 17 nations by the University of Maryland showed two out of three people expected US relations with the world to improve. Such is the reach of the American dream, which casts its light worldwide.

Democracy is a redemptive process of renewal and restoration. The genius of the American Constitution is that it provides a legal and moral anchor for the dream. The separation of powers allows for accountability and the peaceful transfer of power with dignity and respect. With Obama's election, it became easier to be a public friend of America again. His inaugural speech gave hope to Americans and to people all over the world: "To those who cling to power through corruption and deceit and the silencing of dissent," he said, "know that you are on the wrong side of history; but that we will extend a hand if you are willing to unclench your fist." Expectations are high, probably too high, but his speech offered hope for those of us who believe in global public service, multilateralism.

The United States was born out of the European experience of the Reformation and the great thinkers of the Enlightenment, which found its most famous and profound expression in the Declaration of Independence, the Constitution and the Bill of Rights. Together, these reflected Calvinistic thinking that hard work, thrift, and private ownership should be rewarded.

Winston Churchill once referred to Britain and the United States as two nations separated by a common language. Indeed, Britons and many other non-Americans for that matter are confused and uneasy about the language used by many United States politicians, especially their free reference to God, with its overtones of manifest destiny. Such language is perhaps not surprising when research shows that 48 percent of Americans believe the United States enjoys special protection from God, 58 percent believe that its strength and success is based on religious faith, and 60 percent say faith is involved in every aspect of their lives.[1] Twenty-eight percent believe that every word in the Bible must be read literally, 45 percent believe Jesus will return in their lifetime and about 30 percent believe that the September 11 attacks were predicted in the Bible.[2] In short, this is a deeply religious society where two in five Americans report having had a profound religious experience.

The cultural divide between the United States and other nations of the West goes beyond religion. Most people in Western democracies were appalled at the US government's response in the wake of Hurricane Katrina. Most of us see a basic role for governments in civil defense to protect the people from natural disaster. No-one outside America can understand its gun laws or its seeming predilection for the emotional self-mutilation and public humiliation enshrined in TV programs such as *The Jerry Springer Show*. (But even here can be seen the possibility of rehabilitation and redemption through the individual effort and hard work that are the very basis of America's success.)

In a survey of 23 countries, US citizens topped the poll of being very proud of their country, with 60 percent of those polled stating that their culture was superior to all others. (This compared to 37 percent of the British and only 30 percent of the French polled.) Most Americans think they have the best living standards in the world, even though US workers work far longer hours than their counterparts in, say, Britain, Germany, France or Japan, and the United States is one of only three industrial countries that have no legislated maternity leave.

America is different: more people own businesses than are members of unions; more people own shares than actually bother to vote. America's genius is based upon everyone having an opportunity and everyone having the right to a second chance. This right and belief in renewal is a profound social and economic factor in the American success story. US bankruptcy laws are very forgiving, offering companies a chance to trade their way out of default through Chapter 11 protection. They also have a sort of moral Chapter 11, allowing those who have erred or failed to confess, become born again and start again.

Americans prize individual rights and, as a nation, reflect as much unease about international collective rights as about collective social rights at home. George Washington warned against foreign entanglements. John Quincy Adams warned darkly about American agents going abroad "in search of monsters to destroy." The Wilsonian vision of a world run by international institutes and global laws, and the more individualistic Hamiltonian expression of unilateralism, is still being fought out in the United States.

The American author Robert Kagan observed that Americans operate in an anarchic Hobbesian world in which nations have to use military might, while Europeans reflect on their history by moving in a world of laws, rules and transnational negotiation. According to Timothy Garton Ash in his book *Free World*, the new, enlarged Europe is engaged in a great argument between the forces of Euro-Gaullism and Euro-Atlanticism. Much will depend on the outcome of this debate, but the influence of pro-American President Nicolas Sarkozy of France may steer the result toward a more harmonious North Atlantic relationship, except where France's farmers are concerned.

Whenever I am asked whether the United States will still be the major superpower 50 years from now, I answer in the affirmative—unless it returns to its isolationist past and blocks its regular intellectual, economic and cultural transfusion of migrants, or if the popular vote falls so far that zealots of the "left" or the righteous and religious "right" take charge. This would be in no-one's interest, and I don't think it will happen. I side with Churchill in believing that "The United States always does the right thing after considering at great length the alternatives."

24

Climate Change and the Energy Challenge

Anyone who still doubts that climate change is a real issue should talk to any large reinsurance company about the major threat posed to their profits by our changing climate. Of the top 10 insurance losses worldwide in the last 35 years, all but one (the 9/11 attacks) were weather-related, and the number and costs are growing. According to the IAG Insurance Group in Australia, Hurricane Katrina and Hurricane Andrew together cost $70.3 billion in insurance claims; 9/11 cost $20.7 billion. If we had spent $40 billion on mitigation and prevention, we could have reduced global economic losses from natural disasters in the 1990s by $280 billion. If there are any further doubts about the seriousness of the issue, note that the Dutch have just committed more than a billion dollars a year for each of the next 10 years to protect the Port of Rotterdam.

Inextricably bound up with climate change is our use of energy. The United States, which represents just 5 percent of the world's population but 25 percent of energy consumption, is twice as energy-intensive as the European Union and Japan. Japan is the most energy-efficient, industrialized state. China devours nine times as much energy per unit of GDP as Japan, and three times that of the United States. Huge opportunities present themselves to make rapid gains in efficiency, which as we saw earlier is just another word for conservation.

The average American uses the equivalent of 7,500 gallons of oil a year; the average Chinese uses 800 gallons. In the United States, the low cost of oil saw a huge increase in the number of SUVs (only 1 percent of which ever go off-road). Just 15 percent of the energy in a gallon of gasoline ever reaches the wheel of a car, so a gain of less than three miles per gallon would liberate the United States from Persian Gulf imports.[1] The future is in the hydrogen economy, clean-coal technologies, renewables, and the next generation of safer, more acceptable nuclear options that can drive electricity prices down, and provide the security of supply so important to confidence and investment.

Many of the present ideas to handle climate change will hurt the poorest people in the poorest places, who rightly point the finger at consumers in the West who use up to 10 times more energy per person. Global cuts in emissions, as proposed by Nicholas Stern in his 2006 report, could reduce economic growth in China by 15 percent, in India by 13 percent, in ASEAN countries by 12 percent, and in the United States by 4 percent.[2] Many countries that signed up to the Kyoto Agreement have missed their targets, while countries like the United States that have not are closer to the prescribed targets than many of their critics. So-called progressive countries like New Zealand and Australia take the moral high ground while carving out great exceptions for coal mining or dairy farming. Like China and India, they are putting the short-term needs of their economy before their long-term interests of mitigating climate change. Understandably, everyone wants to go to heaven, but nobody wants to die. However, we must find a way to cooperate and to encourage nations to meet targets but allow them to find their own way through a very wide menu of options.

As to the moral case, how moral is it for a rich country like Australia to oppose nuclear energy on safety grounds and yet still find it acceptable to enjoy the huge economic benefits that come from exporting uranium for use overseas?

The Kyoto Agreement, as well-intentioned and as flawed as it is, will have to be negotiated again in 2012. Few issues are more serious. A global carbon tax would do the job and carbon credits and trading emissions systems are a good idea, but I can't see this sort of global discipline happening for another generation at least. None of the options considered so far are universal, have an independent verification mechanism, or a binding disputes system.

Summoning the energy

Energy issues are fundamental to sustainable economic and environmental success. President George W. Bush in his 2006 State of the Union address warned, like many presidents before him, of the United States' addiction to oil. Record oil prices translate into record profits for the oil giants, yet may provide the war chest and enable an economic case to be made for developing renewables. General Electric is investing heavily in sustainable energy projects, and expects its clean-technology projects will earn it $30 billion by 2010. BP has endeavored to position itself in the green market by saying that its initials should now stand for "Beyond Petroleum."

China is showing bold foresight in its investments and research into bio-mass, planning to produce 10 million tons of bio-oil by 2010. As part of this push, Chinese companies have invested nearly $4 billion in one project to develop 2.5 million acres of oil-bearing plants and other agricultural products in the Philippines. Other major bio-mass investments are being made in Africa, and studies are being conducted into the potential of oil-bearing water plants and other bio-mass energy resources in the Indian Ocean.

But history proves that only pricing forces effective alternatives. The only time the major economies reduced their energy consumption dramatically was after the oil crisis of the mid-1970s. In mid-2008 the oil price surged above $140 and the world economy showed the strain. China, 15 years ago, imported no oil; now it's the second-largest importer and will be the world's greatest consumer of energy by 2010. Within 20 years, its energy use will double. That's why natural-gas consumption will increase rapidly, giving space for the fascinating research on hydrogen to expand. But this is a double-edged sword because this will only happen if oil prices stay high.

The confluence of high fuel prices with high food prices means such concerns are understandable, yet the economic arguments don't stand up to scrutiny—unless subsidies are at play. Energy pricing is a convoluted area, in which profits come from using more rather than saving. To developing countries like Brazil, India and China, the opportunity to diversify energy sources seems a no-brainer. The case of nuclear energy is instructive. France gets 80 percent of her electricity from nuclear energy; Finland and Switzerland 40 percent. As our awareness of climate change and resource limitations grows, Greens who once marched against nuclear power will come to embrace it.

Higher energy costs remain the hope of alternatives: only with oil above $100 a barrel do alternatives like solar and wind power make good economic sense. It would take 20,000 wind turbines to power half of London. But the smart money is moving: worldwide investment in renewables leapt from $33 billion in 2004 to $148 billion in 2007.

In 2006, I visited Ukraine to discuss its bid to join the WTO. Anti-Russian feeling was high because the Kremlin had dramatically increased gas prices. Feelings were even higher in Georgia, where gas lines had been sabotaged by mysterious explosions. Russia was also close to joining the WTO, with a major sticking point being European concerns that Moscow doesn't charge market rates for energy to domestic industries, giving them an unfair competitive edge. The same Europeans attack Russia for demanding market rates in energy charges for former Soviet republics, an act of raw politics widely seen as Moscow's payback for their pro-European ambitions.

Had Russia been a member of the WTO, with a high-quality energy agreement, it would have been very costly for it abruptly to cut off energy trade with Georgia or Poland. Taking economic and trade levers out of the hands of politicians into a rules-based system is an important and profound contribution to the civilized management of differences through predictable rules of engagement enforced by legal instruments. This does not deny sovereignty, but allows space, helps prevent kneejerk political reactions, and offers a mechanism for resolution that is less political. A collective cost can be applied to nations that ignore due process and their accepted obligations. This is unique to the WTO.

This phase of globalization is eerily like that prior to August 1914, when experts proclaimed war was impossible for mature economies, such was the nature of economic integration in Europe. What has changed since then are the institutions and instruments we have created to help prevent things spinning out of control.

While the Doha Development Trade Round must remain the priority now, one day the energy industry must be put brought under the same predictable WTO rules as other industries. The same would go for the airline industry. Perhaps men and women with big ideas will appear—the sort of leaders who established the United Nations, the General Agreement on Tariffs and Trade and other great institutions of hope. Perhaps, just as it took a Great Depression and a world war to focus leaders' minds, climate change, terrorism and the potential collapse of a global rules-based trading system will be just the challenge needed to make us reinvent multilateralism.

Mutually assured destiny

As we approach the end of this first decade of the twenty-first century, it is important to remember that we live in a highly complex, highly linked, and increasingly multi-polar world. The choices the world faces, in other words, are not between the Golden Arches or an AK47, and we must avoid the folly of simplifying and polarizing. This does not mean the death of history but the need to share the hard-learned lessons it offers. If we surrender to the urge to simplify and too closely equate terrorism with Islam, we will lose our fight against terrorism and descend into something far graver. The language that pervades some Western (and particularly American) commentary is reminiscent of Cold War rhetoric against communism; an absolutist language that betrays no empathy with Islamic culture, and opens itself to similar accusations that it is a war against nationalism and independence, and for imperial and capitalist privileges. Perception is reality in the political affairs of man.

Recent studies have found that Islamic suicide bombers are more likely to come from well-educated backgrounds than from families in poverty. An examination of 781 terrorist events classified as "significant" by the US State Department reveals that terrorists tend to come from countries distinguished by political oppression, and not just poverty or inequality.[3] The presence of wealthy, revolutionary zealots is a constant through history. When there is an empowered middle class, an aspirational working class, action to address poverty and injustice, and a belief in social mobility, these zealots have no-one to misrepresent. While the Bible says that the poor are always with us, great faiths and philosophers also inspire us to lift the poor, show mercy and be good citizens. This is the defining struggle of our age: not so much a battle between civilizations but within civilizations, between those who believe in the lessons of the Enlightenment and those who think the Enlightenment is the problem.

In a democracy, a small percentage of eccentric extremists do not normally represent a problem. In non-democratic societies, they can take power by acquiescence or force, and can manipulate those who live lives of desperation and humiliation. That applies to Germany in the 1930s, Iraq under Saddam Hussein, or Myanmar today.

Another great folly would be to take for granted our historically high levels of prosperity. Much of this success is based on hard lessons from the past. Most countries now have independent central banks, and a resilient international financial system has withstood severe tests from the 1997 Asian financial crisis through 9/11 to the surge in oil prices. The trading system, so importantly underpinned by the WTO and its rules, needs to move forward, modernize and enlarge its scope; to stand still is to go backward.

Despite the most sustained period of economic growth in history, it is fashionable to attack globalization. Vested interests mobilized by a new generation of NGOs are putting pressure on politicians everywhere. Some even claim that it is globalization that is causing poverty in Third World countries, despite a mountain of evidence to the contrary. The added expenditure of growing middle classes in the BRIC economies is now contributing more to global growth than even American consumers. The IMF has proven that globalization is not shredding jobs in the West; instead, the rich countries are winning out on the whole, despite the widening gap between skilled and unskilled workers. This evidence doesn't stop politicians beating a familiar populist economic drum. Spanish politicians try to stop a fellow European Union member, Germany, buying a Spanish energy utility; the French government engineers a merger of private corporation Suez & Gaz de France to head off an Italian buyer. The United States stops Dubai Ports World buying into American seaports.

Sovereign funds from the Middle East, China, and India are changing the face of capitalism and investment. What now happens when a major mining company seeks to take over a rival and then finds itself up against a bid from China that looks like having a direct credit line from the Chinese government? Is this the competition and capitalism we have known for the past hundred years? This simply underscores the need for transparency, predictable rules and eventually a global set of rules of engagement—all of which are some years off. This kind of competition is causing fear and resentment from countries, consumers and investors who got rich doing the same thing for generations. The longer we imagine economic growth is guaranteed and is the normal course of events, and the more we become smug and self-satisfied, then the greater the possibility for a reversal. With the current global economic crisis and meltdown has come a new set of challenges that may need the kind of rules of engagement advocated in this book.

Prosperity can create complacency, even arrogance, among the "masters of the universe"—the market and the money dealers who have only known good and growing times. As the Marxists used to say, capitalism is inherently unstable. Progress means movement, and that in itself is unsettling for some. Forward movement will require application and vigilance, without which we are in danger of standing still; which, in effect, means going backward.

CHAPTER 25

What We Must Do

Of all the great issues of our age—injustice, intolerance, climate change, nuclear proliferation, terrorism, drugs, inequality, and protectionism— I put democracy and freedom as the most important. Unless people are free to choose, free to argue, disagree and change their minds, then we will never be able to make progress and correct our behavior in any of these areas. That is why we should celebrate, cherish, protect, promote and institutionalize our many freedoms everywhere. Freedom is the opportunity to own our own future, make mistakes, to change, learn, adapt, and seek justice in the pursuit of happiness. It extends the frontiers of hope.

I have been fortunate to operate in a free democracy and enjoy the opportunities of a socially mobile and intellectually open society. Cynicism about democracy is to me deeply disturbing. There is a duty to be skeptical about what politicians and those in public service tell us, and that applies equally to how we perceive advertising or promises made by businesses. But that is a long way from dismissing the international democratic order that humanity has done so much to develop, which to me would be almost tantamount to accepting anarchy. We have seen the cost in human, environmental and financial terms of the failure of the state apparatus.

I served with Ashraf Ghani, who was the Afghani Finance Minister, during the most difficult of times in the UN Commission for the Legal Empowerment of the Poor. His most recent book, *Fixing Failed States* (written with Clare Lockhart), is a textbook for those who care about the world's poorest. He discusses the pitfalls of international bureaucracy in its attempts to build nations. Africa spends an estimated $4 billion every year on 100,000 expatriates; in reviewing UN funding of $1.8 billion for Afghanistan for the period 2002–04, Ghani estimates that up to 70 percent was "spent on the internal costs—for international salaries, white Land Cruisers, satellite communications, and specially chartered airlines—to set up a UN agency presence."[1]

Yet he remains optimistic because examples from recent history and in the more distant past indicate how some solutions succeed while others fail. The core of the argument is that "rules are resources too." In the 1950s, Myanmar and the Philippines were thought to be the developing nations most likely to succeed. Ghana at the time had a higher living standard than South Korea. North Korea, at the time of partition, had the most resources and a better chance to succeed than the South. Just as success is manmade, so is failure. Aid is important: the Marshall Plan pledged 1 percent of US GDP for the reconstruction of Europe. The new European Union pledged more to assist the integration of poorer nations such as Ireland, Spain and Portugal into the wider European market. But aid itself is not enough. Post-war Europe and Japan snapped back into productive progress because they had civil societies, laws, rules and courts ready to function again. Rules were a key factor in their success. Rules are a resource that can be created.

We have seen examples of where the state has too much power in North Korea and Myanmar. In Zimbabwe, a few cronies pillage what's left of the country. More numerous are countries where the state cannot perform its basic duties. These are frequently nations in civil conflict or emerging from conflict—Timor, Afghanistan, Iraq, or the Democratic Republic of the Congo. The evidence of this book argues the need for the rule, predictability and transparency of the law, democracy, property rights, and independent courts. As important is an independent, professional, merit-based, and well-paid public service. Building the capacity of government agencies, from a customs service and honest police force to trusted tax regimes and enforcement mechanisms, is central—without these nothing else will succeed. Roads, ports and schools will not be built, health dollars will be squandered, a cycle of mistrust and perverted incentives will take hold.

It is not enough to attack corruption in developing countries. For many years, governments in the developed world turned a blind eye to bribery undertaken overseas by their citizens. Only in 1997 did the OECD pass its anti-bribery convention, signatories to which agree to outlaw the purchasing of favor by companies and individuals operating overseas. While progress has been patchy, recent cases offer some hope: in October 2007 a court in Germany fined Siemens €201 million after executives at the company were found guilty of bribing officials in Libya, Nigeria and Russia.

Trust in institutions is a central principle of success. That is the experience of the most successful societies. With trust and freedom from fear, an active civil society can reach its full expression in keeping the system honest and expansive, with the engagement and support of the media, creative communities, charities, churches, trade unions and others.

What, then, are the functions of a state? What are the frameworks to handle tensions that always exist in society, and why have a state and a government?

In *Fixing Failed States*, Ghani and Lockhart identify the principal functions of a successful state, which include administrative control, the provision of infrastructure services, sound management of public finances and assets, effective public borrowing, the formation of markets, investing in human capital and creating citizenship rights through social policy.

When a state performs all of these simultaneously, they say:

> ...the synergy creates a virtuous circle in which decisions in the different domains reinforce enfranchisement and opportunity for the citizenry. This supports the legitimacy of the decision makers and their decisions, builds trust in the overall system, and thereby produces a "sovereignty dividend." Conversely, when one or several of the functions are not performed effectively, a vicious circle begins: various centers of power vie for control, multiple decision-making processes confuse priorities, citizens lose trust in the government, institutions lose their legitimacy, and the populace is disenfranchised. In the most extreme cases, violence results. This negative cycle creates the sovereignty gap.[2]

Economic development, optimized by a fair and consistent system of international trade, provides the best hope for the world to address its inequities and environmental challenges. To me it boils down to providing more competition to address problems of poor economic performance, and more democracy when the political apparatus does not deliver. The conclusions of the Commission on the Legal Empowerment of the Poor's final report, *Making the Law Work for Everyone*, emphasize the need to promote and lock in property rights and ownership so that the poor can realize gains on their assets. This only works if the legal system is trusted and courts are independent.

When the Baltic States became free from the Soviet Union in 1991, Estonia had virtually no modern technology. Its Ministry of Foreign Affairs had only two mobile phones. Government offices and most companies were poorly served by old mainframe computers, and it was illegal for private individuals to own a computer. Today Estonia is among the top 20 countries for internet penetration. All its schools are connected, and the vast majority of bank transfers are made by computer. Latvia reputedly has the highest mobile-phone penetration in the world—registering 4.3 million subscribers for a population of 3.5 million. Critics and cynics might point out that the Baltic States and other economies that have opened up most over the past decade have lost a great deal in this current economic crisis. While this may be true, this is because they now have something to lose. My feeling is that the open economies will remain better places to live than countries with closed economies.

Real reformers who are serious about progress sometimes need outside markers to drive internal reform. Taiwan, for example, encountered few difficulties in adapting to WTO membership: for years before it joined it had acted as though it were a member by insisting that both its public and private sectors comply with agreed WTO rules and mandates. Membership of the WTO is making countries like Vietnam more transparent as they adopt the organization's global standards. Turkey has had to change hundreds of laws, advance human and labor rights, and adopt new environmental standards as it battles to join the European Union, a path that has already advanced the juridical framework in Eastern and Central European countries. Some aspirants to EU membership adopt the euro as their currency prior to being accepted. Nations that accept that these international standards are not a concession to be traded off for entry to the WTO or the EU but are a precondition for their own advance, must adapt these disciplines early and reap the benefits.

Ensuring that these advances can be made is akin to a company submitting to the disciplines and rules of a market. Good businesses employ outside auditors, seek international standards and are open in their reporting to investors. Good governance and sound management are vital; without them no business can enjoy sustained success. It is no different for a nation: opening an economy to market forces ensures that governments cannot manipulate currency and inflation for electoral purposes, or marshal the profits for self-reward. The market can be a tyrant: it will move swiftly when a government resorts to deficit financing or makes foolish expenditure promises.

International institutions like the WTO through its agreements, the OECD through its public reporting procedures, and the IMF through its promotion of effective financial management, have played a vital restraining role during crises such as the 1997 Asian economic crisis, helping to lead governments away from failed policies and providing the support for realignment and recovery. Critics correctly point out that the severe prescriptions suggested for the Asian crisis by the IMF have not been so publicly advanced to deal with the current global crisis, which had its origins in the West. The West's version of the black economy was the unregulated, unrecorded and opaque derivative and hedge-fund markets. The moral hazard created by soft loans to people who could never have paid them back would have made any crony capitalist in Asia blush. The system failed and crashed. Democracy allows the people to hold those responsible accountable, and they have and will. Subsequent elections have seen government after government booted out of office. We didn't have these international agencies at the time of the Great Depression, and history shows that the downturn was prolonged by protectionism. They are creatures born from the experience of that economic disaster and the world war that ensued, and in the main they have worked well.

We need more adherence to international rules and norms to prevent the short-sighted and self-interested actions of rulers like Robert Mugabe, who has seen fit to follow the agricultural policies of Stalin and Mao by telling people what and where to farm. Some would suggest that adherence to a global standard marks the end of sovereignty. I follow the counter-argument, that global rules freely negotiated by sovereign governments guarantee the rights of nations.

Globalization is not a policy. It is not regime imposed on the world by some Wall Street conspiracy. It is a process, one that has been going on ever since our ancestors stood upright.

Successful countries live and manage by transparent international standards, and are rewarded accordingly. We must encourage those governments that remain wedded to outmoded ideologies and practices to help their people share in the opportunities and prosperity that result from meaningful adherence to an international order. The worst places in the world are distinguished not only by war, corruption and venal leadership, but by closed economies. Open economies always do better. Competition and trade lead to better economic results while driving out corruption and allocating resources more efficiently.

A free market that lacks trusted institutions, property rights, independent courts, commercial transparency, a professional public service and democracy is a black market, not a free market. Firm, predictable civil institutions are vital, and we must encourage their creation across the developing world—where 40 percent of wealth is created in the informal economy, relegating local businesses to the back streets. When trust emerges, investment increases. After Deng Xiaoping established de facto securitization of property and liberalized agriculture, Chinese productivity jumped 42 percent.

Making the Law Work for Everyone emphasizes that without property rights the poor remain imprisoned in the informal economy, vulnerable to predatory bureaucrats and local mafia. Bringing these people into the formal economy widens the tax base, which in turn encourages voters to hold their politicians accountable for their spending.

Making the changes sometimes requires less-than-ideal means. It's well known that dictators hardly ever quit. They can't: they may be prosecuted, or those who replace them may take revenge. All the incentives are to stay, fight it out, or replace themselves with someone they can control. But compromise in the form of exile or immunity from prosecution can often do the trick. Idi Amin's murderous regime in Uganda came to an end when he was offered exile in Saudi Arabia. Granting immunity from prosecution allowed Chile and Argentina to move to democracy. Think of the thousands of lives and millions of dollars that could have been saved if some such deal had been brokered with Slobodan Milosevic before the Balkans War.

Finding a balance between providing justice for past victims, measured against the knowledge there will be many more if nothing happens, is a daunting prospect. But South Africa showed that there is a way forward from the most intractable of difficulties, moving the nation away from the terror and trauma of apartheid by offering the guilty the possibility of redemption through its Peace and Reconciliation Commission.

Addressing the evident pressures on resources will become a constant of the twenty-first century. We must abandon ideology and work out solutions to ensure provision of enough food to the world's poor. Monsanto has set the year 2030 as its goal for producing corn, cotton and soybean seeds that would enable twice the current yields and need less land and water. Genetic engineering promotes an emotional response in many of us. But like the Green Revolution of the 1960s, GE crops may be essential to feed growing populations. A measured consideration of the facts and transparent decision-making is needed.

Policy-makers and voters both need to be aware that, to use Roger Cohen's phrase, we live in an inverted world, in which the developed world will become increasingly dependent on the developing world.[3] Foreign direct investment by developing nations is already approaching parity with that of the US. In this more multi-polar world, free trade and the rule of law, globalization and democracy are imperative if we are to manage the challenges to our environment.

The short-termism and mercantile attitude toward the Doha Development Round is another great unfolding folly that needs proper leadership to resolve. Just when the global economy could have done with a confidence builder, a July 2008 meeting of Trade Ministers at the World Trade Organization in Geneva failed, again, to make progress.

Such meetings tend to fail because this is where it gets real. Leaders' meetings and meetings of ministers in other disciplines can release splendid communiqués that mean different things to different capitals, but are never binding. WTO agreements must be ratified by parliaments and are subject eventually to a binding disputes system.

Although the Geneva meeting narrowed differences to a remarkable degree, ministers just couldn't swallow the final differences. Matters of process and transparency were, unusually, not a big issue, nor were there any protests. The desire of India and China to have special safeguards against so-called surges of imports from agricultural exporters was a difficult issue, however. This would have undone previous WTO trade rounds, and the severe conditions set for China's membership of the WTO in my time. The proposals would have enabled China to raise its soy bean tariffs on US exports in eight of the past 10 years, and raise poultry duties in six of the last nine years. The US couldn't sell that deal at home and, as usual, many other countries hid behind the US, as some did behind India and China. The conventional wisdom for the collapse of the talks will be the "surge" problem. But this isn't the whole truth: negotiation never got to other serious issues, such as cotton.

Observers suspect that both China and India, which have made spectacular progress under the old conditions, will have difficulty accepting new conditions. China is seeking protection against export surges in her bilateral trade deals, and India will carve out sensitive areas. The reality is that these big nations always have the power, and that is why the multilateral system is the best hope for the small and poor. Trade openings will continue on a regional and bilateral basis, but they seldom advance the issues that stall WTO talks. Rather, they create trade diversion, new privileges, and new, dangerous levers that politicians will be tempted to use. None have a binding disputes mechanism. While the old struggle between rich and poor countries, North versus South, still prevails to a certain extent, for many smaller, poorer players the battle is as much with major developing countries as it is with their old colonial masters.

As we have seen, subsidies—whether through Europe's common agricultural policy or farming subsidies in the US, Japan or India for that matter—do great harm to unsubsidized producers everywhere. For those at the bottom, things have changed. In the early days it was a more clear-cut struggle to get the rich countries to open their markets to poor countries, and for poor countries to establish rules and systems to welcome investment and technology, raising incomes on both sides. As markets open, it won't be just rich American, Japanese or European nations that are in open competition with poor countries. China and India will take up the new opportunities that would have been available to poorer countries. The value of Bangladesh's textile industry increased from a few hundred million dollars to several billion dollars because of the last trade round. As its markets are opened, Bangladesh will see more competition from bigger developing countries. Smaller Caribbean and African nations that had privileged quotas to the US and Europe may see some of this business migrate to other developing countries. Medium-sized powers like Brazil and South Africa will see some of their new industries threatened by these emerging economic superpowers.

Many know that if the Doha Trade Round is balanced, and agriculture is properly addressed, they will gain overall. Yet, for the poorest, smallest, most-isolated economies, the traditional path of development from textiles to manufacturing to service industries cannot now be traveled with the same historic ease. Many have actually gone backwards over the past decade, as a result of lack of trade and good governance. There will not be a Nigerian motor car industry (although an outsourced Tata "people's car" might be a starter). But as wages rise in China's coastal provinces and labor shortages plague other developing countries, there will be some openings: jobs are now leaving China for Africa and Vietnam.

Multilateral trade negotiations are not over, because there is just too much at stake. No trade round has ever failed, but they take too long and produce results that are too shallow. It's iron diplomacy at its toughest. So what now? Even a reckless optimist like me can't see much happening until there are new administrations in place in the EU and India, which are due over the next two years.

Thinkers are wrestling with how to adapt the architecture of international institutions formed in the late 1940s to reflect new realities. The rules, agreements, procedures, habits and management of the institutions such as the UN, the IMF and the World Bank, as well as the WTO, have up until now represented the interests of a small group of mostly rich countries, which found expression in new protectionist subsidies, distortions and imbalances. However, something more profound and historic was happening at this 2008 WTO Ministerial Meeting. Because of the WTO's unique, more democratic decision-making structure, the new economic elephants in the room, like China, India and Brazil, have more influence and are seeking to use that influence.

Eventually a deal will be done: the difficulty in achieving this is a tribute to its importance. Unless we do liberalize trade the poorest countries will continue to find it harder to pull their populations out of poverty. We need to give these people hope and ownership so that the most ambitious are not forced to flee their dreadful conditions, as have Cubans, Zimbabweans and Afghans in their millions.

I came into politics believing that people didn't demand much—someone to love, somewhere to live, something to believe in and something to hope for. But to these I would now add "something to lose and something to leave behind." People without something to lose have nothing to lose and are vulnerable to the most unpleasant of populists and fanatics. If they have nothing to lose, they can be tempted down roads of reaction and violence. That is why this book speaks to the ownership not only of property but of the community and of the direction of their lives through democracy.

I have done my best in this book to explain how we can build a more perfect union in regard to the international architecture to promote the values and standards that have served the world well. The freedoms that have evolved, many of which are now almost universal thanks to globalization, are worth fighting for. If we live by the evidence and judge progress by results, then the road is clearer. I hope that this brief history of the future adds fuel to the fire of ambition and hope that has driven progress down the ages. Not to follow that fire would, in the words of Woodrow Wilson, break the heart of the world.

Endnotes

Introduction

1 Michael Mandelbaum, *The Ideas That Conquered The World* (New York: Public Affairs, 2002).

2 Fareed Zakaria, *The Future of Freedom* (New York: W. W. Norton, 2003).

3 David Wong, "Iraqis Who Died While Daring to Vote Are Mourned as Martyrs," *New York Times*, February 2, 2005. http://www.nytimes.com/2005/02/02/international/middleeast/02najaf.html

4 Freedom House, "Democracy's Century: A Survey of Global Political Change in the Twentieth Century," 1999. http://www.freedomhouse.org/reports/century.html

5 Morton H. Halperin, Joseph T. Siegle, and Michael M. Weinstein, *The Democratic Advantage: How Democracies Promote Prosperity and Peace* (New York and UK: Routledge, 2005).

6 Zakaria, op. cit.

7 Ibid.

8 World Bank, *Where Is the Wealth of Nations? Measuring Capital for the 21st Century* (Washington, DC: World Bank Publications, 2005). Available online at: http://web.worldbank.org/WBSITE/EXTERNAL/TOPICS/ENVIRONMENT/EXTEEI/0,,contentMDK:20744819~pagePK:210058~piPK:210062~theSitePK:408050~isCURL:Y,00.html

9 Ibid.

Chapter 1

1 Centre for Economic and Business Research report, 2006.

2 Bill Emmott, "A Long Goodbye," *The Economist*, 2006. http://www.economist.com/opinion/displaystory.cfm?story_id=6744590

3 Federation of United Nations Associations, "State of the Future" survey, 2007.

4 Sandra Postel, *Pillar of Sand: Can the Irrigation Miracle Last?* (New York: World watch Institute, 1999).
5 Centre for Economic Research, United Kingdom, 2002 Report.
6 Government think-tank, National Institute for Public Finance.
7 Amartya Sen, *The Argumentative Indian* (New York: Penguin Books, 2006).
8 *Wall Street Journal*, "Global Fishing Trade Depletes African Waters: Poor Nations Get Cash, The Rich Send Trawlers; A Dearth of Octopus," July 2007. http://online.wsj.com/article/SB118470420636969282.html
9 Steven Pinker, *The Blank Slate: The Modern Denial of Human Nature* (New York: Penguin, 2003).
10 Federation of United Nations Associations, State of the World survey, 2007.
11 Juan Williams, *Enough: The Phony Leaders, Dead-End Movements, and Culture of Failure That Are Undermining Black America—and What We Can Do About It* (New York: Three Rivers Press, 2006).
12 Dinesh D'Souza, *The Virtue of Prosperity: Finding Values in an Age of Technoaffluence* (New York: English Press, 2001).
13 Niall Ferguson, *The Ascent of Money* (New York: The Penguin Press, 2008).
14 Pew Global Attitudes Project, "World Publics Welcome Global Trade—But Not Immigration" (Washington, DC: PewResearchCenter, 2007). http://pewglobal. org/reports/display.php?ReportID=258

Chapter 2

1 Lester Brown, Founder & President, Earth Policy Institute at the World Food Business Summit, Shanghai, 2007.
2 Will Hutton, *China, The Writing on the Wall* (London: Little, Brown, 2007).
3 Cass R. Sunstein, *Why Societies Need Dissent* (Harvard University Press, 2003).
4 Gerald Segal, "Does China Matter?" *Foreign Affairs*, September/October 1999.
5 The Carnegie Endowment for International Peace, Report 2007.
6 *Financial Times*, November 13, 2002.
7 Hutton, op. cit.

Chapter 3

1 United States National Intelligence Council, "Mapping the Global Future," 2005 report.
2 T. N. Srinivasan, *The Political Economy of Trade, Finance and Development* (New Delhi: Oxford University Press, 2007).
3 The Fabian Society is a British-based "left-ish" think-tank named after the Roman General Quintus Fabius Maximus who, by carefully avoiding decisive battles, helped defeat Hannibal's army by harassing them with ambushes, delays, marches, and counter-marches. Fabian military and political tactics were no stranger to India, where they were probably used before Fabius himself.
4 See Michael Backman and Charlotte Butler, *Big in Asia: 25 Strategies for Business Success* (Palgrave Macmillan, 2003).
5 Edward Luce, *In Spite of the Gods: The Strange Rise of Modern India* (London: Little, Brown, 2006).

Chapter 4

1 Aristotle's constitution of Athens was not a formal constitution; it was an account, a record of the constitution of Athens.
2 UNDP, Arab Human Development report, 2002.
3 Cowell, A., "Zeal for Suicide Bombing Reaches British Midlands," *New York Times*, May 2, 2003.

Chapter 5

1 Amartya Sen, *Development As Freedom* (Oxford: Oxford University Press, 1999).
2 Friedrich Engels, *The Origin of the Family, Private Property, and the State*, 1884.
3 Jim Wallis, *Living God's Politics: A Guidebook for Putting Your Faith Into Action* (New York: HarperCollins, 2005).

Chapter 6

1 Amartya Sen, *Development as Freedom* (Oxford: Oxford University Press, 1999).
2 Raul Manglapus, *Will of the People: Original Democracy in Non-Western Societies* (Westport: Greenwood Press, 1987).
3 Sen, op. cit.
4 Manglapus, op. cit.
5 Laldhos Deosa Rai, "Human Rights Development in Ancient Nepal," *Human Rights Quarterly* 3(3) (1981): 40–1.
6 Minoo Masani, *Our Growing Human Family* (Calcutta: Oxford University Press, 1981), 66.
7 R. C. Majumdar, *Ancient India* (Delhi: Motial Banarsidass, 1982), 25.
8 Radhakamal Mukerjee, *Democracies of the East* (New Delhi, 1923), 197.
9 James Legge, *The Sacred Books of China, the Texts of Taoism* (Oxford University Press, 1962).
10 Will and Ariel Durant, *The Story of Civilisation* Vol. 1: 672.
11 Sister Maria Ignazia Bunuan, ed., *We Chinese* (Taipei: St. Paul Publications, 1982), 25.
12 Durant, op. cit., 799.
13 Miles Dawson, *Ethics of Confucius* (New York, 1915), 20.
14 Durant op. cit., Vol. 3.
15 August C. Krey, *The First Crusade* (Kessenger Publishing, 2006).

Chapter 7

1 Chaim Bermant and Michael Weitzman, *Ebla: A Revelation in Archaeology* (New York: Times Books, 1979)
2 *Times Atlas of World History,* Geoffrey Barraclough (ed.) (London: Times Books, 1993), 74–75.
3 John Clarke Stobart, *The Glory That Was Greece* (London: Sidgwick & Jackson, 1964), 100ff.

4   Simon Hornblower, *The Greek World* (London, New York: Methuen, 1983), 3.
5   Ibid.: 3.
6   Stobart op. cit.: 112.
7   Hornblower op. cit.: 5.
8   Ibid: 6.
9   Stobart op. cit.: 113.
10 Ibid.
11 Donald Kagan, *Pericles of Athens and the Birth of Democracy* (New York: Simon & Schuster, 1991), 47.
12 Ibid.
13 Ibid: 58.
14 Plato, as quoted by Karl Popper.
15 Philippe Gigantès, *Power and Greed: A Short History of the World* (New York: Carroll & Graf Publishers, 2002).
16 Christopher Rowe, *Introduction to Greek Ethics* (London: Hutchinson, 1976), 120; Kagan op. cit.: 142.
17 Stobart op. cit.: 213.
18 Hornblower op. cit.: 10.
19 Douglas MacDowell, *The Law in Classical Athens* (London: Thames & Hudson, 1978), 84.
20 Ibid.
21 Ibid: 75.
22 Ibid: 76.
23 Ibid.
24 Ibid: 79.
25 Ibid: 82.
26 Hornblower op. cit.: 8.

Chapter 8

1   Walter Lacey, *Roman Social Life* (Dunedin, New Zealand: Classics Dept., University of Otago, 1981), 8.
2   Barry Nicholas, *Introduction to Roman Law* (Oxford: Clarendon Press, 1962), 64.
3   John Clarke Stobart, *The Grandeur That Was Rome* (London: Sidgwick & Jackson, 1961), 25.
4   Ibid: 28.
5   Lacey op. cit.: 6.
6   Ibid: 7.
7   Ibid.
8   Ibid: 2.
9   Stobart op. cit.: 25.
10 Ibid.
11 Ibid: 26.
12 *Times Atlas of World History,* Geoffrey Barraclough (ed.) (London: Times Books, 1993), 87.

13 J. M. Ross, Introduction to Cicero's *The Nature of the Gods*, trans. H. C. McGregor, (Harmondsworth: Penguin, 1972), 14.
14 Ibid: 15.
15 Stobart op. cit.: 200.
16 *Times Atlas of World History*: 88.
17 Douglas MacDowell, *The Law in Classical Athens* (London: Thames & Hudson, 1978), Preface.
18 Nicholas op. cit.: 1.
19 Ibid: 2.
20 Ibid.
21 Ibid: 64–270.
22 Ibid: 15–33.
23 Ibid: 64.
24 Ibid: 65.
25 Ibid: 66.
26 Ibid: 67.
27 Ibid: 82.
28 Ibid: 88.
29 Ibid: 69.
30 Ibid.
31 Ibid: 45.
32 Ibid: 46, 48–9.
33 Ibid: 50.
34 Ibid: 51.
35 Ibid: 52.
36 Charles Freeman, *The Closing of the Western Mind, The Rise of Faith and the Fall of Reason* (New York: Random House, 2005).

Chapter 9

1   Sidney Painter, *Feudalism and Liberty: Articles and Addresses,* Fred Cazel (ed.) (Baltimore: Johns Hopkins University Press, 1962), 3.
2   Ibid: 5.
3   Ibid: 7.
4   Ibid: 9.
5   Ibid: 7.
6   Ibid.
7   Jasper Ridley, *History of England* (London: Routledge & Kegan Paul, 1981), 35.
8   Painter op. cit.: 13.
9   Ibid: 14.
10 *Times Atlas of World History*, Geoffrey Barraclough (ed.) (London: Sidgwick & Jackson, 1964), 122.
11 Painter op. cit.: 7.
12 *Times Atlas*, op. cit.: 118.
13 John Roberts, *Triumph of the West* (London: BBC, 1985), 98–9.
14 Ibid: 100.

15   *Times Atlas* op. cit.: 118.
16   Roberts op. cit.: 100.
17   Ibid: 100, 119.
18   Ridley op. cit.: 23.
19   Ibid.
20   Ibid.
21   Ibid: 35.
22   Ibid: 41.
23   Painter op. cit.: 10.
24   Ridley op. cit.: 59.
25   Ibid.
26   Painter op. cit.: 255; Roberts op. cit.: 104.
27   Ridley op. cit.: 61.
28   Ibid: 62.

Chapter 10

1   *Times Atlas of World History*, Geoffrey Barraclough (ed.) (London: Times Books, 1993), 122.
2   Ibid.
3   John Roberts, *Triumph of the West* (London: BBC, 1985), 116.
4   Sidney Painter, *Feudalism and Liberty: Articles and Addresses*, Fred Cazel (ed.) (Baltimore: Johns Hopkins University Press, 1962), 10.
5   Jasper Ridley, *History of England* (London: Routledge & Kegan Paul, 1981),: 71.
6   Painter op. cit.: 12–3.
7   Ibid: 244.
8   Ibid: 246.
9   Ibid: 247.
10   Ibid: 12.
11   Ridley op. cit.: 74.
12   Ibid.
13   Ibid: 73.
14   Painter op. cit.: 246.
15   Ridley op. cit.:74.
16   Painter op. cit.: 251.
17   Ibid: 250.
18   Ridley op. cit.: 75.
19   *Times Atlas* op. cit.: 122.
20   Roberts op. cit.: 112.
21   Ibid.
22   Ibid: 263.
23   Ibid: 235.
24   *Times Atlas* op. cit.: 175.
25   Ibid: 147.
26   Ibid: 146.

27 *Times Atlas* op. cit.: 180.
28 Ibid: 179.
29 Ibid.
30 Ibid.: 180.
31 Marshall Berman, *Politics of Authenticity: Radical Individualism and the Emergence of Modern Society* (New York: Athenaeum, 1970), 30.
32 *Times Atlas* op. cit.: 180.
33 Ibid.: 189.
34 Malcolm Billings, *English: The Making of the Nation from 430 to 1700* (London: BBCBooks, 1991), 111.
35 Ibid.: 106.
36 Ibid.: 107.
37 Simon Schama, *A History of Britain: the British Wars, 1603–1776* (London: BBC Books, 2001), 124.
38 Arthur Herman, *The Scottish Enlightenment: The Scots' Invention of the Modern World* (London: Fourth Estate, 2003), 20.
39 Schama op. cit.: 176.
40 Billings op. cit.: 113.
41 Schama op. cit.: 182.
42 Ibid.
43 Ibid.
44 Ibid.
45 Ibid.
46 Billings op. cit.: 113.
47 *Times Atlas* op. cit.: 180.
48 Billings op. cit.: 118.
49 Schama op. cit.: 312.
50 Ibid: 321.
51 *Times Atlas* op. cit.: 180.
52 Billings op. cit.: 123.
53 Ibid: 124.
54 Ibid: 124–5.
55 Ibid.
56 Herman op. cit.: 6.
57 Schama op. cit.: 402.
58 Ibid: 416.
59 Ibid: 404.

Chapter 11

1 *Times Atlas of World History*, Geoffrey Barraclough (ed.) (London: Times Books, 1993), 174–75.
2 John Roberts, *Triumph of the West* (London: BBC, 1985), 277.
3 Jasper Ridley, *History of England* (London: Routledge & Kegan Paul, 1981), 229
4 Ibid: 281.

5   *Times Atlas* op. cit.: 199.
6   Dick Howard, *The Specter of Democracy: The Rise of Modern Democracy* (New York: Columbia University Press, 2002), xii, 140.
7   Jerome Wilson and William Ricketson, *Tom Paine* (Boston: Twayne Publishers, 1989), viii.
8   Ronald Grimsley (ed.), *Age of Enlightenment 1715–1789* (Harmondsworth: Penguin, 1979), 100.
9   *Times Atlas* op. cit.: 199.
10 Ibid.
11 Ibid.
12 Roberts op. cit.: 281.
13 Wilson and Ricketson op. cit.: 50.
14 Ridley op. cit.: 234.
15 *Times Atlas* op. cit.: 199.
16 Ibid: 222.
17 Ibid: 201.
18 Ibid: 226.
19 Arthur Herman, *The Scottish Enlightenment: The Scots' Invention of the Modern World* (London: Fourth Estate, 2003),
20 Smith, paraphrased by Herman, op. cit.: 202.
21 Roberts op. cit.: 256.
22 Grimsley op. cit.: 7.
23 Ridley op. cit.: 228.
24 Ibid.
25 *Times Atlas* op. cit.: 226.
26 Ridley op. cit.: 231.
27 Ibid: 249.
28 Grimsley op. cit.: 109.
29 Ridley op. cit.: 250.
30 Michael Mandelbaum, *The Case for Goliath: How America acts as the world's government in the twenty-first century* (New York: PublicAffairs, 2006), 246.
31 Ibid.
32 Ridley op. cit.: 271–72.
33 Mandelbaum op. cit.
34 Roberts op. cit.: 295.
35 Ridley op. cit.: 247–48.
36 Ibid: 265.
37 Ibid: 266.
38 *Times Atlas* op. cit.: 240.
39 Ibid: 241.
40 Niall Ferguson, *Empire; How Britain Made the Modern World* (London: Allen Lane, 2003), 217.
41 *Times Atlas* op. cit.: 230.
42 Ibid.
43 Ferguson op. cit.
44 *Times Atlas* op. cit. 231.

45   Ibid: 230–31.
46   Ridley op. cit.: 255.
47   Ferguson op. cit.: xxvi.

Chapter 12

1   Daniel Patrick Moynihan, *On the Law of Nations* (Cambridge: Harvard University Press, 1990).
2   Michael Mandelbaum, *The Ideas That Conquered the World: Peace Democracy and Free Markets in the Twenty-first Century* (New York: PublicAffairs, 2002), 25.
3   Arthur S. Link, *Wilson the Diplomat: A Look at His Major Foreign Policies* (Baltimore: Johns Hopkins Press, 1957).
4   Margaret McMillan, *Peacemakers: Paris 1919, Six Months that Changed the World* (London: Random House, 2002).
5   Townsend Hoopes and Douglas Brinkley, *FDR and the Creation of the U.N.* (Yale University Press, 2000).
6   Gareth Evans, presentation to Folke Bernadotte/Madariaga Foundation Workshop on Conflict Prevention: Creating a Leading Role for the European Union, Brussels, March 9, 2006.
7   Joseph S. Nye, Jr. *The Paradox of American Power: Why the World's Only Superpower Can't Go It Alone* (Cambridge: Harvard University Press, 2002).
8   Philip Stephens, *Financial Times*, October 10, 2008.
9   Alfred, Lord Tennyson. "Locksley Hall," 1837.

Chapter 13

1   Hernando de Soto and Madeleine Albright, *Time*, July 17, 2007, article by commission co-chairs.
2   Source: www.grameen-info.org, March 2008.
3   C. K. Prahalad, *The Fortune at the Bottom of the Pyramid* (Philadelphia: Wharton School Publishing, 2002).
4   Yann Algan and Pierre Cahuc, *La Société de Défiance* (*The Society of Distrust*) (Editions de la Rue d'Ulm, 2007).
5   *Newsweek*, October 29, 2007.
6   Robert Putnam, *Making Democracy Work: Civic Traditions in Modern Italy* (New Jersey: Princeton University Press, 1993).
7   Joseph Heinrich et al. (eds), *Foundations of Human Sociality* (New York: Oxford University Press, 2004).
8   James Surowieck, *The Wisdom of Crowds: Why The Many Are Smarter Than The Few And How Collective Wisdom Shapes Business, Economies, Societies And Nations* (New York: Doubleday, 2004).
9   Marq de Villiers and Sheila Hirtle, *Inside Africa: A Journey through the Ancient Empires* (Toronto: Key Porter Books, 1999).
10 Ashutosh Sheshabalaya, "Eye on the Tigers," *E-Sharp*, November–December 2007.

Chapter 14

1   Matt Ridley, *The Origins of Virtue: Human Instincts and the Evolution of Cooperation* (Viking, 1996).
2   Robert Wright, *The Moral Animal. Why We are the Way We Are: The New Science of Evolutionary Psychology* (New York: Vintage Books, 1994)
3   Adam Smith, *An Inquiry into the Nature and Causes of the Wealth of Nations*, Book 1.
4   Letter to William Eden (Lord Auckland), Edinburgh, January 3, 1780.
5   K. Nyanamaro Mufuka, *Dzimbahwe, Life & Politics in the Golden Age 1100–1500 AD* (Harare: Harare Publishing House, 1983)
6   J.H. Elliot, *Imperial Spain 1469–1726* (London: Penguin Books, 1990).

Chapter 15

1   Charles Kindleberger, *The World in Depression 1929–1939* (Berkeley: University of California Press, 1973).
2   World Bank Policy Research Report, "Globalization, Growth & Poverty: Building an Inclusive World Economy," December 2001.
3   World Trade Organization report.
4   United Nations Conference on Trade & Development (UNCTAD), 2002.
5   Maurice Mandelbaum, *Philosophy, History and the Sciences: Selected Critical Essays* (Baltimore: Johns Hopkins University Press, 1984).
6   Ibid.
7   Richard Florida, *The Rise of the Creative Class* (New York: Basic Books, 2002).
8   Lord Henry Peter Brougham (1778–1868).
9   Dick Howard, *The Spectre of Democracy: The Rise of Modern Democracy* (New York: Columbia University Press, 2002).

Chapter 16

1   Reporters Sans Frontières, Annual Press Freedom Report, 2003.
2   George Gray-Molina, Ernesto Pérez de Rada, Ernesto Yaflez, and Fundacion Dialogo, "Transparency and Accountability in Bolivia: Does Voice Matter?" Inter-American Development Bank, Latin American Research Network, Office of the Chief Economist, Working Paper #R–381 December 1999.
3   Daniel Kaufmann, Gil Mehrez and Tugrul Gurgur, "Voice or Public Sector Management? An Empirical Investigation of Determinants of Public Sector Performance based on a Survey of Public Officials," World Bank Research Working Paper, June 2002.
4   David Upton and Virginia Fuller, "The ITC eChoupal Initiative," October 28, 2003 (revised January 15, 2004).
5   Manobi.net.
6   *The Economist*, October 26, 2006.
7   *The Economist*, "Mobile Phones in Africa, Buy, cell, hold," January 25, 2007.
8   Herbert Walberg, Hoover Institute, Stanford University.

9 *Newsweek Supplement*, August 2007.
10 Aneurin Bevan, *In Place of Fear* (1952).
11 See Larry Lindsay, *Financial Times*, August 2003; Timothy Garton Ash, *Free World: Why a Crisis of the West Reveals the Opportunity of Our Time* (UK: Penguin, 2004).

Chapter 17

1 London School of Economics report sponsored by the Sutton Trust, 2005.
2 Jo Blanden, Paul Gregg and Steve Machin, Sutton Trust.
3 Brink Lindsey, Cato Institute, *Wall Street Journal*, July 2007.
4 *The Economist*, December 23, 2006.
5 KMP Foundation.
6 Juan Williams, *Enough* (Random House, 2006).
7 Will Hutton, *China: The Writing on the Wall* (UK: Little, Brown, 2006).

Chapter 18

1 Giles Bolton, *Poor Story: An Insider Uncovers How Globalization and Good Intentions Have Failed the World's Poor* (UK: Ebury Press, 2007).

Chapter 19

1 Cited in Karen Armstrong, *The Battle for God* (New York: Alfred A. Knopf, 2000).
2 Noam Chomsky, *9/11 New York* (Seven Storied Press, 2001).
3 Fareed Zakaria, *The Post-American World* (New York: W. W. Norton & Company, 2008).
4 ISIS, Malaysia, Islam & Development Conference, 2007.
5 Zakaria, op. cit.
6 Sam Harris, *The End of Faith: Religion, Terror and the Future of Reason* (New York: W. W. Norton & Company, 2005).
7 Mark Lilla, *The Reckless Mind: Intellectuals in Politics* (New York: New York Review of Books, 2001).
8 Michael Sheldon, *Orwell: The Authorized Biography* (Harper Collins, 1991).

Chapter 20

1 Paul M Johnson, *The Quest for God: A Personal Pilgrimage* (HarperCollins e-books, 2007).
2 Cited in Sam Harris, *The End of Faith: Religion, Terror and the Future of Reason* (New York: W. W. Norton & Company, 2005).
3 Darrin M. McMahon, *Enemies of The Enlightenment: The French Counter-Enlightenment and the Making of Modernity* (New York: Oxford University Press, 2001).
4 *Financial Times*, January 8, 2007.
5 Frank Furedi, *The Politics of Fear* (London: Continuum Press, 2005).

Chapter 23

1   Robert Wuthnow and Matthew Lawson, "Sources of Christian Fundamentalism in the United States" in Martin E. Marty and R. Scott Appleby, eds., *Accounting for Fundamentalism: The Dynamic Character of Movements* (Chicago: University of Chicago Press, 1994).
2   Daniel Benjamin and Steven Simon, *The Age of Sacred Terror* (New York: Random House, 2002).

Chapter 24

1   Paul Roberts, *The End of Oil: On the Edge of a Perilous New World* (New York: Houghton Mifflin Harcourt, 2004).
2   APEC Study Centre at Monash University, Melbourne, Australia.

Chapter 25

1   Ashraf Ghani and Clare Lockhart, *Fixing Failed States: A Framework For Rebuilding A Fractured World* (Canada: Oxford University Press, 2008), 93–4; 109–10.
2   Ibid: 163.
3   Roger Cohen, "The world is upside down," *International Herald Tribune*, June 2, 2008.

Index